PRAISE FOR
A ROSIE LIFE IN ITALY

"*A Rosie Life in Italy* is a fun, courageous, madcap account of one family's leap of faith, landing them in a ramshackle Italian villa in the midst of a global pandemic. I was so invested in this story, in Rosie's incredible journey, that I couldn't turn the pages fast enough. The perfect book for anyone who's ever fantasized about throwing reality overboard, in hopes of catching their dream."
—Lori Nelson Spielman, *New York Times* bestselling author of *The Star-Crossed Sisters of Tuscany*

"I love *A Rosie Life in Italy*! Entertaining and funny!"
—Jenny Marrs, host of HGTV's *Fixer to Fabulous*

"I romped through this Italian adventure. Tears of laughter and tears of sorrow were shed. A gloriously entertaining book."
—Angela Petch, bestselling author of *The Tuscan Secret*

"For anyone who's dreamed of uprooting their lives and moving to Europe, Rosie Meleady's humorous and heartfelt memoir brings a fresh twist to the genre made so popular by *A Year in Provence* and *My Life in France*. I personally know how challenging such a life-changing move can be. But *A Rosie Life in Italy* embraces that challenge head on, ultimately asserting that dealing with the harsh reality at hand is as important—if not *more* important—than the

T0188760

dream itself. If ever there's been a story showing how life is about the journey, not the destination, *A Rosie Life in Italy* is it."
—Craig Carlson, *New York Times* bestselling author
of *Pancakes in Paris*

"Meleady's heartfelt and humorous memoir has butterflies in its soul, flying us on the ultimate expat adventure and floating us into a new life in Italy—transformations and bumpy landings included. Grab a glass of wine and soar right into the heart of living la dolce vita without leaving your couch. A wildly fun, heartwarming, and humorous expat adventure! Brava!"
—Samantha Vérant, author of *Seven Letters from Paris*

"I so enjoyed this memoir. Rosie is brave, wise, and funny, and her story is a reminder that fear should never stop us from living our best life—preferably in Bella Italia!"
—Katherine Wilson, author of *Only in Naples*

"*A Rosie Life in Italy* removes the stereotypical veil of a perfect dolce vita, to show the ups and downs, glitches, and satisfactions, of what it takes to say good-bye to your country of origin and follow a life-long passion to live in the land we all know as the bel paese. Highlighting Italy's charms and lovingly surmounting its imperfections, this memoir will likely move you one step closer to following your own Italian dream."
—Raeleen D'Agostino Mautner, PhD, author
of *45 Ways to Live Like an Italian*

A ROSIE LIFE in ITALY

*Move to Italy. Buy a Run-down Villa.
What Could Go Wrong?*

ROSIE MELEADY

This book is a memoir. It reflects the author's present recollections of experiences
over a period of time. Some names and characteristics have been changed, some
events have been compressed, and some dialogue has been re-created.

Published by Sourcebooks
P.O. Box 4410, Naperville, Illinois 60567–4410
(630) 961-3900
sourcebooks.com

Originally self-published in 2020 by Rosie Meleady.

Cataloging-in-Publication Data is on file with the Library of Congress.

Printed and bound in the United States of America.
SB 10 9 8 7 6 5 4 3 2 1

For Annie and Sullivan
My Sun, Moon, and Stars

PART I

Chapter 1

I'M NOT SURE WHEN I FIRST NOTICED THE HOUSE. I DID GIVE THE *vendesi* ("for sale") sign a second glance every now and then when we went to Passignano for an *aperitivo* by the lakeshore of Trasimeno, the fourth-biggest lake in Italy. The sign was A4 size when we first arrived, and now, two years later, it had increased to a meter-long tarp, covering the front gate. The house stands hiding behind two big magnolia trees, its shuttered eyes closed, grass growing up around its ears.

Every time I pass, I am sure I can hear it sigh. I sigh with it. It isn't a sad house; it's just patiently waiting for the right owner to come along and feeling a little exasperated about being locked up all the time.

The inscription above the door reads "1923"—a grand villa built during the Roaring Twenties, elegant but homely, but not the one for me.

My ideal house in Italy has always been on the typical cypress-lined road, peaceful and quiet, birds singing, vineyards for miles around. So the Sighing House is not an option; it's too near the road, it has neighbors, and there is a railway track between the end of the garden and the lake.

The house we currently rent is closer to the description of my dream vision—in peace and quiet, on a private road, with birds singing. It is nice, but when you work for yourself and don't get out much, it gets pretty boring. Also, when I'm getting as excited as our dog seeing her lead at the mention of going somewhere, it's a good indication that the quiet country life may not be for me at this stage.

It was even more revealing when we sat down as a family and separately wrote down our "Must Have" lists for our "ideal home" if we ever were in a position to buy a house in Italy.

My "Must Haves":
Near a train station so I don't ever have to drive on the Italian motorways to get to Florence or Rome.
Near water, because I feel better near water. Maybe it keeps my chakras balanced? I don't really know what that means, but my inner hippy is screaming to get out, so I think being near water will help that.
Near a town so I can go for an Aperol spritz without having to drive home.
Not in the middle of nowhere so I can meet other humans rather than talking to myself all day.

My Husband Ronan's "Must Haves":
Near a train station so he won't have to drive me to Florence or Rome, as he knows I'll never have the courage to do it myself.

Near a town so he won't have to drive me home after an Aperol spritz.

Near water so he can walk our dogs.

Not in the middle of nowhere so he can get away from the house and go for a quiet cup of coffee and a read without me constantly giving him a list of tasks to do as soon as I see him sit down and relax.

Our Teenage Son Luca's "Must Haves":

Near a train station so he can escape from us.

Near a town so he can hang out with people his own age and escape from us.

Not in the middle of nowhere, as it makes it difficult for him to escape from us.

Near water, as it's a good place to hang out with friends and escape from us.

So if we are ever in a position to buy a home to call our own again after our last four disasters, the decision is made that the house will need to be near a train station, within walking distance of a town, near water, and have a garden for our pets.

Our twenty-year-old daughter, Izzy, has left the nest, but when she hears of our lists she adds to the list of requirements for when she's back visiting: Number one, a shower that works better than the dribbling thing we currently have with its two options, scalding-hot dribble or ice-cold dribble. With either option you get a complimentary soggy shower curtain stuck to your backside. Number two on her list is a kitchen big enough for a dishwasher. The kitchen in our current rental is a typical Italian kitchen—tiny.

How the hell they became the masters of the cooking world in these shoebox spaces is beyond me. There's nowhere to stack dishes other than the marble pasta-making table that acts as a worktop, storage space, and coffee machine counter. Nearly every day, Ronan, with his clumsy limbs, knocks over and breaks something by simply walking into the kitchen to make a coffee. If both of us are in the kitchen at the same time, then the whole room is full and there is literally no room to swing either of our cats, never mind have a dishwasher.

Izzy's number-three "Must Have" is a sofa big enough that we can all fit on it, like in the old days, and it needs to be blue velvet. We currently have a red faux-leather two-seater sofa bed that flakes and sticks to our skin, causing us to say casually to each other, "Hang on. Let me dust off your back; you have some sofa on you."

It's an improvement to the initial reactions of: "Jezuz Christ, let me look at your back; you have some hideous rash or disease starting."

So a decent sofa like we used to have when we had a home, which we could all fit and cozy up on in winter to watch TV together with a family-size box of chocolates, gets a thumbs-up. She has not taken into account, however, that Luca now equals Ronan's six foot two rather than being his previous three feet, when we could fit him into a gap. She is the same height as me at five foot two, rather than her previous little four during the halcyon chocolate days, so even with a big sofa it will be squashy with us all on it at the same time.

A cinema room and a pool are also on Izzy's list and are quickly added to everyone else's "must haves," but we were getting off track.

A working shower, a dishwasher, and a non-shedding sofa were good starting points to aim for.

The main nonnegotiable all four of us agreed on was that it has to be "turnkey ready" to move into, with no work to be done other than changing the color of the wall paint perhaps, but absolutely no DIY other than that. The kids spent their childhoods growing up in dilapidated renovation projects—the last house was nicknamed the "Money Pit"—so we've been there and done that and absolutely had our fill of renovation. We just want to walk in, unpack our bags, and be there from day one.

The Sighing House sits in front of Lake Trasimeno, and, yes, it is in walking distance of one of our favorite towns and a train station, but the villa looks derelict and like a big renovation project. It will have to be someone else's dream.

Chapter 2

MY SISTER EILEEN HAD A DOLLHOUSE. MY EARLIEST MEMORY IS of crawling down the hallway, stopping at Eileen's open bedroom door, and staring at her dollhouse, perched high on top of a bookshelf. She sees me, smiles her big smile, follows my line of vision, takes it down, and puts it in front of me.

It was all white, three stories high, with a central staircase, a red satin-ribbon runner glued into place, two rooms off to each side on each floor, and a secret attic space under the orangey-red roof. I didn't know the words for white or orangey red, but they were there in front of me. By the time I was old enough to play with the house, Jim, the nature-loving brother in between me and Eileen—number two of three—had turned it into a home for his pet mice, which had no hygiene manners and chewed through its walls. I watched it burn on a Halloween bonfire and I didn't have the words to say, "Give that to me. I can fix it."

I wanted a dollhouse just like Eileen's but never got one—probably because I never told anyone I wanted one—the same way I never got a rocking horse so I could be like Zorro. If I'd told Eileen, she would have gotten me one. She was the ultimate big sister through my teens, buying me my first bra, taking me to get my ears pierced with my first and only ever pieces of gold jewelry—fourteen-carat ear studs for my thirteenth birthday. She took me to get my legs waxed and told me never to shave. She tried to teach me how to walk in high heels in order to be like the elegant business woman and master of running in seven-inch stilettos, accompanied by tight velvet pants and a satin boob-tube, that she had already become by the time I was six and she was eighteen.

She gave me my first alcoholic drink—peach schnapps, an exotic drink in the eighties, which she brought back from a bus tour around Europe for "guys and girls in their twenties." In our shared bedroom I had no option but to listen to David Cassidy, Johnny Logan, the Bay City Rollers, and Richard Clayderman.

She remained the classy party girl, and I became the backpacker hippy. I failed miserably in anything with a heel and was more at home in patchwork dungarees than a pencil skirt. When we went to choose a dog from the rescue center to join our family, Eileen wanted the shiny new fluffy puppy while I picked Patch, the old mutt with an established personality and one eye. Patch was the best, most loyal dog ever.

As kids, when we drew our dream houses, she would draw a castle or mansion on a hill with millions of windows overlooking the sea, while I'd draw a "more modest" mansion or thatched cottage, hidden by trees, with a pond that had swans, a garden with a peacock, and windows with shutters. My houses always had shutters even though shutters didn't exist in Ireland. Shutters were the hallmark of the perfect house in my mind. I also needed a courtyard with a long table for family dinners.

This idea was inspired by watching TV with my family when I was nine. There was a movie with a huge family dinner under the sun, with profusions of food being passed around and wine being poured. It was a celebration: everyone was laughing; kids were playing around grape vines or olive trees. I can't remember who said it, but I remember the words "Mamma mia." As I stared at the TV, it was my idea of heaven.

I went to Mass on Sunday, and as I knelt in my rain-soaked trousers, I prayed that someday I would live in Mama-mia Land with my family, happy and in the sun. The following Monday, my teacher handed us out pen-pal forms with all the countries in the world listed on them. We were to tick the box of the country that we wanted to have a pen pal in.

"Which country do they say 'Mamma mia' in?" I asked my teacher.

After some thought, my teacher answered "Greece." So I ticked Greece.

My Greek pen pal, Nectaria, and I wrote to each other religiously every second week for ten years without her ever mentioning her long, candle-lit, olive-strewn family dinners, even though I often asked how dinner was with her family that week. One evening I happened to see the scene on TV again, the one I had watched all those years ago, and I realized my teacher was wrong; Mama-mia Land was not in Greece but Italy.

As a child, there were a few things I wanted in life that I felt would make it all perfect as an adult: the dollhouse, a rocking horse, a house with blue-shuttered windows, and, at one point, a treasure chest, an eye patch, and an antique globe to fulfil my inner pirate. As a teenager, an old-fashioned writing bureau became my ultimate desire. If I had that, I would be able to write all the words that would magically combine to make me a best-selling author. The angst, the frustration, and all the things a struggling writer should feel would be worked out at a multi-mini-drawer, roll-top, wizardy piece of furniture.

As one of the oldest grandkids, Eileen set the achievement bar high with a high-level job at Bank of America, and by the age of twenty-two she had her own house and was a fabulous cook with a perm and panache for interior design. Declan was her boyfriend of four years—a guy in sales who cheated on her while on holiday in the Canaries. He apologized profusely, but his giant valentine cards, stuffed toys, and silk-flower bouquets were all thrown back at him.

Eileen went on the rebound, and within a year she'd married Assface Alan. He had no family, no friends, no personality. I still have no idea why she married him—pity perhaps? A project to fix? To be the poor sod's knight in shining armor? God only knows.

Eileen wanted me to like Assface. Assface wanted to be liked. So they'd take me places. When they bought the ultimate house, with a balcony overlooking the sea, just like Eileen dreamed of, they took me furniture shopping with them as a neutral force to prevent arguments, a halfway point between their opposite tastes. While shopping for their dining table, we walked into a showroom of fake antique pine, but a corner of the warehouse had a section of customer trade-ins. And there it stood. I ran my hand over the ridges before slowly easing up the roll top with ease, revealing the studded-leather writing surface, backed by minidrawers and shelves for velum paper and writing ink.

"You like it, haw?" Assface said, seeing my desire for the writing desk.

"I've always wanted one of these. With this I could write the best novels. Imagine its history just leaking on to the pages. I can just picture it in…"

"We'll take the eight-seater dining table over there," Assface called out at the store assistant passing, "and this as well."

My heart skipped a beat: Wow! He was buying me the writing bureau; maybe he wasn't so bad after all. But he was that bad. He bought it for himself and plonked it against the wall at the end of their bed, without velum paper or an ink pen. Just a big, expensive ornament to fill a space. It stood empty, never opened. The only thing on it was the prized fine-china statue of the Madonna and child that belonged to our great-grandmother.

That was how it stayed, until one evening they had one of their many arguments, and to prove to Eileen how much he hated her, he picked up the precious statue and threw it at the wall, where it smashed into a thousand pieces along with Eileen's heart. After that, the bureau stood empty and bare and void of the words of an angst-ridden novel.

My life goals were definitely different from Eileen's. Every year I wrote goals on the first page of my diary. I wrote goals for twenty years' time, ten years' time, five years' time, and twelve months' time.

"To restore a beautiful house in an exotic country near a lake or a river and fill it with interesting things from antique markets" had been on my list of "to dos" since I was twelve years old. I taught my kids to do the same, to set goals without restraint. To think of a life without limits. Luca's were always simply to draw and learn everything. Izzy wanted to be an actor, but a specific type.

"I want to tell stories on TV and in movies, not on stage, and I don't want to be famous."

"Well, being a successful actor on TV usually involves fame. Maybe look at other careers in the industry behind the camera: a director or a writer perhaps?" I suggested, and with encouragement she got a camcorder from Santa that Christmas and soon decided directing wasn't for her. She didn't want to write the stories she wanted to tell the stories of others—she *needed* to be an actor. There were no acting schools where we lived, so she studied movies, pausing each scene, taking notes, and watched *Inside the Actors Studio* over and over, James Lipton quizzing top actors about their acting methods and techniques.

When she was sixteen, she landed herself a small part in a soap opera. As she was a minor, I needed to chaperone. This meant leaving the house at 5:30 a.m. to drive two hours to Dublin, sit around the studio all day, and then drive the two hours home when she was finished. She'd always thank me and I'd joke, "No need to thank me. You can just buy me a villa in Italy when you are a successful non-famous actor."

This kept both our dreams alive.

While things like "Own a camper van," "Restore a house," "Be a photographer," "Learn languages," "Travel the world," and "Do yoga" were on my goals list, having babies never featured. I thought it might happen someday, but it wasn't a "goal." As soon as I met Ronan, I knew he was the one. He looked a lot younger than his age, which turned out to be sixteen years my senior. He had great stories and experiences that guys my age didn't have. I wasn't looking for a baby maker; I was only twenty-two and had a backpacking trip around the world planned to within an inch of its life. He was a photographer and a painter, and I was an aspiring magazine publisher.

He was the first guy I went out with who had a car; a Renault 4 van, with the lid of a biscuit tin covering the rusted hole in the floor of the passenger side and moss decorating the window surrounds. It didn't have a key, just a button he had rigged which, along with a tap of hammer under the hood at a very particular point on the engine, jump started it. He put off meeting my family for months with the excuse that he didn't want to be embarrassed having to get the hammer out to start the engine. Instead, when he dropped me home I would have to jump out of the car while it was still edging along. But it was a car, and Ronan knew great places to explore: forests, beaches, old ruins.

We'd escape to a deserted caravan his family used to use for holidays near the sea, and he'd cook pasta bakes with lemon and hollandaise sauce; introduced me to Ayurvedic cooking for the first time, which he'd learned while training to be a transcendental meditation teacher in Kent twenty years previously.

We'd paint and write and visit antique markets. He went through a phase of buying old radios, the big clunky ones with veneered casings, and rigging them all up together to make a surround-sound system for the caravan connected to his CD player so he could blast the Beatles even louder than usual. It worked well until one day we went for a long walk on the beach and came back to a smoldering heap where our little love shack used to be, the radios with connecting wires still blazing.

Chapter 3

AFTER A YEAR OF BEING TOGETHER AS A COUPLE, I PARKED MY *Work Your Way Around the World* book on the top shelf and replaced it with *Pregnancy and Parenting*. The thought of having kids with Ronan was really exciting; we were both impatient creatives and couldn't wait to see what our combined recipe would produce. It took Eileen six years to conceive, so I presumed, being her sister, it would take me some time too.

Bingo! We conceived the first time we tried.

I wasn't expecting that. I thought we'd have a longer time having fun trying; at least a few years. I was in shock. This was serious; it was no longer an airy-fairy idea. This was a lifelong project that I wasn't sure I was ready for. The idea was great, but now that it was real, I was having serious moments of doubt: Was I ready for this? Was I mad? Did I jump into this too soon?

Ten weeks later, the day after we told my parents about the pregnancy, I woke up with cramps and bleeding. We lost our baby. It was like the universe had listened and said, "That was a trial run. Here's your opportunity to change your mind: Are you really ready yet to handle the soul we have lined up for you?" To which I answered, "One hundred percent, yes."

I no longer had doubts. I knew then that, more than anything, I wanted to be the mother of that soul floating around. Two months later I was in the doctor's clinic for an appointment, as I hadn't had a period since the miscarriage, so a D and C was scheduled.

"As part of the procedure, we'll do a pregnancy test first as a precaution."

It was like they were rubbing the sadness in with salt, but I peed in the jar, the doc stuck the stick test in it, shook it, and left it aside on his desk. I started working through my written list of questions about the D and C; I wanted to be prepared. The doctor started to answer. On the third question, he looked up from his desk.

"Oh, congratulations! It seems you are pregnant."

"That's not funny…I know it's the 1st of April, but that's not funny."

"I assure you I am not joking; there is a very faint line if you look carefully at the test. See."

He handed me the stick. I stared at the faintest of blue lines showing.

"It's probably just hormones left over from the miscarriage?"

"No, that is not how it works," he said, smiling.

My heart felt like it was growing bigger with every breath I took.

We moved into my family's little bungalow and got married that July, in the back garden as my parents had forty years previously. Izzy, the best April Fool's joke ever, was born the following December.

Speed forwards ten years. Ten very full years. Years of business drama, joy, and another miscarriage, followed by another much-wanted baby, this time a son. Travel; two houses; chaos; lots of chaos; addiction; business failure; chaos; despair; gut-wrenching sadness; suicide attempts; depression; chaos; struggle; calm. Ten years of absolute chaos, but also lots of moments of the extreme joy that having children brings.

Ronan's years of bachelorhood had him in the habit of drinking every evening, which gradually grew into not just every evening but every morning and every afternoon also. I thought moving from the pressure and chaos of the city would help, so we bought a nice house in the country. It didn't work.

My parents built a studio in the back garden, and Eileen, who had gone through years of an abusive marriage, left Assface and moved up the road from us.

She too found alcohol a comfort and an emotional crutch. Between the ages of twenty-four and thirty-four, I watched two of the people I loved most in the world being destroyed by alcohol. After a decade of chaos, Ronan gave up drink and never went back. Eileen's sobriety was more sporadic. She would be doing great, but Assface always knew how to push her buttons to bring her back down to despair.

Around the same time, the not-too-shabby career I had grown in print magazine publishing began looking unstable with the rise of the internet, so I started doing some freelance copy writing for a new wedding magazine. One of my first assignments, "The Top-10 Destination Wedding Locations," had me enthralled; Mauritius, Saint

Lucia, New York, Spain, and Italy. I got to explore their luxury venues from my sofa, and after doing interviews with luxury venue managers in each city, they inevitably wrote in their final email: "Thank you so much for including us. Please do come stay a couple of nights as our guest to experience what we have to offer."

Of course, it wouldn't be practical to fly to Mauritius to stay two nights at one hotel, but an idea started to grow. Through the online wedding magazine, I opened an advice section to get ideas for articles based on couples' questions. The more I researched and wrote about weddings, the more I saw a pattern in the questions newly engaged couples had.

"How do I choose a venue without visiting a country?"

"What are the legal requirements for a church wedding in Italy?"

"Can you help me find a venue within an hour of an airport in...?"

I became obsessed. Destination-wedding research fed my love of travel research and logistical organizing. Within a couple of months I became the go-to person online for anything about destination weddings. Then someone asked, "What is your fee to plan our wedding in Malaga?"

I tentatively looked back on the contacts I had made in Spain and reached out to Dyana, an English wedding planner based there. "Sure, why don't you come over for a week. I'll arrange for you to stay at some venues so you can experience what is on offer. Bring your family and then I can be your on-the-ground planner here for any clients you get."

So, within two weeks, even though we hadn't taken a salary in three months from our struggling magazine business, I had booked cheap flights to Malaga for us and our twelve- and five-year-olds. We were picked up by a luxury car and whisked off to a five-star hotel, where we were greeted with drinks and the bell boy instantly called to bring us to our room, which we weren't told the number of at check-in.

In the lift we went past the first few floors and continued upwards, right to the top, where the door of the presidential suite was opened for us, revealing our bags already neatly placed, a bucket of champagne on ice, and a huge bowl of fruit that the kids launched into before running off to explore the expansive suite.

"This is different from the holidays in tents we go on," yelped Luca, out of breath from running from the terrace, looking down at one of the four pools, to each of the two balconies out of sight further down the suite.

Ronan popped open the champagne and poured me a glass.

"Do you miss it?" I asked, feeling a little sad that he couldn't share a glass to celebrate our first ever night in a luxury hotel.

"Camping or drinking?" he answered, joking while pouring. "No, not at all. I'm not sure about this or camping though. Give me a few days," he said, kicking off his shoes and flopping back onto the super-king-size bed in front of the terrace windows.

We had six nights spread over three luxury hotels, with days full of boat trips, tours of churches and beaches, meetings with vendors, and sumptuous meals without putting our hands in our pockets. "I know this sounds weird, and I know I joked about it on the first day, but while this is all amazing, I prefer camping," Ronan said, tucking into his filet steak on the last night. "I mean, they're all just bedrooms after all: you've seen one, you've seen them all."

I was not sold on his argument. "I like camping, but I could definitely get used to five-star luxury. One thing is for sure: if this is what
destination-wedding research is all about, I'm starting a wedding-
planning business."

"Do you really want to deal with crazy brides? I mean, you wanted
us to elope to avoid all the fuss because you said you couldn't stand
weddings."

"It's not a career that has ever been on any of my 'must do' lists,
that's for sure, but we don't have many options at the moment."

Reality was beginning to creep back in after six days of leaving
our troubles in the departure lounge of the airport, but I knew they
would be there to greet us with extra bells on as soon as we landed
back home.

"The freelance work is sporadic, and the only way we're currently
paying the mortgage is with that PR client Sarah sent me, but that
contract ends in May. I don't know how we're going to pay the mortgage after that. Even with a wedding-planning business, it will take a
year or two before we start to make money from it. The potential is
good, but it would be a slow burner."

"Don't be worrying; things always work out... Are you eating
that potato?"

I pushed my plate towards him. I had lost my appetite, and just
as he hadn't convinced me about camping, he hadn't sold me on the
"things always work out" plan either.

While I did appreciate the two years of tranquility after the storm
that had been our lives during the drinking years, living under the
pressure of a high mortgage on a shiny house wasn't how I wanted

my life to be. Life had also become ordinary and predictable. I was restless. This trip had triggered my appetite for adventure again, for a challenge. Something had to change.

Chapter 4

A FEW WEEKS LATER, THERE WAS A STORM WHIPPING UP OUT-side, so I plonked down in front of the TV with a mug of tea and mindlessly browsed through the TV channels.

"This week we are visiting Asturias, on the north coast of Spain," announced the presenter on *A Place in the Sun*, a TV program where people go house hunting for properties abroad. The word "Spain" was enough for me to settle on that channel for some sofa escapism back to warm beaches.

I'd never heard of Asturias before—in front of me there were landscapes of rugged, beautiful beaches and forests. It was similar to Ireland but with bigger mountains and warmer weather. The houses they were being shown started at eleven thousand euro.

"That's unreal!" I pressed record. "Ronan, come look at this."

By the time Ronan came into the room, I had already googled houses for sale in Asturias, gotten one of the kids' school copy books, and was working the figures.

"Sit and look." I rewound back to the start. "How about we move to Spain?" I said enthusiastically.

"No! I liked Malaga but it's all a bit touristy and 'Tally ho, look at my yacht' for us, don't you think?"

"No, not Malaga. Here," I said, using the remote as a pointer I flicked off the pause button.

He watched the rolling hills, the sea, the renovation projects, the stone houses, the beaches, the sun, and the prices and then said exactly what I was thinking. "What are we doing here?"

I stuck my page of scribbles in front of his face.

"My wedding niche can be Spain. Eileen can do the marketing here and we can be on-site there. We sell this house, build a place in Eileen's for Mam and Dad, pay off all our bills, and we would still have enough to buy a place outright in Spain for, say, one hundred thousand euro, put in forty thousand to do it up, and still have twenty thousand to live off for the year while the wedding bookings kick in. I do the planning and you do the photography. What do you think?"

"That," he said, pointing at my page of scribbles, arrows, and numbers, "doesn't make any sense to me, but what you are saying does. I'm in."

And that was the decision made. Like when we decided to get married. Like when we decided to have a baby. One would float an idea and, if the other agreed, we didn't wait around. Life was too short.

Eileen was the only one we told about our plan to move to Spain. We didn't want to upset my parents with the idea of a big dramatic move; we'd ease them into it. Part of our plan was that, with the profit we made from the house, we would buy something we had both always wanted, a dream purchase—a camper van. So we told my parents we were buying a camper van to travel for a few months around Europe before returning to Ireland to find a cheaper house. The return to Ireland was a lie. As far as they were concerned, we were going on a long holiday. We'd gradually let them get used to the idea that we were not coming back other than for visits.

Within three weeks we'd applied for the planning permission for the studio in Eileen's garden. Eileen was as excited as we were, and with her biz-whizz brain, she had spreadsheets done and a business plan for our destination-wedding business submitted for funding.

While Eileen and I differed in lots of ways, other than our similar faces, our voices, and our identical laughs, both our brains connected and got excited about business development and project planning. She would be the elegant front-of-house face of the business while I stayed happily working behind the scenes in far-off Spain. The perfect partnership.

We had cozy evening meetings about marketing and sales funnels, drinking tea and eating cake in front of the fire while listing things we needed to get, from aisle runners and lanterns to business cards.

The website was up in no time and the first inquiries were coming in, which was just as well, as our magazine business fell flat on its face and we closed its doors.

Eileen found an ad on the supermarket noticeboard for "Spanish Lessons in Your Own Home by Native Speaker. Call Victor."

"I know you wouldn't get around to doing it, so I've already booked him. He's coming on Wednesday evening at six o'clock. I'll do them too, for when I visit you; it will be fun," she said.

For an hour before his arrival, Eileen and I debated what Victor would be like. She had been texting him and had established he was from Brazil but his mother was from Costa Rica, so he spoke both Spanish and Portuguese.

"Maybe he'll be like one of those Brazilian footballers. All tanned and muscly," she said, washing the final dinner plate and handing it to me to dry.

"He's probably a student, over here on an exchange and trying to earn a bit of cash."

"Even better; a young Brazilian footballer."

"Hey, he's coming here to teach Spanish to us and the kids, not for you to flirt with," I said.

The doorbell rang and we both hurried to the door and threw it open like a big makeover reveal on TV; I was still holding the plate and tea towel.

Both our eyes dropped from the tall level we were expecting. There stood what looked like a slightly tubby politician probably canvasing for the next local election.

"*Hola, buenas tardes. Soy Victor*, and you must be the signoras?" said the gray-bearded but perfectly groomed face with smiley eyes behind dark-blue rimmed glasses. He took Eileen's hand and kissed it.

"This is the first lesson of how a Spanish gentleman greets a lady," he said, winking at Luca, who was standing by my side. "I recognize you. We are members of the same club."

Neither Eileen nor I knew what he was talking about, but we

led him into the kitchen, where we all sat eagerly around the kitchen table, ready to receive the gift of fluency.

"I teach a little differently. Some words are the same or very similar in Spanish to English, so when I tell you a word that is similar," he said as he looked at Izzy and Luca, "I want you to imagine a lot of spaghetti on top of that thing."

Ronan pulled a face at me, and I threw back a "give him a chance" glare.

"So Izzy, I have heard you want to be an actor?" Eileen had been texting him a lot, it seemed.

"The word for actor is the same in Spanish, so let us all imagine a lot of spaghetti on top of Izzy's head."

The kids were in convulsions.

"The same is for 'taxi.' I want you to think of lots of spaghetti on top of a taxi. Got it?"

We all nodded. Tears rolled down Luca's face from laughing at the thought of Izzy with pasta on her head.

"So now you already know two words in Spanish. Next I teach you through song and dance. Everybody up."

Ronan looked horrified.

Half an hour after Victor had left, the kids were still walking around the room chanting and clapping:

> *Treinta días trae septiembre,*
> *Con abril, junio, y noviembre.*
> *De veintiocho solo hay uno,*
> *Y los demás treinta y uno.*

He had not only taught them some Spanish but also the number of days each month has. He was booked to come back on Wednesday; we were going to do three lessons a week. "I can't come on Tuesdays, but I'll see you at the club, Eileen." It clicked with us both; he was in AA.

"Why haven't I seen him before?" Eileen said after he'd gone. I caught the twinkle in her eye that had been missing for so long.

"Because you are not going there to date; you are going there to stay sober, remember?"

Building the business had taken her mind off her personal battles, the always-bubbling conflicts with Assface, and her ongoing battle with the bottle. And now there was this new interest, Victor, whose family's vineyard was his Achilles' heel. He was in Ireland to escape from it and rebuild his sobriety. This whole move to Spain was not just a new start for us but for Eileen too.

Within three weeks of putting the house up for sale, we had two bidders fighting for it. We closed the sale early in the peak month for house sales in Ireland's Celtic Tiger economy boom. We signed the deal, and the deposit was paid, contracts signed, and a close date fixed for Midsummer's Day. There was no turning back now.

To celebrate, we went to look at camper vans, put a deposit down, and gave a post-dated check for the balance on a midrange van big enough for the four of us. We would soon be on our way to Spain, and it was all becoming very real.

We began clearing clutter, donating to charity shops, and packing up boxes that would go into storage until we found a place in Spain. Mam and Dad moved to the holiday caravan they had on a small plot further south, while the building of their new place would be completed by the end of the summer.

The business, under Eileen's stewardship, was flying along. She was networking and doing stands at wedding shows and being a new, improved version of her old self again. Victor had nearly become part of the kitchen furniture. Three times a week he was there to give lessons, and he called in for a coffee two other days a week before he and Eileen went to their "club" together.

He taught us to tango to the words of the nursery rhyme:

> *Bailaba la niña alegre, en una noche estrellada.*
> *Moviase al son del aire, bajo la luna de plata.*

> *The cheerful girl danced on a starry night.*
> *She moved to the sound of the air, under the silver moon.*

> *Con el corazón muy blanco,*
> *Y mariposas en el alma*

> *With a very white heart,*
> *And butterflies in her soul*

> *Danzaba la alegre niña,*
> *Bajo la noche estrellada*

> *The happy girl was dancing,*
> *Under the starry night.*

The kids and Eileen were naturals, rhyming off the songs and ditties after he left. However, I was sure Eileen was cheating and getting additional lessons outside class hours. All I remembered after each class was a random phrase he taught us: *El burro es malo* (The donkey is bad), which I was sure would come in handy at some point in our life in Spain.

Victor left for a three-week visit to Brazil to see family. He would be back before we left, just in time for our going-away party, at which he had already "booked" the first dance with Eileen.

"Luca, you must practice the tango with your aunt while I am gone, because the next time I go to Brazil she will be coming with me to show off her tango skills."

Eileen was delighted and I was jealous.

"Why won't you whisk me off to Brazil to dance the tango," I whined at Ronan. "Because I am not Brazilian and I have two left feet. I'll whisk you off to Spain and let you relax, how about that?"

There was just one thing left for me to do before our going-away party, and that was to sign off the PR contract with the client, which was coming to an end. The client had no idea what their contract meant to me. To them, it was just the successful launch and conclusion of an educational event, but we had timed the end of our lives in Ireland and our new lives in Spain to match the end of this contract. Once this was done, I was free.

I drove to Dublin for the wrap-up meeting with Sarah, the owner of the PR company I had been freelancing for. I planned to stay in town after the meeting to get a few final bits and pieces for the trip and then take the evening train home.

As I shook the client's hand at the end of the meeting, I started to well up. He looked at me a little oddly but was flattered that his event meant so much to me. I didn't care that he didn't realize I was furiously shaking his hand because as soon as I let go, my life was going to flip to another chapter, a whole new exciting volume for me and my family. As he released my grip and opened the door to freedom, my phone buzzed. I ignored it.

He walked us down the steps, and after Sarah's less enthusiastic handshake, my phone buzzed again and I ignored it. A woman walked by pushing a buggy. Pink pajamas clashed with the red teething cheeks of the cranky baby inside, biting a soft ball made up of multicolored hexagons. The mother's face told of sleepless nights and lonely days. A little girl in navy uniform skipping alongside was twirling her doll around, her elasticated school tie wrapped around the rag doll's waist, turning her into a bird or a plane or perhaps an angel.

As I dodged a man jogging past, just as I got into Sarah's car, my phone buzzed again. This time I answered it. It was Ronan. "Hey, sorry, we were just finishing the meeting, so couldn't answer."

"Are you on your own?"

There was a car coming up the cobbled road towards us faster than permitted.

"No, Sarah is here. We're in her car; she's dropping me in town. What's up?"

The baby propelled the ball from the buggy in a fit of temper, and the little girl ran after it as it bounced onto the road, but the car didn't see her. "Something's happened…" Ronan's voice was shaking. I was holding my breath at the scene unfolding in front of me. I could hear Ronan was somewhere he shouldn't have been, an echoing corridor, an announcement, "Will Doctor…", a faint siren in the background.

In a split second the jogger grabbed the little girl's arm and pulled her back, the mother scolding her for doing something so stupid. "It's Eileen. She's…"

If they had been in a different place, the mother would have been praising her for picking up after her baby sister. If that man had not been there, things would have gone differently. The girl's life could have been very different, and the sister's life changed forever.

Ronan's words claimed back my full attention. "Eileen is…dead."

Chapter 5

RONAN HAD FOUND HER. THE NEIGHBOR CALLED HIM, AS Eileen's dog had been barking for hours. Her loyal dog, Toby, was lying on the bed by her side. She had her dinner cooking on the steamer. She'd gone in to have a lie down and just never woke up. A brain aneurysm.

The day before, Eileen and I were choosing whether to buy a red or cream aisle runner for our wedding business. Now I stood in a room full of coffins, choosing one for my only sister, ironically wishing she were here to help with the decision. She was such a better planner than me.

All the coffins were so ugly and morbid, except for one. It didn't have religious pictures all over it, or shiny lacquer, or elaborate handles—it was plain, natural, simple, and kind looking. I chose that one. The undertaker said it wasn't finished, but Eileen would have liked it, if you can like your own coffin. I put her makeup bag and Opium perfume in the casket with her. She never went anywhere without them.

I went into auto mode, organizing the funeral, the wake, dealing with Assface, being the strength my parents needed. The day after the funeral, Maurice the estate agent called, "The buyers are wondering if we could bring the move forwards a week to two weeks' time." I had forgotten the house sale.

"Oh, Maurice, I… Eil…my sister…she died last week… We need more time."

Maurice was apologetic, but I wasn't listening. I could see a shadowed outline of a person through the fogged glass of the front door. Luca ran to answer the bell before I had time to think what to say. I knew the shape.

I walked away out of sight into the conservatory, the phone still to my ear, Maurice still talking. "Hello, are you still there?"

"Yes, sorry Maurice. Please ask the buyers for more time. I've got to go, someone is at the door."

"Mammy, Victor is here; he's back from holiday. I'll get Izzy and our Spanish books from Nanny's."

"*No*, Luca. Go over to Nanny's and stay there until I call you. There won't be Spanish classes today. Where is he?"

"In the sitting room."

"Oh God, the cards."

I ran to the sitting room and froze at the door. Victor stood in front of the fireplace, holding one of the sympathy cards open, reading someone's nice thoughts in the card titled "Sorry for the Loss of Your Sister." His eyes were glassing quickly.

"I got back last night. I tried to call her but she did not answer then or today. I thought she might be here. What happened?"

"Aunty Eileen is gone to heaven," piped up Luca from behind me.

"I told you to go to Nanny's *now*." I opened the front door and pointed around the side of the house. Luca jogged off, kicking his ball in front of him.

I was back in the sitting room within seconds, but Victor was already sitting on the sofa sobbing, leaking big, juicy tears, which I was envious off. No one had even cried like that at the funeral. He had no business being so…so vocal. How dare he? How dare he cry so much about my dear sister when he'd only known her a wet week? I'd known her all my life and I had only cried… I hadn't cried at all… and here he was sobbing so much he was finding it hard to breathe.

"It was an aneurysm," I said, standing in the door, wary of entering the room in case the intensity of the grief was contagious.

"I don't know this word."

"It means a bleed in her brain. She was asleep; she's okay." What a stupid thing for me to say. "I mean it will be okay." Another stupid thing for me to say.

He looked at me in disbelief. "She was the most beautiful soul I ever met. I know I only knew her a small time, but she was so kind. I had seen her at the meetings for months, listened to her stories, watched her help everyone. So when she opened the door here, I couldn't believe it was her. At the meetings she was everyone's rock."

"That was her problem; Eileen was everyone's rock but her own. She looked after everyone and put herself last."

"Problem? It was not a problem; it was a gift. '*Con el corazón muy blanco y mariposas en el alma.*'"

I didn't know where to look, my body twitching. I picked at a drip-lump of paint on the doorframe with my nail. I tried not to remember what the words meant, but I did. *With a very white heart and butterflies in her soul.*

"Victor, I'm sorry but you've got to go. I have a lot to do." My nail broke.

"I understand; I am being so selfish." He dried his tears on his sleeve and stood up, composing himself. "I am so sorry for your loss…"

He pulled me into an involuntary bear hug and walked quickly out the front door but paused while his foot was still in the way of my closing the door.

"Call me when you are ready to start classes again."

"There won't be any more classes, Victor. We're not going; we can't go now. My parents need… Goodbye, Victor, okay." I hastened.

He nodded and at last his foot moved enough for me to close the door and slam my back against it and against what had been brought into my house in the last ten minutes. Victor brought big, sobbing grief. Maurice had brought realization: I had no sister, no income, and in three weeks I'd have nowhere for my family, including my elderly parents, to live. Without Eileen I had no business, and there was no way I could move abroad and leave my parents. They had just lost one daughter; I couldn't let them feel they had lost the second also.

Trying to catch my breath, I ran from the front door as if the hall floor were a crocodile-infested river I needed to cross, with the bedroom door being the safe bank. I slammed that door too, locked it shaking, and with my back against it, tried to grab air into my lungs. My knees gave way and I succumbed to the infection of Victor's sobbing grief.

I awoke to knocking. The room was dark. I was still on the floor and I could hear Ronan's voice close to the other side of the door.

"Rosie, Rosie."

Slowly, I picked myself up, unlocked the door, and found my way to the bedside lamp. "What time is it?"

"It's half past eight, I thought you might want to have something to eat?" he said gently, sitting down beside me on the bed and putting his arm around me. "Are you okay?"

"Half past eight?"

I'd been on the floor for over six hours; my gluey eyes told me that I'd probably cried for two and slept for four.

"You needed the sleep; you've been going like a robot for the last couple of weeks."

He didn't know I had been on the floor the whole time. I cuddled into him, hiding from the overwhelming sense of fear that was sweeping over me.

"She was only forty-six, here one day and gone the next. She's not coming back. It's so final." He pulled me closer, but it didn't ease the empty void I could now physically feel, a void I felt my equally fragile human body and mind could be sucked into at any moment. I was never scared of death before, but now it terrified me.

The next morning there was a text waiting from Maurice. Even after they heard our news, the buyers were unwilling to move the date. We were to be out in three weeks' time, as agreed. A "Plan B" needed to be thrown together. As if they could read my thoughts, Mam texted me and asked us to come to theirs for breakfast. We followed the smell of sausages and bacon mingled with fried tomatoes and mushrooms and freshly brewed tea across the garden to their studio.

"We've been thinking: we know you can't keep this place, so we'd like to get this." Dad handed Ronan a brochure: *Mobile Cabins, Your Instant Luxury Country Home.* Dad continued, "We saw them at a trade show a couple of years ago, and we were thinking of putting them on our plot before we built this place. They're really fantastic, well insulated, kitted out, fully furnished."

I looked at the brochure. "Yes, they look nice, but why not build a little house instead? It would hold its value better."

"Ah, will you stop," said Dad impatiently. "We're not interested in value, and we're too old to be waiting on planning permission and something to be built. We want something now that is comfortable. This is the perfect solution."

"We called them this morning and got prices for a fully furnished two-bedroom cabin. It's sixty thousand. They're very swanky, and they can have it to us within a week of ordering," said Mam, pouring coffee for Ronan. I gulped my tea; our original plan and calculations would have left us enough to buy a place in Spain, restore it, and still have enough to live on for twelve to eighteen months. But the mobile home was double the cost of the studio build for which we had initially budgeted. Mam's face looked more relaxed for the first time in weeks, and Dad seemed a bit more animated. It would be a great distraction for them, and there wasn't really any other solution.

"Well if that's what you want, then let's do it!"

As soon as the money for our house came through, we bought them a two-bedroom, fully furnished mobile cabin for sixty thousand euro. We paid off our bills, the solicitor's fees for the house sale, and all our loans. The fund was dwindling fast.

Two days before we were due to hand over the keys of our house, Mam and Dad's land was finished being prepped, their old caravan was crushed, and the spanking new mobile home put in place just in the nick of time for them to move into.

For the first time since the chaos of finding Eileen's body, Ronan and I were alone with our kids. There were no visitors and no family staying. At last we had some silence, with forty-eight hours left in our home and no plan. We packed up boxes like robots, minds blank. The only thing we knew was that a removal van was arriving the next day at nine o'clock in the morning to take our stuff to a friend's garage for storage.

As we packed, a car horn beeped. I could hear the driveway gravel crunch under heavy tires.

"Bloody hell, did I get the day of the removal van wrong?" I looked out the window. "Oh, it's the camper van! Everyone outside."

In the blur of the last few weeks, we had completely forgotten about its arrival day. The sales guy was a jolly man, unaware of what had happened as he handed over the keys.

We didn't tell him; I'd had enough pitiful looks to last me a lifetime.

"There you are now. I've filled it full of diesel for you. Where you off to first?"

The kids climbed into it, excited, followed by me and Ronan. Side by side, watching the kids giddily discovering the tiny spaces, Ronan's fingers entwined mine and gave me a squeeze; a gush of warmth ran through my body. We had a home.

Chapter 6

I'D BOOKED OUR FERRY TICKET TO THE UK THE DAY WE AGREED on the sale of the house. The time had just flicked past us, and our leaving date was now in three days' time. The story we originally told Mam and Dad about us touring Europe for the summer and returning to find somewhere smaller had become reality. We just had no plan now.

We packed what we needed into the camper, took the road map of Europe out, and tried to work out what to do.

A long-term Facebook friend, Karen Craven, had seen my post about Eileen and had been messaging me ever since.

"If you are not going to Spain then why not come stay at ours in Italy, or you can stay in the rental we manage next door if it's free. The owners let us use it for friends and family at a cut rate."

It seemed like a good option. It was the only option. So an immediate plan emerged: travel through France, stopping in campsites along the way, and by the time we got to Italy, we may have thought of a plan for our futures. The removal van arrived the next morning and they set to work. We lifted the kids out of their beds and sat them at the breakfast table for the last time. When they went back to their rooms to get dressed, their beds were gone, and when they returned to the kitchen to tell us that their beds were gone, the kitchen table was gone.

I gave the floors a final sweep and stepped out of the house, pulling the door behind me. I didn't look back. The last ten years had been filled with sadness and chaos; stepping away from this house and looking forwards at my children was a step away from the negativity of the past and a step into a more positive future.

We stopped overnight at Mam and Dad's on the way to the ferry. It was the first time we saw their cabin, and the first time they saw our camper van.

As we drove through their gates, it looked like the cabin had been there for years. They had already planted roses and geraniums along the front, and a nameplate, "Daisy Dell," was secured by the door. They didn't hear us come in over the banging of a hammer.

"What you building, Dad?" I called out, following the sound of hammering behind the mobile.

"Ah, you made it! I'm building a deck for your mother to sun herself on. I'm going to build a pond there and put gnomes around it to catch the goldfish. Your mother is in there; go on in to her." He didn't make eye contact with me but walked quickly past, taking Luca's hand. "Izzy and Luca, show me this camper van of yours. I'm dying to see if our new home on wheels is better than yours."

I found Mam in the sitting room with her sewing machine out.

"Hey you! What you making?"

"Oh, you've arrived! I didn't hear you come in with all the banging your father is doing. I'm making new curtains for in here and matching cushions for the chairs."

"But Mam, it's beautiful the way it is," I said, looking at the tastefully furnished room in cream and the taupe three-piece suite with matching curtains.

"Ah no, I hate browns; too drab for my liking," she said as she sewed the bright orange fabric. "I'm going to paint a mural of sunflowers all around the room."

"Oh Jesus," I said, not meaning to be audible.

It has been the story of my life, Mam painting madcap wall murals all over the house, with outlandish decor ideas, and Dad helping her follow them through, with the structural side made from recycled wardrobes, chipboard, and straightened rusty nails. Although they were constantly redoing our home, I don't think they ever bought a piece of wood or a nail. Everything was remodeled from something that was no longer needed. Homebuilt wardrobes became flooring, and floorboards became homebuilt wardrobes. Even now, with a spanking new cabin, which was probably created by an interior designer, they were pulling it apart to put their own gaudy stamp on it.

"Here, what am I thinking? I'll just finish sewing this side and I'll show you around, and then we'll make dinner, or do you want a sandwich and some tea first? You must be starving."

The cabin was impressive—a large kitchen, a walk-in wardrobe, a large bedroom with more built-in storage than we had in our house growing up, a small utility room, and a decent-size bathroom with an entrance from the main bedroom and hall.

"So how are you doing?" I asked while I peeled spuds and watched my dad play lawn darts with the kids. I was mentioning the unmentionable.

"Will I make gravy?" She opened the fridge and stuck her head in, rooting in the vegetable drawer even though the broccoli was already prepared on the counter.

There was a silence between us.

"I go to ring her about five times a day still." She stopped rooting but remained behind the open fridge door.

"Yeah, me too. She was always ringing, at least three times a day to both you and me. I don't know how she had time to do anything else... What about Dad; how is he?"

She closed the fridge and started putting the chicken in the oven.

"He seems to just want to pretend it didn't happen. He won't talk about her, won't let me put her picture up. When you called yesterday..."

"I know; he called me Eileen... I could hear him pause afterwards. I know you both have called me Eileen most of my life, and Jim, Peter, and Peter, Tony or Jim."

Mam laughed a little.

"It's hard to believe she's not here anymore."

"Only physically not here; she'll still be around us," she said, fiddling with the knobs of the oven more than necessary. I couldn't swallow and turned my back to look out the window. "So Dad said he's building you a deck to sun yourself on?"

"I haven't sunned myself a single day in the fifty-five years of being married to him. He says these things to make it sound like we are living a life of luxury on a yacht in the Bahamas."

We laughed harder and longer than the joke deserved, so the tears could freely run from our eyes disguised as joy.

But, it was true; Mam wouldn't be able to sit still long enough to "sun herself." She was always too busy baking something, making tea, finding someone to feed with multiple offers of soup and sandwiches, painting, or sewing something. The coming months of waves of grief were going to be hard for them both, but at least they had each other. And the new cabin would keep them busy as they made it their own palace through the summer.

Early the following morning, Dad and I stood side by side, watching Mam stuff cellophane-wrapped sandwiches into every orifice of the camper van and hug the kids goodbye for the fifteenth time.

"She lives for those kids. Come back, won't you?" he said.

He knew me too well. Perhaps they'd known our Spain plan all along.

"Of course, Dad." I grabbed him and hugged him tight, even though he resisted. "We'll be back soon."

"Take care, and don't eat all those sandwiches at the same time." He walked back to the door of the cabin; his face was in the shadow, but we could still see him wave. "Come on, Mary," he shouted at Mam. "Let them be off; they'll miss the boat."

We put on a brave face saying goodbye, but we were none the wiser of what our future plans were. Ronan and I tossed out ideas about what we could do all the way to the ferry port, and then from the ferry port all the way through France and down into Italy. All the way I was grieving without crying, but arriving in Italy was a great distraction. The drivers were bloody crazy.

Chapter 7

RONAN HAD BEEN DRIVING FOR EIGHT HOURS SOLID; WE NEEDED to find somewhere to stop for the night, eat, and have a shower. We traversed over dizzying Scalextric-style motorways with coastal towns dotted below.

"How do we get down there?"

The GPS TomTom thing wasn't working. I flicked around the map to try to find a town to exit into.

"I need to pee," groaned Luca.

"Take this exit, not that one, the next one, the one for Nervi," I shouted.

"Are you sure?"

"Yes!"

I wasn't, but decisiveness was called for. The road wound down around at what felt like a seventy-degree drop. With a right-hand drive car in a left-hand drive country, I was on the inside, with cars and trucks whizzing at me around precarious bends. *Thunk*; one clipped the wing mirror.

"Move out a bit."

"I can't. The drop below is ridiculous, and I am already hanging over the edge of it."

I glanced and felt sick. "I can't look."

"Neither can I."

"You keep your eyes open. You are doing great," I lied. I didn't know how he was doing, as my eyes were squeezed shut.

Finally, we reached the end of the drop and wiggled our way along an ever-narrowing road lined with cars, scooters, and Italian-style three-wheeled rickshaws. Everyone in the town must have been in the store on the left, with the peeling paint facade and no name, just "Supermercato," toilet rolls and bottles of water stacked in its windows, separated by some hanging brooms and dustpans.

A selection of stalls beside the building, packed into a small car park, explained why everyone needed to park along the street. Nonnas with their grandchildren jumping around their feet chattered away loudly to each other while haggling over the price of fish. A group of old men playing cards in the shade of the store's awning. My window was down, and the warm air drifted in and filled the van.

"I smell oranges. Can we stop and get oranges? I'm starving," said Izzy, lifting her head from her book.

"No, the smell is the sea, and I still need to pee," countered Luca, not taking his eyes off the umpteenth monster drawing he'd worked on since the start of the trip.

"Soon you'll get to pee. You are doing great—just hang in there," I shouted back.

There was nowhere to turn around, but Ronan somehow managed to do an eight-point turn between the scooters and bikes, while I just sweated and made unhelpful gasping noises.

"Well, there's nothing here, so I presume we go back to the main road and find another town?" He wasn't asking my opinion. He was already driving back along the road we came down, which was easier than arriving since we were now on the inside, beside the cliff, so only faced the danger of tumbling rocks, which the road signs warned of, rather than of our tumbling down off the road edge. Back at the motorway intersection, the traffic was flittering along without a break.

"How the hell are we supposed to join in the stream?"

"I can't see; tell me when we are clear to go," he said to me, now that I was sitting on the outside. I felt like I was being asked to shout directions at a blind man to help him cross six lanes of traffic at rush hour. Ronan gave up on me and somehow merged onto the motorway. He was wrecked and we were all starving. We needed to find a stop soon.

"Take this exit."

"This? Are you sure?"

"Yes!" I was doing it again. I had no clue. I should have known by the name; first I brought him to Nervi, and now we were doing the same perilous descent with no result to a town called Sori. My eyes were closed and my head was in my hands. "I'm sorry, I'm sorry, I'm sorry I made you take the turn for Sori!"

He was silent.

Another eight-point turn to get back towards the motorway, but then we spotted a sign for Recco. After about five minutes I saw a hotel on the roadside. Villino Miramare.

"They have one family room left and they have parking," I was glad to announce after hopping out and running in to the reception ahead of everyone else spilling out of the van.

We collapsed on the bed for a few moments while Luca had his long-awaited pee, but there was no time to waste; the hotel's restaurant was closed, so we had to walk to the sea front in search of food. We bought four slices of pizza and some ice tea from a takeaway place and sat on the beach gobbling it down so fast that Ronan was off to buy more before the guy had another pizza out of the oven.

The sun was setting, and the kids were happy skipping stones on the water against a backdrop of oranges and pinks flaming the sky. I needed to walk after sitting for so long, and so I took myself down the beach. Alone, I breathed deeper than I had done in weeks, filling my lungs with salty air. I took off my shoes; my toes melted into the soft sand and were wrapped in warm water. I could live here, I thought.

She was with me—Eileen. I could feel her there, walking beside me, whispering on the breeze, "Everything is going to be all right."

The next day we were on our way to the Cravens' *casa* in Tuscany. Karen and John had moved to Italy from Devon five years previously with their two children, and from the pictures Karen posted, their lives seemed idyllic, living in the Tuscan hills surrounded by forests and uninterrupted views of rolling vineyards and wildflower fields.

While we were planning our move abroad, Karen had Skyped

me several times offering advice and gentle encouragement. Her suggestion that we come to stay in the holiday rental was the only solid thing we had to hold on to, and the only reason Italy ended up on our itinerary; it was somewhere to aim for in our plan of nothingness.

They lived between the beautiful towns of San Gimignano and Volterra. Finding their place would have been a challenge had they not met us on the road so we could follow them to their Hansel-and-Gretel-style house, two miles up a white track surrounded by forest.

Getting out of our cars, Karen and I hugged each other tightly. Although it was the first time we had physically met, we had been friends for years. We discovered we were the same height, had similar dyed hair color, and were wearing very similar clothes and exactly the same sandals.

"That's freaky," said one of the kids. "You look like twins."

John was a quiet giant of a man, with Kiwi blood flowing through his protruding veins. The long scars on his leg helped him explain why his professional rugby career was halted twenty-five years previously following a motorbike accident.

His shyness evaporated almost immediately when Ronan mentioned rugby season. While the men bonded over unusually shaped balls, and the kids competed for the highest bounce on the trampoline, Karen and I discovered we had yet another thing in common: we both liked getting sloshed on red wine while cooking epic dinners.

The following morning, I was up before everyone else, as usual. We opted to stay at the house rental a little further along the track rather than impose on our new friends. They were the only two houses for miles around, previously hunters' lodges, but had been purchased by an American who Karen and John had a cut-rate, long-term rental agreement with in exchange for looking after the short-term holiday rental we stayed at.

I was wondering why anyone would want to stay so far into the wilderness of Tuscany, but the uninterrupted sunset and sunrise from the pool deck soon explained it to me. I lowered myself into the pool and floated; a falcon circled far above in the blueness, playing with the wind. I stretched out my arms, mimicking him.

With the sun on my face and my eyes closed, I breathed in the scent of mint and surrounding lavender, floating, floating, then *boooom*. A massive explosion in the distance vibrated the terrace and caused ripples in the pool. My heart was thumping fast. I tried to stand but had drifted out of my depth, so I coughed and spluttered to the side and whooshed myself clumsily out of the pool, grazing my knee on the rough volcanic stone surround.

I tried to run but instead waddled to the house as both my legs had gone to jelly. Karen pulled up her car just as I reached the door; thank God she was here to save us.

"I'm off into town for a few errands; do you want to come?"

"What was that explosion?" I gasped, creating a puddle of pool water at the entrance.

"Oh that! That's the quarry on the other side of the hill. Sorry; we're so used to it at this stage, we forgot to warn you. They dynamite once a week, and sometimes flakes of plaster fall off our ceiling," she said, casually walking towards the front door. "Something else I forgot to show you…this," she continued, pointing at a small haversack inside the door.

"I left you an earthquake bag. If there is one, grab the bag as you are running out the door; it has all the essentials in it—change of knickers, crackers, water, nuts, bandages, cigarettes, and a small bottle of wine."

"Okay," I said faintly. "Give me a moment to get dried off and dressed."

"I'll make us a coffee."

Everyone was still asleep in the house, so I felt if they slept through that explosion, they'd sleep through an earthquake. No need to wake them to warn them and tell them about the emergency earthquake bag. I got dried, dressed quietly, and headed into town with Karen.

"Oh, sorry, I forgot to leave coffee in the cupboard for you guys, so we'll stop at a bar on the way."

Although it was not yet eight o'clock, the bar was busy, a meeting place for a quick espresso and a catch-up on news and gossip. A policeman in his immaculate Armani-designed uniform was being served before us. Karen noticed my astonished look as the barista took a bottle of grappa from the counter and added a dash to the coffee cup before handing it to him.

"It's called a caffè corretto, sets you up for the day ahead," she said, winking at me. "Do you want one? Might ease the head after all the wine we drank last night."

"No, I'll stick to a cappuccino, thanks."

He downed it in two, ciao-ed goodbye, and drove off in his police car.

As we wound our way up the road to the hilltop town of Volterra,

I noticed the imposing fortress high above the town. "Wow, that castle must have some great views. I'd love to check it out for weddings."

"I don't think you'd want to. It's a maximum-security prison. Although they do have a restaurant in part of it operated by the prisoners."

"Maximum-security prisoners running a restaurant and with the best view in the area?" I found myself saying for the first of many times, "Only in Italy."

Karen needed to go collect blood test results at the hospital, but rather than just go directly to the hospital car park, she parked a distance away so we could walk through the cobbled streets of Volterra. She also needed to pick up a school book for Chloe, so while she was at the bookshop, I lingered outside one of the alabaster workshops and watched a sculptor absorbed in smoothing the leg of a fine, mineralized woman among a crowded cavern of white, translucent bodies.

A couple and their two pet dogs walked past, the dogs' eyes a piercing ice blue. On second glance, I realized they were not normal pet dogs; they were wolves.

"You'll see that now and then, people with pet wolves," said Karen, catching up with me. "There are also wild wolves in the mountains. We see tracks near our place from time to time. We also have wild boar and the deer."

Wolves, earthquakes, and explosions; Karen and John's rustic life in the Tuscan hills didn't seem so idyllic after all.

"Oh, I know where I have to take you! As you are into weddings, I need to show you the town hall."

Up the steps of the medieval building, Karen's explanation in

Italian that I was an international wedding planner (even though I was not) got us into the *palazzo*'s civil ceremony room for free. Its powder-blue-and-gold vaulted ceilings and twelfth-century frescoed walls looked strangely familiar.

"They filmed one of the scenes for that vampire movie here, what's it called... *Twilight*."

"Ahh, that's how I know it. Izzy had me watch it three times."

"Oh, bloody hell. Talking of vampires, I need to get to the bloods clinic before they close for lunch. Come on."

We hiked to what appeared to be the back of the hospital, surrounded by woods, but with an imposing ghostly building on the left. Shards of glass lay beneath the tall, arched Victorian windows made up of individual rectangular panes; some were shattered, and those still intact were streaked with gray scum. The light breeze was amplified through the empty corridors and came our way through the creaking windows as a horror-movie howling wind. It was a warm day, but a freezing shudder ran up my spine.

"You get it too? I always get a horrible feeling passing here, but it's not surprising: that's the old mental hospital. There's horrible stories of how patients were treated, and there's still baths and beds and wheelchairs in the rooms where people were basically tortured."

"Jeez, you don't read about that in the Best of Italy guidebooks. Please tell me we're not going in there?"

"No, the clinic is in the new hospital just around the corner. I always say to John, 'If I ever get sick, don't let them bring me to this hospital.' I'd never heal looking out at this and getting these negative, shivery vibes. They need to get a load of Shamans in to clear the air or just burn it down with a lot of sage involved."

As we drive back up the bumpy white track to the house, a large truck came towards us.

"Oh God, it's Davide. He was supposed to do that delivery yesterday. Hang on tight." Karen whacked the car into reverse and high-sped it backwards, expertly avoiding the deep pot holes and small boulders until she swerved into a small grass recess that just about fit a car before a steep, wooded drop. I was just about to ask Karen about it but got distracted by a Hello, how are you? text from my mam.

The large silver tanker bumbled past with a wave from the driver. Karen swerved in behind him and cavorted down the rest of the track to her driveway.

Back at the house, the kids were wrinkled in the pool and the lads had lunch made.

"Why were you getting heating oil delivered when summer is just starting?" I asked over lunch.

"Oh, that wasn't oil," explained John. "That was the water tanker. There's no piped water up here, so we have to buy water in and fill up large tanks in the garden. It's expensive, so we try to minimize its use by filling up those large glass wine jars from the drinking fountain in town each week for drinking water."

The simple life in the Tuscan hills is not as simple as it seems.

We ended up staying a week, with day trips to Florence, Siena, and Pisa.

We had never been to Italy before. I don't know how I had missed this paradise of history, food, wine, architecture, and culture on my previous travels.

We spent the week discovering cathedrals, gelato, pasta, pizza, statues, piazzas, and the joys of Aperol spritz aperitivos with my new sister from another mother. We cooked sumptuous meals on their terrace in the evenings, watching one fabulous sunset after another. I found myself breathing deeper and growing distracted from the grief and the "What the hell will we do" conversations that we'd had all across France.

During the whole stay, the Cravens hadn't pried into our lives. They gave us time to just be. But, from the drip-feed of information we gave them, Karen had gathered that we hadn't got a home to go back to and that we were at a loose end over what to do.

Until the final night.

"Why Spain?" Karen asked, when the topic of our original plans came up.

"It's where a lot of Irish and English choose to get married, on the beach in the sun."

"I was an au pair in Galicia in the north of Spain in my early twenties. Did I tell you that?" said Karen.

"Oh, that's close to where we were thinking of, Asturias."

"You know it's quite wild up there on the north coast, that the sea is rough and the weather is more like the UK's rather than what people expect sunny Spain to be? There's a lot of drizzle and rain, which keeps it green, like Ireland I suppose. You would be better off moving down to the south of Spain if you are after the wedding market."

"Oh no, the south is too touristy. Lacks the authentic Spanishness we are after; it's not for us. Anyway, the houses would be too expensive. Up in the north they are dirt cheap, so we could buy there and travel down to the weddings in the south."

"You do realize that is a full day of driving non-stop? You would probably be quicker flying from Ireland."

Karen had a point. I hadn't thought of checking the distance and how to get from the north to do weddings in the south. I also hadn't taken into consideration that the north of Spain was not what people had in mind when they considered having a wedding in Spain. How stupid was I? What if we had sold everything and moved to a barren part of Spain without doing the proper research, without visiting first. What was I thinking?

But the fact was that we *had* sold everything, and we were not going to Spain; we were not going anywhere. All the thoughts rushed in at the same time: What am I doing? I'm such a bad mother, bad sister, bad daughter. I started to feel the room closing in on me and grief bubbling up. I was just about to excuse myself from the table when John threw in a distraction.

"Why not move here?" he said, passing the platter of roasted vegetables picked from their garden. "You can get some real bargains on houses if you have cash."

"You could go to our school, Luca," piped up Chloe.

"Could we, Mam?" asked Izzy, smiling.

"I could talk to our landlady about renting you the house next door while you're looking," said Karen. Ronan stopped chewing. I could see it would just take my saying yes and he'd be in and so would the kids.

"Thanks, but no. It's beautiful here, but life is tough, the water, the wolves, the earthquakes and explosions."

"Wolves, earthquakes, and explosions?" Ronan asked, chewing quickly again.

"You missed my morning."

"Don't listen to Karen," said John. "Has she shown you her apocalypse cupboard? I'm serious—she does have one; she's stopped just short of asking me to build a bunker in the back garden."

"Once you get used to all that, it's part of living in the Italian countryside. It's great," said Karen, ignoring John while taking the platter. "And once you have a routine, it's easy, idyllic actually, and the kids' school is great."

Ronan was convinced, "Rosie, we could…"

"*No!*" I said, louder than intended. "Can we not talk about this at the moment?"

As smoothly as she passed the platter, Karen turned the conversation on to the two wolves we'd seen in town that day. Everyone was instantly distracted, except for Ronan, who looked into me, trying to read my thoughts from across the table.

Chapter 8

AFTER A LONG GOODBYE, WITH THE KIDS NOT WANTING TO leave, we headed on south. I'd spent a day planning the route this time. I didn't tell Ronan what was ahead. I was hesitant, as I'd heard the Amalfi Coast road is one of the worst roads to drive in Europe. We reached it on a bank holiday weekend: the road was flooded with Vespas, motorbikes, cyclists, cars, and buses, all with death-wish drivers. It was another jaw-dropping drive along a cliff-face road, but Ronan had now developed a technique. "Drive at them, like a game of chicken. That seems to be the way of beating these mad bastards at their own game," he said.

We collected sea glass and sea ceramics on the beach and watched the sun creep towards the Amalfi Coast peninsula while indulging in king prawns and deep-fried zucchini flowers. We sat on the beach; the kids were swimming as the sun started to set.

Ronan brought me a spritz and sat beside me. For the first time since leaving Tuscany we were without the kids in earshot. "That was interesting, what Karen said about the north of Spain. What are your thoughts now about it?"

"I don't know." I watched the waves crash and soften, pulling the old layer of sand away at the frayed edges. "I mean, what was I thinking getting us to sell everything to move to a barren part of Spain miles away from everyone and everything without doing the proper research, without having even been there? What was I thinking?" I began to choke on the anger I had towards myself.

"I was so caught up in the whole stupid idea I took my eye off her. I should have noticed something was wrong. She would have noticed if it had been me. I should have been there for her; I should have called her that morning. She needed me and I wasn't there and now I've dragged us all here and we have nothing, nothing."

His arms were around me and I sobbed into his bare chest.

"Hey, hey, hey, come on, you didn't make all these decisions by yourself. I was there too, and what happened to Eileen is not your fault. She passed the night before, while she slept. You couldn't have done anything; there was no way of knowing." He lingered a kiss on my forehead. "And as for dragging us here, come on! Look at this place." He lifted my chin gently. "Look at how happy our kids are."

I heard them screeching with laughter as Luca chased Izzy through the waves, the silhouette of a crab between his fingers.

"Thank you for getting us to come here. Seriously, if it was left to me we would all be sitting at home watching *The Simpsons* on the sofa, eating chocolate, and complaining of the miserable weather."

"But we have sold everything and we're not going to Spain. We're not going anywhere. I don't know what I'm doing. I should be giving them stability."

"Rosie, come on, we're not destitute! We have a big wad of cash sitting in the bank waiting for us to decide where is best for our kids to be. How great is that? What we did was courageous; it took guts. We now have a blank canvas to paint the best future for our kids on. In Spain, Ireland, or…"

"Italy." I finished his sentence.

We walked to the shore where water swished over the dull, dry pebbles, tumbling them and leaving them behind brighter, smoother, and renewed.

"Definitely Italy…but not yet. I promised Dad we'd come back. They lost one daughter; I can't let them feel they've lost us as well."

"Oh Rosie, come on. Your Dad will be okay in a few weeks; he's just feeling fragile. He'd want you to be happy. They could come over for long holidays or even move over; it would be fantastic. They'd love it here. They're always complaining about the cold."

"But I promised… Anyway, what would we do for money?"

"We'd have as good a chance of making a living here in Italy with the lump sum behind us as we would back in Ireland. The cottage beside Karen and John would be a perfect base, the kids would have friends, you can grow veg with Karen, hang out at the school gates together, and we'd find a place in Tuscany to call home. They said they need very little to live on here as they grow their own food, and John said he could do with a hand doing garden maintenance work, which is how they get the money they need. I can do that. Let me take over the breadwinner role and you can live a life of leisure for a change. They've done it; so can we."

He was painting me the perfect picture. Perhaps, for once, I should leave the decision to him and the kids rather than being the domineering force in the family.

"Maybe you are right. But don't say anything to the kids yet. Let's sleep on it. My head is feeling muffled. Let's get the kids and go back to the hotel and de-sand them."

He bent and kissed me on the lips and then ran up like an excited child to the kids with bounding, great splashes.

Italy had absorbed us both. It was very much starting to feel like it should be home. The world had been swept away from under my feet. But it seemed Italy was as good a place as Ireland to start again from scratch. My tattered edges could be sewn back together; I'd never be the same again, but with some strong stitches I would be more resilient.

Walking back to the hotel, I let my family walk ahead a little and I watched them slurping on their favorite flavors of gelato as they melted in the last heat of the day.

They were happy, laughing; the sadness was lifting. Ronan was right; we had done the right thing coming here, and perhaps we didn't have to go back: we could get Mam and Dad to come here for a long holiday or even move here. I could be the stable, good mother and good daughter here; I just needed to figure out how to make an income. But this was not the time to be practical. It was time to live in the moment and enjoy my family's laughter and happiness, not to try to fix everything at once. Italy was healing me, and I needed to give it time to work its magic.

As I washed the sticky gelato remains off my hands in the hotel room, my phone rang: Sarah was calling, and she had news.

Hanging up and leaving the bathroom after the call, I didn't know how I felt about what she'd just told me. Ronan was also just finishing a call and was hurrying in from the balcony to tell me, "I was just talking to John, and he was talking to their landlady and she said we can have the house for two hundred and... What's wrong?"

"Nothing's wrong. Quite the opposite, I think." My eyes were filling a little. "That was Sarah on the phone—she's split from Jonathan. It's been a long time coming, they were always arguing. Anyway, she needs a new partner in the PR business, and she was wondering if I would be interested."

"What did you say?"

I didn't need to answer, he knew by my face. "She's offering me three thousand euro per month plus expenses, and as Jonathan did all the photography, there will be regular work for you too," I said, trying to be upbeat. There was an audible pause.

"When does she want you to start?"

"As soon as possible." I had taken the baton from him again and run with it without looking back to see how he was doing.

"Lucky we didn't tell the kids then." He slumped back out on the balcony for another cigarette.

It was three in the morning and I still hadn't slept. I lay in bed trying to figure out what I was feeling; I had built up Ronan's hopes and destroyed them within a couple of hours, but there was a certain comfort in the idea of returning to Ireland. It made me feel "safe."

I felt if I was there among familiarity and family, things would stop spinning for a while and we could get off the merry-go-round of doom. This was a positive thing, I told myself as I finally drifted off.

It would stabilize our lives. I wouldn't need to worry or think so much. It would give me and my parents time to recover from the grief, and when the time was right, in the future, we now knew where we wanted to be: Italy.

Chapter 9

"CAN WE JUST GO BACK TO TUSCANY?" MOANED LUCA AS WE packed up the next day. Ronan looked at me and knew he had to take the lead on this; without his support, our lives would be adrift again with nothing solid to stand on. "We need to go back to Ireland for a while. Mam has a new job, and, hey, don't you want to see Nanny and Grandad?"

"I suppose so."

"We'll come back to Italy soon and maybe to live, won't we, Rosie?"

"Yes, for sure. We just have some things to do in Ireland first."

It was reassuring to know Ronan had come around to believing that returning to a stable job in Ireland was the right thing to do, so we both perked up and talked optimistically about what a regular income for us both would mean again during the full day's drive back to France. There, in a campsite, we started the search online for a new home in Ireland. We discovered rents were crazy high, especially for the current tourist season months in the coastal area where we would need to live, close to my parents and new job.

"When did rent get so high? Two thousand to four thousand per month for a three bed? That's just not doable. How about we try to buy again?"

"As we are self-employed, without even a current business operating, a regular mortgage is not an option. We'd need to go for one of those subprime mortgages for the unmortgageable that we keep hearing ads for on the radio. It means higher interest rates, higher penalties if we miss payments, but with the pay Sarah is offering, we would be fine. Let's fill in an online application and see what they say."

Money was still flowing in Ireland, the bubble getting bigger. We were approved within twenty-four hours for a mortgage of one hundred and twenty thousand euro. The fact that we had a lump sum in the bank of ninety thousand helped. This meant we could look for a house to the sum total of two hundred thousand, leaving ten thousand as a rainy day or renovation fund.

We googled "Houses for sale in Ireland" and applied the filters: "three bedrooms," "Under €200k."

"Can you believe in all of Ireland there are only two houses sale for under two hundred thousand?" I said, double-checking that I hadn't selected a five-bedroom filter. "There is one terrace house in the middle of nowhere, and one near the town where we just sold a house… It's within the area we want, and the cheapest, at one hundred and ninety thousand."

We looked at the photos. There were none of the interior, but the outside had potential.

"We can be back in Ireland within two days," said Ronan, examining the road map. "Let's book a viewing appointment and hope it's okay, as it's our only choice."

While we waited for the estate agent to arrive, we explored the overgrown garden of mature trees leading to a wood and a gentle stream running the boundary. I fell in love with the garden, and we agreed to buy it before we even saw inside the house.

The estate agent looked at us in disbelief. She didn't realize this was our only choice and how relieved I felt that I at least liked the garden.

The house had one tap. It was previously lived in by Paddy, an old farmer who had bad knees, so he hadn't been upstairs in five years. The toilet seat had broken, but instead of buying a new one, he'd hacked a hole in the plastic toilet lid and used that as the seat. His pillows were silage bags stuffed with other silage bags. There were dodgy electrics and no heating, but it had a solid roof.

We felt sorry for Paddy until we found his bank statements while clearing the place out. He had seven hundred and ninety thousand euro in his account. Why didn't he buy a pillow or a toilet seat?

Ireland was still in boom time, so every tradesperson was completely booked out for months. It was nearly September and we were working against the clock. Izzy was starting secondary school and needed somewhere to get ready and study, so she agreed to go down to stay with my parents for a couple of weeks until we found someone to install a water tank, septic tank, and heating system before the winter.

When we dropped Izzy off, my mother was piling up sandwiches on the table, and I noticed my dad's *Reader's Digest DIY Manual* on the bookshelf. I flicked to the plumbing section. There was a one-page diagram of a basic water system in a house. "Can I borrow this, Dad?"

"Of course," he said, looking over my shoulder. "Ah, plumbing. You could do that; you probably remember stuff since Abbeyfield."

Indeed I did remember; I was always at my dad's side as he fixed pipes and cisterns, installed sockets and fixed wires. He converted the attic from scrap wood and made his own roof window. I never knew what a tradesman was. Why waste money when Dad could figure it out, roughly, himself? I vowed never to end up with someone like my father, but I did.

So, with me doing the mapping and Ronan doing the heavy work, we installed the water pipes, septic tank, and heating system connected up to a wood-burning range within two weeks. It was in no way perfect, but it meant we could move out of the camper van just before the one of the coldest winters in history hit. During the four weeks of snow, we all slept in the sitting room until we could get insulation and heating upstairs.

"This is like camping in France," Luca said, getting cozy between me and Ronan on the mattress on the floor.

"It's better, Luca, because we can watch the TV and I can do this." Izzy stretched into a star shape showing how much potential room she had if she got tired of cuddling into us. The very cold weather also meant pipes would freeze: this was particularly drastic when the toilet backed up. "We didn't go down far enough with the sewerage pipe. It's not only frozen but cracked," explained Ronan, coming in from outside with his new beard covered in snow. He wasn't trying a new look; he just couldn't stay in the freezing bathroom long enough to have a good shave, and he said it kept his face warm.

"I've tried pouring hot water on it, but I think we'll need to make a hole in it, clear the blockage, and pour hot water on the backup." So while the kids kept the pots refilled for the hot water on the stove, I poured while Ronan prodded and squished the solid contents of the open pipe outside our back door.

"Over a bit," he instructed. I bent closer to see where he was talking about. And with one final slam of the pipe rod, the blockage was cleared along with a fountain of liquidized poo straight into my face. Ronan froze; Luca, who had come out to indulge in every six-year-old's fascination with poo, also froze. I froze. Did that really just happen? The drips of brown sludge from my face onto the white snow answered the question.

A high-pitched wail came from the pit of my stomach up my throat to my pursed-closed mouth, while my feet did some sort of little peddle dance, revving up to do the mad dash into the bathroom. Splashing my face like crazy in the hand basin while still making inner wailing noises, I watched the backed-up toilet empty its load in a whirlpool and secretly hoped the force would splash the lads roaring with laughter outside.

We bought our kitchen from a secondhand-goods newspaper. Its previous owner was an architect; the kitchen was beautiful, with solid-wood cabinets with a black marble top. While Ronan was out collecting it, I got a sledgehammer and knocked down a wall so that it would fit perfectly. As Ireland's economy was booming, people were refurbishing when they didn't need to, so dumpsters, or "skips" as we call them in Ireland, became renovating gold. We found high-grade tropical radiators, French doors, and all our windows and floorboards, all thanks to people trying to keep up with the Joneses. Ronan went out for cigarettes early one Saturday and came back with an amazing claw-footed bath. "Look what I got."

"That's like the one in my friend Suzy's bathroom," said Izzy.

"Yeah, I think it was from outside their house all right."

"Oh no, Dad, you didn't take it from their skip, did you? Please tell me you didn't… Oh no, you did, didn't you? I'm never going to live this down in school." Her face was flushed with the thought of the embarrassment. "Why can't we just be a normal family and buy new stuff?" She left the room, and the homemade door slammed behind her.

"That wasn't me," she shouted back, making the point that door didn't slam because she was in a temper but because we had hung it a little off.

I followed her to her room, and I knocked on the doorframe that held her temporary curtain door up. "I've brought hot chocolate."

She sat on the bed with her back to the door. I approached with caution and gave her the silence needed. "Are we poor?"

"No, sweetheart, we are not poor. Even if we had no money, we still wouldn't be poor, because we are a family, and as long as we have each other we have all the richness we need. We just don't believe in waste. I always wanted a bath like that, and why buy a new one when there is a perfectly good one we can take for free that is going to be dumped in landfill?"

"Suzy's horrible. She gives everyone a hard time and says her dad's a millionaire. If she says anything to me I will hit her. I'm just warning you in case I get suspended."

"Well, if she's like that then she won't ever be coming into this house, and there was no one home when Dad took the bath, so they won't know it was us, don't worry."

"I hate that school. Everyone is so mean to each other. And I have to put my hand up and ask to go to the toilet. What's that about?"

Her previous few years of homeschooling had bypassed the things that most kids take for normal.

"Can we just go back to Italy?"

"We will, just not yet; we need to be here for Nanny and Grandad, and, hey, how about that acting school we found in Dublin? You wouldn't have that in Italy. I think you are old enough now to travel up and down on the bus by yourself if you want to start the Saturday classes?"

"Can I?"

"Sure; let's give them a call."

Our ten thousand euro went a long way, but not quite far enough. There were always things to be done to the house. The following year, we pumped another sixty thousand into the house, mostly paying for an extension for our bedroom and office, which in hindsight we probably shouldn't have done.

We built it with the help of a cowboy builder, who we stupidly listened to when he convinced us the expensive metal roof we had just bought didn't need to be at the recommended angle. As a result, the underside became a secret gathering place for pools of condensation, which joined forces on top of the plasterboard and caused the expansive forty-by-twenty-inch ceiling to cave in with a torrential, dramatic crash just as I was listening to a news report on the radio downstairs about a tsunami happening in Japan.

We couldn't afford to replace it, so we stapled black plastic bags to the beams to keep the insulation in place and to keep the condensation from dripping on our heads. We became experts in puncturing holes where condensation pooled and had five collection buckets dotted around the room.

We lived in the house for two years, with the nice downstairs and horror-story upstairs, while I worked in PR with Sarah, until Ireland's bubble finally burst.

Clients began dropping like drunks in a bar. After a few months, there was not enough work for both Sarah and me to take an income and keep on staff. I couldn't keep traveling to the office without a salary coming in, as we were barely getting by and the house needed so much work. The ceiling was still plastic bags, the sewerage system frequently stopped working, and rats had taken up residence in the ceiling above our bed—did you ever hear rats mating? They screech a lot.

We were at that point again: no income, a business failing, no savings, and no idea how we were going to meet the next mortgage payment.

"I could sell my camera equipment; that would get us through a few months," said Ronan, adding another final demand to the pile already in the hall.

"That's like a fisherman selling his nets."

"There's nothing happening, I haven't done a shoot in two

months. By the time I get more work, the camera will be out of date. It's better to sell it now while it still has value."

Reluctantly, we put it up on eBay and got a decent offer, which would get us through a few months. We accepted the offer on the day we were literally down to the copper left in the coin jar. There was just one problem: the funds would be paid into a PayPal account, which would take three days to transfer into our bank account.

"Shit… Three working days? That means it won't be in until Monday." I moved my keyboard across the desk, away from the splashes starting from the leaking roof.

"It's okay, we have enough food in to last until Saturday, and Jim and Ingrid have asked us over to dinner on Sunday, so that's that covered."

"But Izzy won't be able to go to her acting class on Saturday; we don't have the bus fare." I couldn't believe things had gotten so bad. She hadn't missed a single class all year. "I'm going to bed."

"But it's the middle of the day?"

"Who cares? What else is there to do. Maybe when I get up this nightmare will be over."

Here it was: rock bottom.

I remember a mother of a friend of mine used to say, "Little pigs have big ears," a horrible saying about children being able to hear everything, but it's true.

A couple hours later, I was woken by Luca and Izzy bounding into the room. "Luca and I went on a treasure hunt."

"And look how much we found." Luca spilled a load of coins onto my bed as I sat up.

"We searched down the back of the sofa, under the car seats, there was a jar on the kitchen shelf with ten euro in it, and then our old piggy banks that we had forgotten about. Luca also added the money he got from the tooth fairy last week."

"How much is there?"

"Fifty-four euro and sixteen cent."

"Wow, you did well, guys."

"I don't need to go to my class on Saturday. Let's get some chocolates and watch a movie instead."

"There's enough here to do both. You'll go to class and Luca will take back his lucky two euro from the tooth fairy."

As they walked down the hall, I heard Luca ask Izzy, "Are we poor?"

"No, bro, our family are the richest in the world."

An emotion bubbled up inside from the pit of my stomach into my chest and throat. It was not sadness or anger or disappointment in myself; I knew what they felt like too well. It was new; it was determination, a stronger, more potent strain of it than I had ever felt before.

"Never again," I whispered out loud as I got myself up out of bed and unlocked the side of my wardrobe where I kept my business suits.

Chapter 10

I NEEDED SOMETHING SOLID, SOMETHING THAT COULDN'T BE affected by recession. I took a pen and paper to bed and began to mind-map. I tried to find a new business idea by looking at the inevitables that can't be affected by change: everyone is born, but births are too messy. Everyone dies, but funerals are too sad. And many get married in between. Everything led me back to the same spot. It was time to put on my big-girl pants, take my wedding business out of hibernation, and start networking again.

"Business Speed-Networking Morning. Tuesday 7:00 a.m. in the Lyonscarrig Hotel. New Members Welcome."

The posters were plastered on every second lamppost in town. I hated that kind of thing, but with the determination coursing through me, it was as though I had superpowers, so I rooted out the business cards Eileen had gotten printed, put on a suit, and showed up.

"You have one minute to pitch your business. If you hear a pitch you like or you can help, use the blank cards in front of you to pass on the lead or to arrange a chat during coffee after this session. We're here every Tuesday, and new members are always welcome."

There were thirty people around the horseshoe table setup, and I was number twenty. The people before me were used to this. They stood up and presented a perfect elevator pitch, and cards with leads, and secret "Meet me after" messages were flying around the table. I took up a pen and pretended to take notes, perfecting my elevator pitch like everyone else. My heart thumped louder than I thought possible, and then the sweat started. I could feel the puddles starting in my armpits.

"Drink some water," my brain instructed, sensing my panic. I went to lift the glass, but my trembling caused the glass to vibrate and the water splashed over the side onto my cards. I placed it back down quickly with a loud clunk. The guy beside me looked at me and gave me a polite smile.

Thankfully, everyone else was too busy paying attention to number eighteen's funny pitch to notice my sweat, spilled water, and red face. This would have been right up Eileen's street, one of her favorite things to do. Just as I was sending her a telepathic "You're such a bitch for dying" message, my name was called. I stood up, for once thankful for fat thighs, as they stopped my knees from knocking. A bell signaled the start of the one minute.

I took a long, deep breath and looked down at the notes I'd jotted beside the geometric design doodle I'd scribbled so hard it had made a hole in the card. "Rosie. Wedding Planner."

Bloody hell, is that it? Why didn't I write more?

"Hi, I'm Rosie. Sorry, I am new to this," I fumbled. The bell dinged twice to signal thirty seconds left, and I completely lost my train of thought and looked at the card again.

"I'm a wedding planner." Silence.

"I just started the business, well not really…I started it with my sister, but…"

The bell dinged three times. I stopped talking. Everyone gave me a polite nod and I sat back down.

"It's difficult the first time, but you get used to it," the polite guy reassured me. I wanted to respond "I will never get used to this as I won't be coming back" but just gave him a nod back.

By number twenty-five, the thumping blood in my ears subsided enough for me to start being able to hear what people were saying. I find the mantra "I never have to ever do this again" soothing. When number thirty stood up to speak, his chair fell over as his round belly tried to fit in the space between the table and chair. He joked and everyone laughed. They all seemed familiar with him. I was tempted to start packing up my bag but noticed another woman was glared at by the MC for doing the same thing, so I decided to count down the sixty seconds left before I could skedaddle out of this hell.

"I'm Derek. I work with the Department of Science for this area. We're having an exhibition of a local artist, John Whitley, at the castle on Thursday evening, and I'd like to invite you all to attend. There'll be refreshments provided by the great Phil O'Sullivan." He nodded in the direction of number eighteen, and everyone chuckled again as Phil, the catering comedian, took a bow from his chair. "It's free, so come along."

It was over, thankfully, the longest half hour of my life. In my rush to pack my paper and pens, my business cards scattered all over the floor. Everyone except the scolded woman, who was already out the door, was ambling over to the breakfast buffet and coffee table.

"Excuse me, Rosie?" Someone was talking to my ass as I scrambled to pick up my "Go fish" display under the table.

"Yes?" I bumped my head on the way back out. It was Derek, the round exhibitionist.

"Forgive me for asking, but were… are you Eileen's sister?" He stumbled on his tenses, but I forgave it. I don't even know what tense to use when speaking of her.

"Ah, you are very alike. When you walked in I got a fright." He laughed a little and then blushed. "I'm sorry; that was completely inappropriate." I was blushing for him but smiling at his fumbling.

"Look, umm, you mentioned wedding planning. Eileen had talked about it with me before, um… Well, we had a discussion. You see, I have a castle. Well, not me exactly; it's owned by the government, but I have been managing it for twenty years. Johnstown Castle—do you know it?"

"No, sorry."

"That's the trouble; no one knows about it!" He threw his arms open as if it was the best punchline ever. "It's not being used. Well, it is for the odd exhibition and government meeting, but it might be good for weddings?"

"I'm sorry I didn't do my pitch very well. I do destination weddings, not weddings in Ireland."

"Why not come to the exhibition on Thursday and have a look?"

"I'm sorry." I was apologizing a lot but I desperately wanted to get past this small roundabout of a man and make it to the door. "I can't come on Thursday."

"Well how about now? It's only five minutes away."

A voice in my head was screaming, "*Stop making excuses. Go!*"

"Okay, if it's only five minutes away." I smiled a little. I liked his determination and found him charming, but on the verge of being annoying.

Down a tree-lined path with a forest ahead, I followed him around to the right and suddenly braked while he drove on. Before me was a long, majestic avenue broken by a central fountain and framed by manicured lawns. Beyond the fountain was the most beautiful fairytale castle I had ever seen, complete with turreted crown-tops of symmetrical Rapunzel round towers.

Derek's car was at the fountain before I could close my mouth. He parked beside the castle's front door.

"This is fifteen minutes from where I live, and I didn't even know it existed," I said.

"Well, the grounds are popular with the locals, but the castle itself isn't open to the public. The last owner was a scientist, and he left the estate to the state in the early part of the century to be used as an educational facility for agriculture. That's why, on the top floor, you'll find the rooms kitted out as labs, but as the years went by, labs needed to be more advanced, so the department built a high-tech facility in the grounds and the castle itself was left empty."

He turned the iron key and the big wooden door creaked open, leading us down a walkway of Gothic windows and into a large entrance hall that was open to the three floors above. The landing of each was balustraded all the way around the four walls. From each wall led a door.

"I'm not sure how you could use it, maybe photos or something, but I remember Eileen saying her sister was very creative, so perhaps you could come up with an idea. It's just a shame it's left lying here not used for anything."

"How did you know Eileen?"

"We were in the same 'club,'" he said, winking at me. "She was such a driving force for us all, an inspiration. When she arrived at a meeting, you could see everyone's spirits lift, no matter how bad a week they had. You know, she really helped me through a bad patch. I don't know if I would still be here without the help she gave me at a very low time. She's still sadly missed at the meeting and talked about often." I was touched by his words as we stopped outside giant double doors.

"This is called the Flag Room," he said, opening the doors into a room that was disappointingly decorated with 1970s wallpaper, large, drab, dusty flags hanging around the walls, and a vast conference table in the center. "We use this room for meetings sometimes."

The next door led to a storage room with more seventies wallpaper peeling from the top of the far corner.

"Who on earth thought it was a good idea to restore a sixteenth-century castle with seventies wallpaper?"

"My predecessor, I'm afraid. They used these rooms as offices for the department, and he thought they could do with a revamp."

"Is that a wasp nest in the window?"

"Oh yes, I must get someone to look at that." He quickly closed the door as three wasps headed our way.

"I'm afraid all the rooms are too small for wedding receptions," I said, feeling deflated—what the outside promised, the interiors didn't live up to.

"Oh no, you couldn't have parties here; the grounds close at seven o'clock sharp," said Derek.

I wasn't too sure what he was expecting me to do with the place, but I just decided to be polite and make a suggestion, "Perhaps you could..."

I was desperately trying to think of an idea to make him feel good about my visit as he opened the final door from the entrance hall, and I found myself saying "Wow!"

The original wallpaper was untouched, and above the grand fireplace to the left was a giant mottled mirror.

"That was one of the first mirrors in Ireland, brought over from Paris no less," Derek said proudly.

Reflected in it was the giant picture of the Fitzgerald family on the opposite wall. The husband in his white, spandex-looking, eighteenth-century pants with his pretty, pale-faced wife. She wore a dress straight out of a Jane Austin novel and that was the same pattern as my own wedding dress. Both looked proud, with their pretty little daughter playing with a ribbon and a waiting dog.

"That's Kathleen. She died tragically falling off her much-loved horse a week before her own wedding. The horse is buried beside that dog in the pet cemetery on the grounds."

I might have given more thought to the fact that he didn't mention where she was buried, but I was too distracted by the view through a magnificent Gothic bay window that stretched from the floor to ceiling of the end wall. A peacock fanned his tail under an ancient oak tree that stood to the side, guarding the perfectly manicured lawn. Beyond the lawn, the still lake reflected the autumn colors of the changing mature chestnuts, maples, and sycamores surrounding the almost sacred scene. Two swans glided on the mirror surface towards the fairytale turreted boat house.

"No one died during the famine in this area because the family kept the lake stocked with fish and helped anyone in need. The castle has a history of helping people."

It all came to me at once, the answer to the many similar questions I had received during my time as the wedding expert on the wedding website: "Where in Ireland can I have a romantic, non-religious, legal wedding ceremony?"

The law had just recently been changed to allow civil weddings to happen at registered locations rather than just in registry offices, which were just that—offices. Ronan and I had been lucky and gotten married in a reasonably nice Georgian building, but I had heard of couples getting married in public government buildings with the public health dentist in the next room pulling out some poor kid's tooth while the couple were saying their vows. Here I only had the low buzz of a wasp nest in the next room, but we could drown it out with a harpist.

"I could use this room. We could do wedding ceremonies here," I said.

"Ah, now there would be no 'we' in this deal," said Derek, clearly marking his boundaries. "I wouldn't be involved at all; I'd just give you a key and you could get on with it and pay a fee towards the upkeep of the castle from each wedding, but you'd look after the cleaning, setting up, and all that sort of stuff. You just tell me the dates you need it, and I'll make sure it's not being used for anything else that day."

"Are you serious? It would be that easy? Does it not have to go before a committee or something?"

"Not at all. I've been in charge of this place for twenty years. They call me the king of the castle," he said, proudly pushing out his chest a little. "What I say goes, as far as this place goes. If you want it, it's yours."

He unlatched the duplicate key to the castle's front door from the ring and held it out to me.

"This all is a bit too good to be true. I mean, you don't know me and you are entrusting me with this?"

He smiled, "I lost a friend who saved my life. You're her sister, so I can only imagine it was so much harder. You look like you could do with a bit of a lift."

I had caught my reflection in the mirror as I was walking in, and could see my resting bitch face was showing; I looked as pale as the woman in the portrait. I knew I had barely enough petrol in the car to get home and back to the ATM in the morning to withdraw the money from Ronan's camera sale, and here was a—not quite—knight in shining armor handing me the key of a fairytale castle to use as I wished.

"Come back to the business meeting next Tuesday morning. As soon as word is out locally that you are doing weddings here, you'll get your first bookings in no time," he said, waving me off from the car park.

He was right. Once I had done the paperwork to get it registered as a ceremony venue, the bookings started to come in. I created a package including Ronan as a photographer and comedian Phil to do the champagne and canapés after the ceremony on the lawn. I went back to the weekly Tuesday morning business meeting, and it did become easier. Through it I soon found a florist, a baker, and connections with local hotels for the wedding receptions. Within weeks, deposits were coming in. Ronan and I were back on our feet.

I revamped the dormant website Eileen and I had toiled over. Now I was not only offering destination locations like New York, Spain, Malta, and Italy but a fairytale castle in Ireland.

Chapter 11

TWO YEARS LATER, WEDDINGS AT THE CASTLE WERE OUR MAIN income, and my destination-wedding brand had grown.

I had wedding planners on the ground in each country who looked after my couples from the point they arrived, saving me the expense and hassle of traveling each time, but I still took familiarization trips to each country at least once per year to check out new venues and meet with vendors.

Things were looking very promising. However, the one-year gap between the end of the PR salary and the start of a steady income from the wedding business came back to haunt us. We had missed eight mortgage payments in all during that period. And the sharks decided it was time to come out.

Those eight missed payments accumulated interest at a huge rate. In four years, our subprime €170k mortgage had increased to €230k. They wanted us to make double payments—which we could not do. So they handed our account on to a collecting agency, who called me four times a day, harassing and threatening. English Greg was the most persistent.

I tried to reason with them, deal with them without involving Ronan, as I didn't want to give him a reason to drink. I logged the number they called from as "Do Not Answer" and ignored them for a while, but then they would just start again from a new number, and soon I wasn't sleeping. I lay in bed working out that within two years we would be able to pay off chunks; the business just needed more time.

A wedding-familiarization trip to Venice was a good distraction. I'd never been before, and even though it was in November, in off-season, it was still a welcomed break all the same.

I had gotten a second phone: "Just for weddings," I told Ronan. Really it was to separate the vampire debt collector calls from my business so I wouldn't have to answer any "unidentified" calls on my personal number.

It worked. I sat waiting for my personal driver to arrive in the Venice airport when my phone rang with a number I didn't recognize, so I let it ring out.

For some reason, it was a surprise to me that Venice was surrounded by water and that my private driver was not in a luxury car but a speedboat. Exhilarating as it all was, getting on and off boats in heels—never mind the choppy November water—was not an elegant sight. It took two men to grip me in a chain-like system, getting on and off each taxi ride to hosted lunches and dinners over the weekend.

On the Saturday night, I was sitting at one such hosted dinner at the Aman Canal Grande Hotel—a seven-star hotel—admiring the frescoed ceilings on the mirrored tables around my plate, when my wedding phone buzzed.

"Hi, Rosie; it's Greg. Could you verify your name, date of birth, and address for me please?" He had done his research and found me.

Instead of saying "Greg, what the hell are you doing calling me on this number?" while surrounded by wedding industry people in classy suits and evening gowns, I simply said, "No."

"I'm sorry, but for data-protection purposes you need to verify your name, date of birth, and address for me please."

I had automatically done this on every call up to that moment; why hadn't I thought before to simply say "No, I'm sorry; I don't know who you are, and I am not going to give my personal information to you, a stranger, over the phone." He was a bit lost for words. "Right then, I will send you the request by mail then."

"Fine," I said, and hung up.

That evening, after eating the most delectable dinner overlooking the Rialto Bridge on the Grand Canal, I consumed a large amount of very fine wine and then insisted that the venue's event manager show us the room where George Clooney's wedding night had been. She agreed, and in front of twenty strangers who excitedly followed, I promptly jumped onto the bed and rolled across it shouting, "Woo woo, I was in George Clooney's wedding bed." About five of those strangers joined me, and we remain good friends to this day. Needless to say, I never got invited again on the Venice familiarization trips, but I couldn't do weddings there anyway: not my cup of tea—too much water.

"What's this?" asked Ronan, handing me an opened letter the

day after I came down from the high of being back home. In the seven-star luxury of Venice, I had temporarily forgotten the refuse-bag ceiling and dark shadows waiting to pounce on my return. As soon as I opened the letter and saw the signature—"Gregory"—reality came with a jolt. It wasn't just a letter but a long list of the times and dates of calls made to me, plus a statement with "Final Notice" and "Eviction Pending" stamped in red.

I broke.

"Why didn't you tell me?" Ronan was not annoyed but upset that I thought he was still so unstable that he couldn't be trusted with such information.

"Listen," he said, lifting my face up towards his as he held my crumbling body, which no longer had the strength to carry the family. "You don't have to control and look after everything anymore. I am here and I will never go back to that place again. We are in this family together. It's you and me, not just you anymore. Leave these assholes to me; I'll deal with them. Do you think they go to bed thinking about our missed mortgage payments? No, they just move on and make the next threatening phone call to the next poor sod." The ball of tension between my shoulders began to unravel as Ronan continued to talk sense to me.

"We are not the only ones. You've seen the newspapers: thousands of people found themselves suddenly redundant after the crash with massive mortgages they will never be able to meet. Even that girl Suzy in Izzy's class, with the bath, they're gone."

"But her father was a crook, building dozens of houses on credit and taking money from people and not finishing jobs; that's why they ran back to her granny's house in Manchester," I argued.

"Okay, true, but every day I am reading of suicides caused by debt, families breaking up, families being thrown out of their homes as the debt collectors bring in the heavies. Things are different for us; it shouldn't affect us—we've been through worse."

He was right; we had been through the chaos that addiction brings to a family; we had learned not to sweat the small stuff and to laugh easily. I had grown an invisible barrier so nothing could break my heart again. We had figured out what was important in life, we knew what real stress was. For Ronan, dealing with these assholes on the phone would be easier than our previous life's roller-coaster ride. Why had I let them get to me? Now Ronan was going to take on the burden, I started to feel lighter again.

"We are paying our current payments. No court would have us evicted as long as we are paying something," said Ronan. He knew his stuff after years of us dealing with people on the brink of homelessness. It was hard to believe we were now facing that ourselves.

I gladly handed the baton to Ronan while I worked fourteen-hour days hustling for more bookings.

A few weeks later, on a mid-May morning, I woke up in every way; my brain was less fogged by emergency chaos and was able to think logically again. I was thinking the same thing Ronan had said when looking at *A Place in the Sun* a few years back: "What are we doing here? What are we doing in this house?"

By the time Ronan's alarm went off, signaling me to get ready for that day's wedding, I had been awake for an hour with a pen and paper.

I waited until he'd had a coffee before I pounced. "Every penny we earn goes into this money pit. I have worked it out that it will take another five years of blood, sweat, and funds to finish it, and at that point, Izzy will be twenty and have probably fled the nest, with Luca close behind."

He was watching the birds on the bird table, sipping his second cup of coffee, and not saying anything.

"What are we doing here, Ronan? Rents have plummeted now, so what if we told the bank they can have the house, give them the keys, and we rent somewhere for half the amount our mortgage currently is? We could save and eventually move to Italy. If we stay like this we are never going to have money to do anything other than patch up this house."

"I've been thinking the exact same; I just didn't think you would go for it."

By the end of that day's wedding at the castle, the plan was in place. On the way home I googled houses for rent nearby and one popped up. Ronan passed the turnoff for home.

"Let's go have a look to see where it is."

We drove around the little seaside estate and there it was, the front door open with a woman sweeping the hallway. Ronan stopped the car and was out and over talking to her before I could think of an excuse for him not to. He waved at me to come over.

"The previous tenants have just left, and I just put it on the rental site an hour ago," she explained as she showed us around.

It was a fairly new build, a holiday home, no wires hanging from walls, no ceilings falling in; the plumbing and sewerage were in place—the decor was boring, but it was clean and functioning. "We'll take it," said Ronan, shaking on an agreed rent of five hundred euro per month—half our mortgage.

We moved in the following week. We had a roof—without rats—over our heads and were in a safe position to negotiate with the sharks.

The lending agency we originally got our mortgage from had gone bust. Our debt was then owned by a second collecting agency, which Ronan found, with a little investigating, had bought the debt from the first collecting agency for a fraction of what we owed. The next time they called, Ronan, the clever hound he is, asked them to send over the agreement we had about the debt we owed them. They couldn't produce it, because it didn't exist.

After several senior managers got involved, with a lot of threats and negotiating, they agreed that in exchange for the keys to the house they would write off our debt in full.

It would take a while for the repossession to happen, so we still had access to the house. We gradually sold or gave away our furniture and belongings that could not fit in our new, small rental.

Renting was a new experience for me. I can't deny there wasn't a feeling of disappointment in myself that after fourteen years of paying mortgages, I had nothing to show for it, nothing to "leave" my kids. But what was that about? Was I raising my kids to rely on me to provide them with a lump sum to live off after I died? Didn't I want to bring my kids up to be financially independent and not rely on anyone else, including us, for financial support? Did I want my kids to be tied to four walls because of memories, like I was with our family home, the idea of leaving being heart-wrenching? Didn't I want to bring up my kids with the freedom to choose anywhere in the world to be their home, based purely on what was best for the life they wanted to lead?

From the start I paid three months' rent in advance before the last payment expired. The Irish law was in favor of the landlord rather than the long-term tenant, and no matter how nice the landlady seemed, I was nervous. Nervous of the horror stories circulating about people being asked to leave at short notice, nervous that one day we would get a call that would leave us without a roof over our heads. She seemed nice, so I squashed the worry down, but I continued to pay three months in advance, just as a safeguard.

I've always believed in following my intuition, and I was right.

Chapter 12

RENTING WAS AMAZING. A YEAR INTO IT, I WAS STILL NERVOUS, but by continuing to make advance payments I was able to relax and discover the benefits—no repairing or hard labor to be done. If there was a problem with an appliance or the sewerage, one phone call and the landlord fixed it. Bliss! For the first time I began to see money build in our account.

Derek retired from his post at the castle and had an afternoon party in the Flag Room. I had become Cinderella of the castle, dusting antiques, hoovering, mopping, and cleaning toilets before and after each wedding, but I loved it. Most of the time, I had the castle to myself to hang out and daydream while cleaning and setting up. I had the cream aisle runner, chair covers, and lanterns from when Eileen and I were setting up our business, which made the weddings at the castle as fairytale as they could be, all done under the approving eye of little Kathleen.

Sally took over from Derek. She wasn't so lax about things like my having a key; instead I needed to make an appointment to collect the key from her and bring it back every time I needed to do a viewing with potential couples or prepare for a wedding. It made things difficult, as she didn't work weekends, which was when I had most of my viewings and weddings. So instead I would still need to book things through her and then she would arrange for one of the groundsmen to let me in and lock up after me.

It was no big deal; it just meant a little more planning on my part as I couldn't approve a viewing or wedding without approving an appointment with Sally first. She sighed every time I made a request; being in charge of the key seemed a major difficulty. I think it was the opening and closing of the drawer she kept it in that drained her vital energy sources.

During one call to make an appointment, Sally asked for me to come in for a "review" meeting. I had guessed this would be coming, as I was sure she would want an increased fee per wedding, which to me was okay as I had worked hard at promoting the castle and I knew the following year would be a bumper year for bookings.

"Isn't the castle doing well?" She smiled, tapping her pen against her red-winged spectacles. "How many weddings have we done now? About one hundred?… The businesses in the area are happy too, as the castle is now attracting lots of visitors from… Where are they coming from again?"

"Mostly the U.S., UK, different parts of Ireland, Australia, Canada, and we had a wedding from the Lebanon last year; everywhere really. And yes, with an average of eighty people coming per wedding, it's about four thousand new visitors per year to the area."

I'd prepared with figures and had surprised myself with the amount of contribution to local tourism the weddings at the castle had made. "I think next year will be when it really takes off, as word is spreading and the last two years have really been about getting the word out there and marketing and all the hard slog of getting it up and running. But next year will be the year that…"

"Yes, well that's why I called you in. The committee has decided that this will be the last year we are doing weddings at the castle. They decided that the castle is attracting so many visitors now that it's time it's refurbished and made into a museum. You can finish out this year's weddings, but no new bookings beyond this September."

"Committee? But I don't understand; the castle has been lying unused since the seventies. Why choose to refurbish it now, when something good is just starting to take off in it? You just said that the weddings are doing so well and…"

"No, I said the castle is doing so well. It would be a shame not to make the most of it and refurbish it to its former glory so that all these new visitors can enjoy it even more, don't you agree?"

"Yes, the castle definitely could do with some TLC, but the reason why these visitors are coming is because they are being dragged here as guests of a wedding in a castle in Ireland. They aren't finding the castle in a guide book and deciding to come to Ireland because of it; they're not given a choice. They need to buy a bloody suit, come for the wedding, and stay for a week because that's what is asked of them by the friend getting married. Many guests have never been to Ireland before, but after having been to the weddings, they plan to come back again. The committee is missing the point. Can I…"

"It has been decided: they are already putting the work out to tender. It's been great having weddings here, but now it's time to…"

"Turn it into a museum? The same as every other state-owned building? Why not weddings? They will bring in so much more money than a museum."

"Because it's what you just said: it's state owned, they are not interested in profit. We—I mean they—just want something easy to run. Museums are easier to run than weddings." There was no talking to her or the mystery new "committee."

Rather than driving straight home, I decided to take a walk around the lake. I knew the grounds so well now that I felt part of the castle, part of its history, as did all the lovely couples who had had their weddings there.

I sat on my favorite bench, which gave a central view of the castle reflected perfectly in the lake. I was in disbelief that this pattern was happening again: just as money was starting to gain momentum, the carpet—or aisle runner in this case—was whipped away from under my feet yet again. I was giving myself time to cry if I felt the need, but I found myself taking deep breaths and smiling just as Ronan called. "So how did your meeting with Sally go?"

"I'm not too sure. Well, I think terrible, but in another way… they are doing up the castle and turning it into a museum, so they're stopping me doing any more weddings from the end of this season."

"Oh wow, that's a bit of a blow. How are you feeling?"

"It's strange. I don't feel upset; I feel relieved for some reason?"

"That's because of that wedding inquiry you got last week, the one for three years' time, remember?"

I thought back to the excited girl who had just got engaged and requested the castle for August 2018, and how I had broken into a cold sweat when I realized Izzy would be nineteen by then and Luca fourteen. There was no way I wanted to still be in Ireland, tied down doing weddings at the castle. We hadn't much time left in which to travel with our kids before they started doing their own thing. "Something like this needed to happen. It was too good an opportunity for you to ever give up yourself. As you always say to the kids, nature will support you and push you in the right direction. Things will work out, love; don't worry. They always do."

Sometimes swallowing your own medicine is the hardest. I could of course fight this with the "committee" and get local businesses involved to back me up. but I was smiling because I was relieved. I wanted to be in Italy in a few years, not here in Ireland, and to make that happen, I needed to start focusing all my effort on growing my destination-wedding business in Italy. A breeze picked up and rippled the middle of the castle's reflection, making it look like it was bowing over. I bowed back. It was time for us both to move on to new things.

While it was going to be a blow to our income, it wasn't going to devastate us as before. I could easily fill the gap. The "never again" determination had turned me into a workaholic. I had been working twelve-hour days, seven days a week, developing my expertise on weddings in Italy, while on the side I developed online courses teaching what I knew: how to become a wedding planner; how to create an online magazine; how to create a location-independent business. In my spare evenings I had done a two-year diploma in photography so

I could act as backup and assistant to Ronan for wedding bookings that didn't require me to do the planning.

I also had a secret. I was going to blurt it out to Ronan there on the bench, looking at the castle, but it wasn't the right time. I was never very good at keeping secrets, especially not from Ronan, but circumstances had changed, my businesses had taken off, and I was doing solo travel trips to Italy to network with venues and explore new possible locations. I was the breadwinner of the family. I couldn't tell Ronan about it yet, maybe never—time would tell.

I already had an established wedding brand, and from all my site-inspection trips over the years, I had developed an expertise about Italy, and I had fallen head over heels in love with the place, each region a new treasure box waiting to be opened.

By the time I got home from the castle, I already had a plan in place.

"We'll do the same in Italy as we do for the castle. Stress-free wedding-planning packages, easy to book, with photography included. Now that I'm not tied to having to be at the castle for weddings, we can go to ones in Italy. Why not? Flights are cheap if I work it well and group two or three bookings together for each trip. We can travel back and forth, make a good profit, and enjoy Italy."

It worked: by the following year we had fourteen weddings neatly grouped into five trips. As Luca was homeschooled, he came with us, falling in love with Italy as much as we did. Izzy stayed in Ireland, as she was working on the soap opera and had gotten herself a lead role in an indie film. As I knew the dates well in advance, I became a master at finding cheap flights and accommodation.

It was during one of these trips, while staying at a little hotel overlooking Lake Garda, that it happened. I was sitting on the terrace with a glass of wine while Ronan had a coffee. "This is the life," he said, pulling on a cigar. We could see Luca down in the pool from the balcony.

I felt maybe this was the time I should tell him my secret, or perhaps it was too soon. "Ronan, I need to tell you…"

"Oh feck, do you know where I left my phone? I can hear it ringing somewhere; hold on." He got up and went inside. "Oh here it is… Hello?"

I watched the cigar burn down in the ashtray. I love the smell of cigars, so I lifted it and took a pull. The hot, burning smoke lingered on my tongue and then hit the back of my throat. Immediately I was coughing and spluttering. "Oh that's disgusting," I said, jogging past Ronan into the bathroom to rinse my mouth out.

From the open door of the bathroom, I watched Ronan leaning against the bedpost. He looked solemn. "Yes, I understand."

He was nodding a lot, so I sneaked over beside him and he pressed the speaker button. "So there will be a lock on the gate from today, and if you go past that it will be considered breaking and entering," said the calm, somewhat apologetic voice of the woman on the other end. "We will have the right to have you and your wife forcibly removed and to call the police to arrest you, do you understand?"

"Yes, yes, I understand."

"I am sorry to have to be the one to tell you this; it's not a pleasant job. Thank you for being so understanding, but you have my number now, and if you wish to go into the house for any purpose, such as to remove personal items, furniture, or post, please do call me first on this number and I will arrange something for you. I wish you and your family all the best. Goodbye."

"So the repossession of the house is complete," he said, slowly closing his phone. "After two years, they are finally taking over our home, the rat-infested, money pit, and signing the document I sent them releasing us from the debt."

We both looked at each and simultaneously screamed, "*Yes!*" I threw my arms around his neck and Lake Garda whizzed past my eyes several times as he swung me around. We were now completely debt free. A new start, again.

Later in the afternoon, we took a walk down to the town of Malcesine and happened across a cute shop that sold vintage metal signs. Ronan thought the owner was posing at the door while he took a photo, but then I pointed out the "No photos" sign, and when we zoomed in we could see he was scowling at us, not smiling, so I bought a sign with incorrect grammar: "Our home is where our heart is."

We didn't see ourselves as having been made "home*less*"; we were just houseless. Lots of people rent for life; we could too.

Chapter 13

THE FOLLOWING WINTER IN IRELAND WAS ITS USUAL HORRENDOUS self. I woke up one morning to rain pounding off the window and to another confirmed wedding-photography booking for the Amalfi Coast. It was all the encouragement I needed to approach Ronan with my long-festering plan. "I'm looking at our wedding calendar, and we have ten weddings between August and September, so I'm thinking we should find a central location to stay and go over to Italy for the full six weeks."

"What about the dogs?"

"We'll get a dog sitter. It shouldn't be too difficult to find someone who wants to stay in a coastal village in Ireland for six weeks."

"Hmm, it's a long time to be away from them. Can we not bring them with us?"

"No! We'll be working and traveling around the country. We'll find someone nice to look after them; don't worry. Look here. I found this house and pet sitter website. Let's fill in our details, put it out there, and see what response we get. No harm?"

We uploaded photos of our dogs, of us, of the house, and of the beach.

> Wanted: Friendly person or couple to watch over our German shepherd and bichon frise in a beautiful seaside village on the coast of Ireland for a six-week period starting in April. Both are house dogs and are easy to care for. We have a large field behind our house where they can exercise, so no need for dog walking beyond the house. It's okay to leave them for a few hours if you want to explore the surrounding area, and my brother, who lives nearby, can look after them from time to time if you wish to go out for the full day. Nice house with big bedroom and en suite.

The most time we'd been away from the dogs was two weeks. That evening I put on Pavarotti and made spaghetti bolognese to get into the Italian mood. After I'd had a few glasses of wine, Ronan decided to call it a night, but I was wide awake—what better time to start planning our Italian adventure? Out came my laptop: I input the dates we needed into an accommodation booking engine.

Two pages came up, of places from all over Italy. The cheapest also looked the best: an *agriturismo* in Umbria on Lake Trasimeno. There were photos of the friendly owner on his tractor and of his daughter hugging goats and petting chickens.

The apartment had a lake view, two spacious bedrooms, and an open-kitchen living room, but the big selling point was the little terrace overlooking the lake. I double-checked the price.

"Is that per week or for the whole five weeks?" I muttered to myself. I checked again, and then again. The true test would be when I pressed "Book now." With wine courage, I did it. It was booked, and it was seven hundred and fifty euro for five weeks. A gush of excitement ran through me. Perhaps the owner's daughter would be a friend for Luca; they looked about the same age.

I checked flights and worked out that we could fly into Naples and spend the first week in Sorrento, as we had two Amalfi Coast weddings that week. Then we could drive up to the place I'd just booked, using it as our base for our remaining weddings. I checked the flights to Naples and got a €9.99 special one way, which became about €100 each by the time tax, bags, and seats together were added. I booked it and clicked to add on a car hire deal.

"Woohoo!" Excitement was rising again with my wine consumption. I was on a roll.

I searched for places to stay in Sorrento, scrolling for ages and stopping at a photo of a terrace surrounded by lemon trees.

Cozy apartment with terrace, situated in the middle of a lemon grove in a quaint hamlet only five minutes from Sorrento Centro and train station.

The price was fifty euro per night. The only photos were of the terrace, a lemon, and Sorrento Centro. I gulped down the last mouthful of wine from the glass in one hand while I pressed "Book" with the other.

"*Daa naa!*" I lifted the bottle and poured, but nothing came out.

"Oh, that's not good," I said out loud.

Bing. "David has responded to your posting on House Sitters" popped up on my screen.

Making a cup of my hand to keep my head from wobbling so that I could see straight, I clicked the link to the house-sitting website.

"Hello my name is David. My wife Maureen and I are currently pet-sitting a German shepherd and a cat in the West of Ireland. We are English and South African and retired, and have been enjoying seeing the UK and Ireland for the last two years through house and pet sitting. We like to take on long sits so we can really get to know the area and bond with your pets. The sit we are currently doing ends in April, so it would be perfect timing to do yours."

"I've arranged every—hiccup—thing," I said as my head hit the pillow. "Flights, houses, things, everything."

"Great, but it's after midnight; we'll talk about it in the morning," Ronan mumbled, turning over.

"Ronan, I have something I have to tell you, a secret."

My drunken mind needed to tell him everything. I could no longer keep it to myself, I needed to come clean. I blurted it out, but he didn't hear; he was already snoring.

Ronan was already on his second cup of coffee when I got up with a cardboard mouth and dry eyes stinging from not wearing my reading glasses for the hours I was on the computer before bed.

"How's the head?" he said, handing me a cup of tea. I responded with some sort of elongated vowel-like noise.

"So, what did you arrange?"

"Oh umm." I searched my foggy head for a reminder. "I found a great place in Umbria that would be a good central spot as a base. Here, I'll show you." There was a confirmation of the booking in my inbox from the agriturismo, so I followed the link easily.

"Oh, that looks fantastic, and what a great price. Send me the link so I can read more about it."

I was so glad he was happy.

"I also booked outgoing flights, but not return flights, as I haven't worked out where the nearest airport would be on the last week yet... Oh and car hire." I just about remembered, adding that before things got a bit muddy.

"You booked car hire? What did you get? I'd have liked to be involved in that decision. You know I like picking the car hires."

"Ohh, it's eh," I had no clue what I'd booked when I was skipping merrily along the "continue" links with every slug of wine. "It's ehh—it was a deal." I was searching for the confirmation to sound like I knew what I had done. "Here it is."

"Rosie, that's a one-liter engine, not much better than a lawnmower."

"It's fine! It's a car, isn't it?"

"I'd rather something more sturdy on the Italian roads if we're doing so much driving."

"Look I'm sure we can upgrade with no problem. I'll figure it out later and do it." I saw a confirmation of booking from a property in

Sorrento, but the details were a blur. I decided to wait until later to check on it, when Ronan wasn't around.

"Have we had any response from the house-sitter ad?"

"No. I mean yes." I had a vague recollection of something. The tea was helping clear the fog. "Yes, sorry, I forgot, a guy responded." Ronan logged into the site and read aloud the message from "David."

"Sounds okay?" I said. "A bit weird that they have been doing this full time for two years, but we'll wait until we have a few more responses."

"Too late," said Ronan. "You've already booked him."

"'So glad to have found you, David.'" Ronan read my response from the screen. "'You and Maura sound perfect'… You could have at least got her name right." He continued reading: "'Let's do this! We leave on the 15th. How about you and your Mrs. come stay the night before, we'll have dinner, and you can settle in and meet the pets.'"

"I wrote that?"

"How much did you have to drink?"

Chapter 14

WE PACKED UP OUR ROOM, FRETTING ABOUT THE DOGS, FILLING our holiday suitcases and work bags. We'd boxed and bagged all our personal stuff and crammed it into the office room.

"We seriously need to declutter when we come back," I said as we squeezed the door shut and locked it.

The house was spotless. Thankfully David and Maureen turned down my drunken offer of a pre-night stay, but they were to arrive at any moment. We'd have some tea and cake, a chat, show them around, let the dogs meet them, and then, in about two hours, leave for the airport. They had some really good reviews on the house-sitting site, so my choice didn't seem too bad.

A bashed-up Ford Estate pulled up, packed as tight as our office with bags and boxes. David unfolded from the car. He was taller than Ronan, perhaps six foot four, with wrinkled skin hanging from previously muscular, pale arms. "Hello, doggies," he said enthusiastically, jumping around with Looney and Asha in the front garden.

"I'm Ronan and this is Ros—" David wasn't listening; he was still jumping around with the dogs, his comb-over flapping in the wind. It was getting awkward, until Maureen ordered, "David, stop. Come inside."

They seemed friendly. They both took a coffee. Maureen didn't stop fiddling with her expensive gold, jeweled earrings. Her wedding band had thinned and her finger knuckles now looked too big for it to be removed. In the meantime, David was expertly sloshing his lower dentures around his mouth to get at a bit of stuck cake. I guessed this was his long-term habit after eating, as Maureen seemed oblivious, while Luca stared, horrified, at the roaming teeth.

We showed them around the house, the kitchen—demonstrating how the cooker worked, the heating—the bathroom, their bedroom; Maureen appreciated the new linens and fresh flowers.

Ronan brought David out to the garden to show him the back field where he could take Asha for a run in the evening. "It's connected to the garden, so there's no need for a lead; just a stick or a ball and she's happy."

"So, did you have dogs in South Africa?" I asked Maureen, looking at the men outside.

"No, our daughter was very scared of dogs growing up. She was attacked by a German shepherd when she was little. It tore up her face."

"Oh my God, that's terrible."

"Yeah, she had twenty-one operations. She's twenty-eight now and okay, but it took a lot of psychological therapy."

I looked at my dear Asha, who wouldn't hurt a fly.

"Emm, if you don't mind me asking then, why do you choose to sit German shepherds?"

"Oh, we love dogs. I'm more fond of the smaller breeds," she said, petting Looney, who had happily made a bed for herself on Maureen's lap. "But David loves German shepherds. We know they are good dogs; that was just a crazy guard dog my sister had."

"Your sister?"

"Yes, she had the dog in her yard to keep trouble out and had it trained to attack anyone that came into the yard without them. She had left the door open and our girl wandered out when my sister was looking after her. It's a necessity in South Africa to guard your property. There's a real problem of white genocide going on there, you know?"

I was too distracted by the idea of how traumatic that whole dog-child ordeal was to let the last sentence sink in. But Luca heard it and went to the back garden to tell Ronan. Ronan was telling David his usual joke that Asha, being a German shepherd, only followed commands in German, which somehow led to David saying, "Have you ever actually read *Mein Kampf*? It actually makes some very good points."

"Right, so I think it's time we head off. Is there anything else you need to know before we go?" Ronan asked, coming in looking a bit startled.

"Oh, just the dogs' leads. Where are they?" David asked.

"They are hanging up here in the hall. The pink ribbon one is Looney's obviously. And the heavy chain is Asha's. But you don't need them. As I said, you just need to bring them for a run in the back field. Actually, we don't want you to bring Asha out beyond the gate; she's all muscle and gets quite excited when she sees other dogs, so just giving her a run in the back field is fine. Rosie's brother, Jim, will call up once a week and bring them to the beach."

"Oh, don't worry; leave her with me. I know German shepherds very well."

We gave the dogs a hug goodbye and said an awkward farewell to the two strangers as we handed them the keys to our house.

"She's weird," I said, while Ronan said in unison, "He's weird."

"They're bloody racist Nazis," shouted Luca over both of us. "I don't think we should leave the dogs with them."

"They'll be fine with the dogs," I said.

"But Asha is black. She might be cruel to her."

"No, Luca, that's not how racism works."

"But they're crazy!"

"They are weird," said Ronan, not helping. "They've been traveling around house-sitting for the last two years, with all their stuff with them. Like they don't have a home in South Africa anymore."

"Well, what can we do? We can't arrange an alternative now. It'll be okay. They were good with the dogs and that's what matters."

I spend the rest of the journey to Dublin thinking of my Nelson Mandela shopping bag under the stairs and our gay Nigerian neighbors, who had said they'd call in and check on the dogs while we were away.

Everything was going to be all right, I told myself as I took up biting my nails for the first time.

Chapter 15

AS WE STEPPED OFF THE PLANE IN NAPLES, THE WARM BLAST OF air reminded me of why I wanted to leave Ireland. I immediately shed a layer into my hand luggage. By the time we were through passport control and lifting our last bag off the luggage carousel, I had shed a second layer.

"So, what did you upgrade the lawnmower to?" Ronan asked.

"Emm." I had completely forgotten to change the car hire from my original drunk booking. I used the best defense: lying. "I thought you wanted to do that. You said you wanted to do it. Did you not do it?"

"No, I didn't—"

"Oh for goodness' sake, Ronan; there's no way we are going to fit us all in the car with these five bags." I knew that's exactly what he was about to say, so I pipped him to the post. "Never mind; we'll sort it out at the car hire desk. Come on," I said, hastily pushing the luggage trolley swiftly to the exit.

"I'm sorry, but we have no other cars available because of the holiday weekend."

"But that's a bubble car. Three of us couldn't fit in that, never mind our five big bags."

"But that is what you booked. I am sorry, Madam."

"Look, my husband is outside having a cigarette. He left the booking to me and I messed up. As a woman you understand what this means: he will constantly remind me of it in every future argument about anything."

"Well there is one car that came back this morning. It is a two liter and was due to go for some maintenance, so I shouldn't really–"

"Okay, great, we'll take it. Here he comes—act normal."

"Hey, there you are. Have a nice cigarette?" I would never ask him this in a million years. I constantly nag him to give them up. I needed to act normal.

"This is my husband, Ronan. Ronan, this is…" I read her name tag. "Roberto."

Even less normal. Why would I introduce him to the car hire assistant as if we were at a bloody cocktail party?

"It's Roberta," she stated. "Roberto is for a man."

"Oh, right, yeah, sorry. Umm, anyway, me and Roberta have sorted out the car hire and she has kindly upgraded us to their best two-liter ca–"

"It is not an upgrade, it will cost extra," she interrupted.

"That's fine, Roberta, thank you. Thank you for telling us that. You have my card details there; just give me the documents to sign and the keys and we'll be away."

"Okay, but it has not been cleaned yet."

"That's fine, just the documents and keys, thanks."

"Can we get some food?" asked Luca.

"No, let's hit the road and get a nice big slap-up lunch in Sorrento. There's a great pizza place there in the square," I said, knowing how much Luca loved pizza.

"Jezuz, what were the last lot doing, rally driving?" Ronan said as we approached the car. It was coated in mud and dust.

As we pulled out of the car park, the gear box clunked with every shift.

"It will just take getting used to," I said reassuringly.

The owner of the Sorrento property sent directions to meet a "Tina" at the Sorrento train station. We could follow her to the property, as it would be easier than trying to direct us there. A lady called Enza would look after us when we were there. I hadn't looked at the property again since booking, but I remembered it had a lemon grove terrace.

"Tina" met us and we followed her to the entrance of a labyrinth of an ancient village. She didn't speak a word of English.

"*Parcheggi*," she shouted to us as we pulled in off a busy bend beside her.

"She's telling us to park over there," I said, pointing to a spot beside the steep cobbled slope leading to the entrance of the village, where there was barely room for a car.

"I hope the handbrake on this car is better than the clutch," sighed Ronan, maneuvering onto the precarious slope of the hamlet's cobbled road.

The boys off-loaded our five heavy bags while I glanced around looking for an entrance to our digs. But no, Tina loaded our bags into the back of her skinny Jimny jeep and hand gestured for us to pile in, Ronan with his long legs in the front and me and Luca in the back. There was no room for error and no room for a pedestrian, never mind another car, as she accelerated up the meandering road through netted lemon groves.

Beeps and strategically placed mirrors stopped collisions around blind bends in alleyways that were only meant for donkeys, not cars. She was flying along; it was more impressive than any roller-coaster ride or ghost train I'd been on. We stopped at the top of the hamlet and followed her example of unloading our bags.

"Is this it?" Ronan asked. I could sense his hangriness rising; we hadn't eaten since Dublin, and it was three o'clock. We were also thirsty.

"Oh, don't start complaining before you even see it."

We dragged the bags up a steep incline, through a gate, and up some steps. Tina signaled us up some more steps and into a tiny room the size of a cupboard, with a sofa and a sink. Beside it, through a makeshift door, was a dark room with a double bed squeezed in.

The lads looked horrified. I was horrified but trying not to show it. Make the best of a bad situation and all that. Tina hot-footed it out the door with a quick "*Arrivederci.*"

While Ronan bellowed "I'm not staying here," I shouted "*Aspetta, Tina, aspetta,*" after her.

Ronan broke into his best broken English. "We need to eat, where? Get water, where?" I tried to translate.

"*Dove pranziamo? Dove supermercato?*"

"*No, no supermercato, no* eat, *ciao.*"

"*Dove Enza?*" I shouted after her.

"Enza is sleeping for two hours. She is very old. She will be here at five," she shouted back in Italian. I didn't translate. She dumped us on top of the lemon mountain with the weight of all our worldly possessions in five heavy suitcases; her duty was done, and she was not waiting around.

Considering our location, Ronan was aptly turning into a bubbling volcano ready to blow. "Why the hell did you book this place? We're not staying here."

"Well you find something better then. Stop blaming me for everything that goes wrong."

"Okay, I will," he said emphatically and began to google.

I took a moment to see how we could make the best of it, but I was struggling. The two-seater sofa bed looked too small for Luca's growing limbs unless he slept with his head in the kitchen sink, and that was if he could get to sleep with the loud buzzing of the small antique fridge with the flickering light in the corner.

"The lemons are nice," I said weakly, looking out to the terrace in among the lemon grove, spotting the angle they had taken the photo from to hide the pile of agricultural equipment beside it.

I called the owner's number. "Enrico, this is Rosie. We are at the apartment, but it is not suitable. We have not eaten and there are no shops nearby. We don't even have water."

"I will be there at seven and I will bring you water."

"Seven? That is four hours away. We haven't eaten since eight this morning. You said there would be someone here to call on if we needed anything."

"Yes, my mother, but she sleeps until five; then you can ask her for some bread, but you cannot disturb her now. So please don't make noise."

"Right. I've booked somewhere for three nights," Ronan said. "I'm sorry, Enrico, but this is not for us."

"No, please do not leave; I will be there at seven o'clock."

"The ad said it is five minutes from the centro?"

"Yes, the entrance of the hamlet is five minutes from the centro."

"I think you should have mentioned the apartment is twenty minutes from the hamlet entrance and up a bloody mountain." Now I was hangry.

I hung up. Thankfully it was a pay-on-booking, so I canceled it immediately, just as Ronan stuck his phone in front of me; he'd found a small three-star hotel on a beach, further out from the center, with Wi-Fi and a restaurant. A last-minute booking offer with a 50 percent discount brought it to just five euro more per night than where we were, and it included breakfast.

"Good find—let's go." I couldn't fault it. Anything was better than the lemon prison I had brought us to.

We took our chances with the tap water and I texted Enrico, I am sorry, we are leaving, it is too remote.

Ronan was already marching away. The two biggest suitcases he was dragging thudded down the steps behind him, his camera bag strapped to the top, followed by Luca, who had one case in each hand, leaving me to trot after them with my camera bag belted onto my wheelie. Ronan marches when he's hangry; he was way ahead. I winced watching the wheels of our suitcases bounce along the sloping cobbled laneways, flipping from time to time; twisting Ronan's arm with it; causing him to stop, adjust, and restart his war path; and giving me time to catch up a little.

Although my stomach rumbled, I still noticed how pretty the lemon groves lining the small valley next to the road and the crumbling facades of the stone homes facing it were. I stopped for a moment and breathed in mandarin from a grove in bloom, hidden below the road. We were hungry, tired, sweaty, and disappointed by our lodgings, but I still felt happy and full. Full of Italy.

We drove the magnificent coast road out the other side of town and followed the GPS to a small hidden exit that looked like a private gated entrance. The road wound down a series of hairpin bends with the inviting, sparkling sea getting closer until we found ourselves at its level. A faded car park sign with the hotel's name welcomed us.

Hotel Baia di Puolo was tucked away to the right, with the beach and sea stretching out to the left of the path. Our room was a triple with a balcony terrace overlooking the sea. We opened the windows and let the salty freshness pour in. Lunchtime was over and it was too early for dinner, but the restaurant happily whipped us up mozzarella and tomato panini. Later, we had pizza as promised, while watching the sun set beyond Mount Vesuvius.

Waking to the sound of waves lapping against sand is one of the best experiences ever.

"I want to live by the sea," I whispered to Ronan. He was still asleep, and so was Luca. They are both night owls who prefer not to meet my energetic morning larkiness.

From the balcony I watched two guys sieving the sand through a machine; a group of fishermen were gathered by nets further up the beach. It was too tempting to wait until the lads were up and ready to go, so I slipped on a cotton sun dress and sandals and snuck out to explore.

"*Caffè?*" the waiter asked just as I was leaving. I hadn't intended to have breakfast on my own, but why not.

"*Cappuccino per favore.*"

Perhaps the mix of salt air and the sound of waves had somehow woken my taste buds; it was the best-tasting cappuccino I've ever had.

I took a stroll along the water's edge. While the April sun was hot, the water was still too cold for me to contemplate a swim. As I walked, I texted David to see how their first night with the dogs had gone. I'd reached where the fishermen were and watched them weave a new net, their faces bronzed and creased with smiling lines. They spotted me and one ushered me over. I approached shyly, embarrassed; I couldn't speak their language. He handed me the spindle and showed me the motion to make a new loop.

"*Sí, sí, perfetto!*" he said as I clumsily added a second new loop to his net.

Click.

I turned and saw Ronan with his camera, capturing my moment as a fisherman's assistant.

"So, do you want to go into the town?" Ronan asked as we strolled back up the beach hand in hand to the restaurant terrace, where Luca was eating his second helping of cereal, cheese, and croissants.

"I'd be just as happy to chill out here for the day. How about you?"

"I was hoping you'd say that. We have a busy few days ahead, so it would be good just to relax and read a book on the beach or something."

I had a second cappuccino and looked at my forgotten phone. There was a response from David.

"Oh my God, no!" I said out loud, reading his response.

Not too good. I am in the hospital, getting stitches in my head. I fell over while bringing Ash for a walk. The lead snapped and I fell backwards. Your brother Jim is with me.

Chapter 16

"WHAT THE HELL? WE TOLD HIM NOT TO BRING HER FOR A WALK. Ring him," urged Ronan.

"*No*, you ring him. I can't deal with this." My stress levels had gone through the roof. What if he had to leave—what would we do with the dogs for the next five weeks? Both of us had to be there for the weddings.

"I told you he was crazy. I'll ring Jim."

"I knew he was crazy too, but I didn't see you flooding the table with options."

"Flooding the table? What's that supposed to mean?"

"I don't know but it sounds… You know what I mean."

"Hey, Jim," Ronan said, putting him on speaker phone. "What's the story? We just got a message from that guy David that he was in hospital and you are with him?"

"Ah, we're home now. Yeah, it's all okay; don't worry. He decided to bring Asha for a walk, and Asha pulled on the lead just on the path right outside the house. The lead snapped, and he fell backwards and banged his head on the pavement. His Mrs. called me in a panic, as his head was gushing blood and she couldn't find a first aid kit. So I went around, patched him up a bit, and brought him to the hospital and they put five paper stitches on it. It just looked worse than it was, but he's okay now and he's taking it well."

"How the hell did her lead break? It's a thick chain."

"No, he had the thin one on her."

"Looney's ribbon lead? On a big German shepherd? The man is bloody crazy! What was he thinking?"

"Anyway, don't let it spoil your holiday. How's Italy?"

We told him about the lemon prison and showed him where we were staying, feeling pretty guilty that he was at home dealing with all the crap.

We flipped a coin to see who would call David. Even if I lost, Ronan was going to be doing it, but he lost so we didn't have to have that conversation.

"I'll put him on speaker phone."

"No, don't. I don't want to hear. I want you to filter what he says. Break it to me slowly if he says he's going to sue us or if they are packing up and leaving. I'm going for a walk down to the beach. Follow me down, and remember, break it to me slowly." The second cappuccino was making its way back up my gullet. The idea of David suing had instantly brought back the same stomach tension the debt collector's number appearing on my phone screen used to conjure up.

Instead of going to the beach I went to the restaurant bar and ordered a chardonnay. I was on my second by the time Ronan came down.

He sat down beside me and looked out at the sea without saying anything.

"Well?" I slurped my wine.

"Well what?" He knew how to drive me nuts. "Oh come on, Ronan. What did he say?"

"Well, he thinks Asha is the most amazing dog he ever met. He realizes he used the wrong lead, but when he fell back, Asha sat beside him and barked until Maureen came out. He thinks he was knocked out for a bit, as Looney got to him before Maureen and was licking his face when he came around lying on the pavement."

"Are you serious?"

"Yep, they both think we have the most amazing dogs in the world."

"So they are not suing or leaving?"

"Nope, they feel they have 'bonded.' I told him the first aid box is under the sink and reminded him that we told him not to bring Asha for a walk, she's fine with just the field."

"Oh, thank the Lord."

I spent the rest of that day and the next one napping, paddling, reading on the beach, ignoring emails, and being eaten by mosquitoes.

The next morning, on the way to our first wedding of the season, I noticed I'd missed a call from Jim. "Oh no, he's dead."

"Who is?" Ronan said, startled.

"David. He must be dead; otherwise why would Jim be calling me so early?"

"Are you sure he's dead?"

"No, I'm not sure. I'm just guessing."

"Bloody hell, Rosie. Don't do that; just ring Jim back."

Jim picked up the phone.

"Is he dead? Tell me he's not dead."

Jim was laughing before I'd even asked. "No, he's not dead, but I was driving to the shop this morning to get milk, and I saw him walking along the road with Asha pulling him along with what must have been every bandage you had in the first aid box wrapped around his head and underneath his chin like a mummy. He only got five paper stitches in his head. And I am sure he was wearing Ronan's long black coat."

"What is he doing, bringing her for a walk again? Oh, look, I've got to go; we're working today. Ronan, pull over here. I need to go to the pharmacy. Chat later, Jim. Please don't call me before nine tonight when we're finished work, even if he is dead."

"*Scusi, parli inglese?*" I asked the white-coated pharmacist.

"Yes, certainly. How may I help you?"

"I need mosquito repellent."

"Ah yes, we have two types: we have this one that works, or we have this much more expensive natural one, which is like food for mosquitoes. Which would you prefer?"

The day just got better and better from there. The wedding was beautiful: a civil ceremony for a sweet Irish couple under the ancient willow tree in the San Francesco Cloister in Sorrento's center, with beautiful sea views and fabulous carved doorways for the couple shots after. Ronan and I were in photography heaven. And people are so kind in Italy; they see couples twenty times a day during the summer in Sorrento, and yet they still stop for a moment to clap while they pass and shout "*Auguri!*"

We were invited to join the wedding dinner at O'Parrucchiano, a restaurant that has been in Sorrento since 1868 and that is famous not only for being the birthplace of cannelloni but having a sprawling lemon grove where branches entwine to form the ceiling of a huge outdoor courtyard. Other than taking a photo of the cake cutting, we were finished work for the day, so while the guests enjoyed time together, we had a table to ourselves and time to savor a nice meal after a long working day.

"I could live here, what about you?" Ronan said, tucking into his first course.

"What, here in Sorrento?"

He nodded. I understood why he was enthralled: the sea; the buzz of the scooters going around as parents did the school run with kids sitting on the front and back, weaving their way through traffic jams; the fresh market stalls; the hustle and bustle of daily chaotic life in the small, oblong square that was Sorrento. I had been there several times before on familiarization trips. It was the only place I'd sung karaoke, after spending the day swimming from a sunbathing deck that jutted into the sea facing the high cliff face. I'd browsed lazily among the ceramics shops and experienced the somber, eerie chants of the hooded priests carrying the cross to the church on the eve of Good Friday.

I'd also spent a week here in November, when the tourist season was over. There was Tony in the café bar where I'd go for my morning cappuccino and cornetto. By the third morning he was testing me on my Italian and helping me along so that I could order with a "proper" southern Italian accent. But there were also the shut-up souvenir shops and hotels that would not open again until March. It was all a bit derelict.

"Maybe, but in winter it's—"

I was interrupted by a lemon falling from a tree above and plopping directly into the mother of the bride's dinner, knocking over her wine glass and smashing it on the floor. There was a moment's silence before the waiter shouted, "That is very lucky! *Auguri!*"

The whole restaurant shouted "*Auguri!*" and clinked their glasses. Perfectly timed, the accordion player entered serenading the couple as they walked to cut the cake. A passing waiter told us, "That happens at least once every night. We go through a lot of wine glasses."

Our stay in Sorrento came to an end. We regretfully left the little hotel tucked into the cliff edge and followed the road to Positano, where we would stay for three nights. We pulled into one of the car parks and handed our keys to an attendant. Only they know how to squash in every car to maximize the space in the tiny car parks layered on the cliff face. We traversed up and down flights of steps again, pulling our wheelies behind us through lanes and alleys until we found the entrance to our accommodation halfway up a flight of steps.

"Oh my God, my arse is killing me" were the romantic words Ronan woke up to the following morning.

Not only my ass, but my thighs and calves were talking to me from the previous day's endless flights of steps workout. Ronan wasn't much better. We got a taxi from the road to the hotel perched on top of the cliff, where the bride was getting ready. We took the preparation shots before jumping on the guest bus down to the town for the ceremony. Luca was happy to stay at the apartment, reading and eating the supplies we'd got him the night before.

Our favorite videographer, Mario, was working with us that day. He had brought along a drone operator.

"You would think he was too fat to work, but he is the best drone operator in Southern Italy," Mario explained proudly and loudly.

The drone guy was indeed a large chap and thankfully didn't understand English. The Italians don't hold back with their blunt descriptions. In every "Learning Italian" book there's a chapter on how to describe someone. They have umpteen ways of describing noses, *naso francese* being one of the most desirable, illustrated by a pretty female with a long, elegant nose. Then you have the *naso romano*, with a side profile of a handsome man with the typical hooked nose. Then you have *naso a patata*, which is a button nose, illustrated by a picture of…Shrek. There's also the *naso schiacciato*, which is a mashed nose, and *naso adunco*, meaning "falcon nose."

The town was full of tourists crowding in and out of the gelateria, art galleries, and pretty boutiques. Down on the beach we finished the shoot and went for a coffee at one of the beach bars. I checked my Fitbit; it had already recorded twenty-five thousand steps, most of them being actual steps, and we still had to get back to the car park.

"Do you remember the last time we were here?" Ronan asked, looking at the beach.

"Of course. We were sitting right over there and we collected sea glass with the kids, and then we had the best gelato in the corner shop we passed on the way down."

"And you said you could live here. Do you still feel like that?"

"In Italy? Yes, for sure. In Positano? God no, I'm not fit enough."

"I know it's not practical, and it will be a long time before we can do it, but if you were to pick a place in Italy to live, where would it be? How about Venice?" he asked, finishing his coffee.

"Oh no, too watery. I was ready for pretty canals, but for some reason I didn't realize it was surrounded by the bloody sea, which was rough when I was there. All that on-and-off-boats malarkey, with my sense of balance? And having to wear wellies when it floods? No, not for me."

He did his low chuckle that I love to hear. I followed his gaze to the kite surfer taking giant leaps into the air and down again to skim the surface before flying high again.

"Listen, I have something to tell you." It was time for my secret to be told.

But he hadn't heard me; his mind was roaming around beautiful Italy. "Lake Como would be too posh for me. Anywhere north that gets snow would be off my list also—I'm not moving to Italy for cold weather; I've had enough of that in Ireland to last me a lifetime."

The moment was lost, so I joined in his fantasy trip. "I think it would either be Tuscany or Puglia. Puglia for the sea."

We waited to watch the sunset but didn't see it. Nobody does in Positano, as it sets on the other side of the cliff, but the pastels melting into crimson with two bright orange wisps of clouds were satisfying enough as we stopped at the gelateria and ambled back to the apartment. It was a perfect evening except for our aching glutes. Too perfect for me to disturb it by telling him my secret. The right time would come soon, and then our lives would change forever.

Chapter 17

THE FOLLOWING DAY WE DID THE SIX-HOUR DRIVE WITH LUCA TO Lake Trasimeno, to the agriturismo that would be our home for five weeks. The car's air con just blew hot air, so we kept the windows open, which also helped block out the clunking noise of the clutch.

We were nearly there but got a little lost, so I called the owner, Emanuele, who gave me directions and told me his daughter Lucia would be waiting at the car park to show us around. "It seems a lot of responsibility to give a fourteen-year-old," I said.

We rounded the bend, saw the sign "Agriturismo La Dogana," and drove slowly up an idyllic cypress-lined stone path. With the windows down, I smelled barbecue and heard a high-pitched screech of "*Bree, die, nooo, die die!*"

Ronan slammed on the brakes. "Stay here," he ordered us, jumping out of the car to go save some woman called Bree from being murdered. A Jack Russell with a cartoonlike length of sausages shot past his feet.

"Stop her!" shouted the same voice of the murderer. Ronan stood on the last dragged sausage and pounced on the dog.

Luca and I were also out of the car at this point and saw a young teenage boy jump over the wall. He lost his baseball hat to a branch, and long, silky black hair tumbled down onto his skinny, sallow shoulders. As he got closer, I recognized that he was the girl from the goat-hugging photo on the website and not a boy at all. A golden retriever bounded after her.

"I'm sorry—this is the second time she's robbed the guests' barbecue sausages this week," she said, catching up with the dog. "*Breeee sei una ragazza così cattiva!*" she bellowed like a ship horn at the dog, now sitting on Ronan's lap.

"It's a bit late now," said Ronan as the bigger dog took the other end of the sausage string and tugged it from Bree.

The girl was not as young as I thought, perhaps sixteen or seventeen. It was hard to figure out.

"I am sorry. This is not the normal way I greet my guests. *Buonasera*. I'm Lucia, the thief is Bree, and the big one is Big Boy."

"Well hello, Big Boy," I said in my sexiest voice for the laugh, realizing too late how inappropriate it was.

"Jeez, Mam, that just doesn't sound right." Luca pulled a face. I wasn't sure if Lucia was laughing at us or Ronan, who was getting his face licked, post sausages, by Bree.

"They are both rescue dogs, so they still rob food when they can. All my animals here are rescues or were abandoned. Did you have a nice trip?"

"It was long, from Positano. We had a wedding there." I groaned

ROSIE MELEADY

a little, as my left buttock had gone numb and my calf had gone into spasms after sitting for so long.

"Oh Dio, that is long. Yes, I saw on your information that you are a wedding planner. I am too." Okay, so perhaps she was eighteen or nineteen?

"We had a beautiful wedding here last week for a German couple, but let's not talk about work. If you want to park in the car park around the corner, I will show you to your apartment so you can relax. Bree, get off the guest. *Dai!*"

"Why are you telling her to die all the time?" piped up Luca, amused by the crazy woman.

"I am not telling her to *die*," she laughed. "*Dai* means 'come on' in Italian. You will hear it a lot when people are walking their dogs. I never thought of it as '*die*'; that is so funny," she said, laughing loudly and walking towards the old farmhouse.

Our apartment was in the center of the building. Symmetrical flights of steps from each side led up to a small terrace at the entrance covered by a stone porch.

The rooms were even nicer than in the photos. Spacious and quaint. The most amazing feature was the uninterrupted view of the lake over the tops of the olive trees.

"I have left some water and a bottle of local wine in the fridge for your enjoyment. Now I show you where the pool is."

We walked with Lucia up an incline behind the building. "My great-grandmother first bought this farm. There are four thousand olive trees, and she had prized cows that were housed in the lower level of the building you are staying in. My father turned it into guest apartments, making it one of the first agriturismo in all of Umbria.

And I agreed, after studying marketing at the American University in Rome, to take over the business from my father, as I am the only heir, and to start doing weddings here."

"Ah, the American University. So that is why you are so good at English," I said while recalculating her age. She must have been twenty-two or twenty-three. Due to my miscalculations, she was aging fast, and I searched her face for lines.

"Indeed."

At the top of the incline, a wooden gate led up some steps and through an herb garden buzzing with bees. On the terrace just below the herb garden stretched a thirty-foot-long infinity pool with a perfect view of the lake.

"Wow!" We all gasped at the same time. I couldn't stop myself clicking into wedding work mode. "Woo! What an amazing space for a wedding."

"Oh, we don't do the weddings up here; we do them down at the restaurant."

"*What?* No? You need to use this space… I think we are going to have some interesting conversations in the coming weeks."

We walked slowly back to our apartment through the terraced olive grove fringed by a field of poppies.

"I don't know how to say it in English, but I am a doer but not imagination?… But I have to confess, after you booked, I have researched your work and I would love your advice on how I can make here better for weddings."

"Of course, I'd love to help, but only if you can answer one question for me: How old are you?"

"Oh don't worry, everyone asks. They think I am a young sheeps, but they do not see me in the government building being a wolf about stupid f-ing taxes and charges where I tear off all their heads and leave them for dead… But to answer your question, I am twenty-six."

Lucia joined us for a glass of wine on the terrace, a practice that became a regular occurrence, with long chats into the evening.

Even though we had no weddings for the rest of the week, the next day I was up early for a walk across the estate. I spotted Lucia taking food to the horses, trailed by not just Bree and Big Boy but also by a baby fawn she had nursed back to health after it had been hit by a car. She looked like a pre-transformation princess in a Disney movie.

The following week, Luca went to stay with Karen and John while we prepped for our seven-hour drive to Puglia. By nine o'clock in the morning we had the car packed and ready to go. I was dreading the idea of another long trip with the gears clunking and no air con. Ronan turned the key in the ignition and nothing happened. The lights worked, so we knew it wasn't the battery. He tried again, but again nothing happened.

"This bloody car. I knew it was going to cause problems." He popped the bonnet and searched for a missing connection. I began to panic. "What are we going to do? We have to get to Puglia today for the wedding tomorrow."

As if by magic, Lucia walked past with her dogs. Ronan was telling her what had happened just as I got an answer from the car hire company. "Let me talk to them," she said, taking the phone from my hand. I didn't know what she was saying, but it was very fast and loud, involved hand gestures, and I'm sure the air turned a tinge of blue around her. The wolf had appeared.

"Okay, it is fixed. I will bring the dogs back to my house; then I take my car and drive you to Perugia with your luggage, where they will have a new car waiting for you rather than this piece of shit."

Within an hour we were sitting in a shiny, brand-new car with working air con and thanking Lucia profusely. Now relaxed, we could enjoy the coastal road down the full inside-leg measurement of long-legged Italy.

Puglia was a completely different flavor of Italy. Its whitewashed buildings, Greek-blue shutters, and pale blue sea are in stark contrast to the terra-cotta reds and the green shutters of Tuscany and Umbria. We arrived the day before the wedding and had booked into a mas-seria near the "White City" of Ostuni.

The communal lounge area was set out like a living museum and included a working gramophone with a full collection of records. Dinner was made by the owner and ran to five courses of "peasant food." Every ingredient was from their farm; it included what others would call weeds, but to the Puglianese, dandelion, poppy, wild chic-ory, borage leaves, and wild fennel are additional sparks of unidentifi-able color to an already rich art piece of tastes on the palate.

Cheese was subtly flavored with the fig leaves it came wrapped in and was made from their own sheep milk and fresh burrata cheese. It was all served with red wines deepened by the southern sun on the vines I could see from the window. The use of olive oil was encouraged to enhance the flavor of everything and ranged from the early, peppery green to the subtle, extra-virgin liquid gold. The meal was the best I'd ever had, heightened by the owner Armando's descriptions and stories at the start of every course.

"All the oil is from our own olive trees, some of which have been carbon-dated as two thousand years old, some of the oldest in Puglia, which has sixty million olive trees. We say in Puglia we have an olive tree for every citizen in Italy.

"In peasant food, nothing was thrown out. This has led to flavors and dishes such as the sauce *cime di rape*, made from turnip tops, which was the sauce on the orecchiette pasta you just had.

"Also in the dish you are about to eat, you will taste the nutty flavor of *grano arso*. Food was scarce in Puglia. If the grain burnt, you invented something to make it delicious, and that is what happened with grano arso, which means 'burnt grain' and is now purposely made and features on menus of Michelin-starred restaurants."

"The Irish also discovered one of their favorite dishes by accidentally burning grain…Guinness," I told him.

"But Guinness is not a food?"

"That is debatable. It's a good source of iron. Three pints will fill you like a three-course meal."

"It sounds like you miss Guinness like I would miss the oil from our trees should I ever leave this place. I traveled when younger, but this is now my paradise. I have no want or need to be anywhere else."

We could understand why. This was Ronan's first time in Puglia, and he was falling for it as much as I had. "How about Puglia? Could you live there?" he asked as we drove back to Umbria.

"Absolutely."

Between Tuscan weddings we spent days exploring the

surrounding picturesque towns near La Dogana—Cortona, Castiglione del Lago, San Feliciano, the island Magione, Tuoro, and Passignano sul Trasimeno—interrupted by long, leisurely, tasty lunches, snoozes, and swims in the pool to cool off in the evening. At night we sat on the terrace chatting with Lucia. The other guests would come and go. A low, thudding beat in the background wafted up from the Ciao Ciao Club down on Tuoro's beach, accompanied by the lilt of young love's laughter, the scent of jasmine heavy in the air.

September was fabulous. Lucia volunteered us to help a neighbor gather their grape harvest. We thought it would be fun and a great experience to see the process. When it came to it, we were all a bit freaked out by the number of insects crawling over the bunches of grapes as we picked them. We tried to do our best without getting attacked by ants, earwigs, and spiders. None of the other elderly pickers seemed bothered, throwing the grapes into crates along with the surfing insects.

When our crate was full, we brought it over to an antique-looking, giant mincing machine that had been wheeled out of a shed and given a quick hose-down by a guy with a head of thick white hair—not a sterilizing tablet in sight. This ancient open-top machine, with its red paint chipped away to expose the metal underneath, was hooked up to a generator, and the large metal coil churned around, squashing the grapes as the crates were emptied into it, cleverly spitting out the separated stalks into a grubby bucket. The resulting profusion of juice was shunted down an equally discolored, dirty-looking tube from the back of the machine into a basin, where it was left to ferment in the shed.

We stood in a row and watched in horror as they emptied the crates of the freshly picked grapes into the machine, along with the accompanying earwigs, ants, and spiders that had failed to escape.

"I'm never drinking wine," said Luca, watching the grapes and crawlies being minced.

"I'm definitely never drinking that wine," I responded.

"I'm just happy that I don't drink anymore." It was the first time I'd laughed at a Ronan-related drink reference. Italy was helping me heal.

On our final evening in Italy, we sat on our terrace at Agriturismo La Dogana and watched the full moon paint the lake orange and silver. Ronan had his feet up and was enjoying a new Italian coffee brand he'd discovered and of which he'd packed fifteen packets to bring back to Ireland. "To me, this place comes close to perfect. You've got the rolling olive groves down to the lake, the fields of sunflowers, and lots of lively little towns."

I felt completely at peace; a waft of Opium perfume lingered and then passed.

"Maybe it's time to revisit that dream we had of living abroad. Why don't we look into renting a house here for next year's wedding season, to use as a base where we can leave stuff instead of lugging it over with us on each trip?"

"Here or Puglia?"

"I'm not sure," I thought aloud. "Puglia is not so central for our work. Most of our weddings are in Tuscany. Luca could get a train to Florence or Rome if he wanted to just go for a day himself. And Puglia doesn't have a Lucia."

I'd grown attached to her. She had become like an adopted

daughter, and I enjoyed helping her develop her wedding-venue business. She had been an invaluable help to us, letting her inner wolf come out when we needed action fast.

"Okay, so Umbria it is. But realistically, can we afford it, Rosie? We would need a deposit for rent, a car here, backup money…"

It was time to tell Ronan the secret I had been keeping from him.

"Well, here's the thing; I've been putting aside the money from the online training courses I've been running for the last few years. So I have an 'It's too bloody rainy in Ireland so let's go to Italy' fund."

"Oh yeah?" he laughed. "How much do you have?"

I knew he thought I was going to say a couple of hundred, or perhaps one thousand at most. So, watching his facial expressions go from jaw dropping to absolutely ecstatic when I said "Forty thousand" was quite amusing.

"Why didn't you tell me this before?"

"Because I knew that every time we needed something, like to upgrade the car or camera equipment or whatever, you would persuade me to dip into it. You're like my mam: the idea of having money burns a hole in your pocket. Also, to be honest, it gave me comfort to know I had a runaway fund in case you ever started drinking again…"

Things became silent between us. "But I don't have that fear anymore. I'm ready for us to move on to the next stage of our lives, together."

Chapter 18

ARRIVING BACK IN IRELAND WAS A WHIRLWIND. THE WEATHER was awful and Ronan developed a proper flu on the way home, which I didn't delay catching from him. For two weeks we both passed in and out of consciousness, while every joint hurt and our energy remained at a level just enough to allow us to reach for a hanky and blow our noses before passing out again. The kids kept their distance, and my mam and Jim took turns dropping off casseroles and stews so none of us would starve. Ronan was a week ahead of me in recovery, so he was up and about before the really bad wintery weather struck.

As soon as I was less contagious and had enough strength to stay vertical for an hour, Izzy started to come in to sit on the end of the bed for the long chats I missed so much during the weeks we were away from each other. They had become frequent in the past year, between her jobs and my trips to Italy, but I sensed she was hiding something.

"What's up, chuck?" I asked, not wanting to beat around the bush any longer. I had a flashing thought that she wanted to give up acting because she was sick of the rejections, tired of getting to the final two for dream parts only to lose to someone else they found slightly more suitable because of size, shape, or eye color.

"I have good news," she said hesitantly. I was equally hesitant, as good news in our family always meant there was bad news to follow.

"One of the best agents in London wants to take me on their books."

"That's brilliant news." I couldn't see how this was going to lead to bad news.

"*And* I'm up for a lead part in a three-part series which the agent thinks I will get."

"That's even better news!" Maybe there was no bad news. "The thing is…" Oh, here it comes, I thought.

"The agent says that for him to take me on I need to move to London. I need to be based there for meetings and auditions. I can't progress my career from here, and now that the soap opera is finished, I need to get something soon."

"Oh… Okay, so when are you thinking of going? In the new year?"

"No, sooner. In four weeks actually. I've already organized a sofa to rent in a friend of a friend's flat. Just until I get on my feet, and then I can find my own flat."

"Apartment?" This was no longer sounding like just a temporary trip; this was permanent. I knew this day was coming, but like a death, when it's finally announced you feel like you are in the hollow center of a whirlpool. I put on a brave face. "That's great. You better start packing."

"I already have. I'm so excited, Mam."

"Have you told Dad yet?"

"Yes, I told him this morning."

So that was why he'd been avoiding me.

An hour after Izzy dropped the bombshell that she was flying the nest, I got a call from Wendy, our landlady—she said she had "forgotten" to tell me two months ago that she was upping the rent to one thousand from the end of the month. So just as we thought we had everything sorted, that slippery carpet had raised its corners again, ready to be whipped from under our feet.

With foggy flu head and an aching heart at Izzy's news, I was in no mood for this second crash landing.

"You forgot to tell me?"

"Yes. In fairness, we haven't done a rent increase in the two years you've been there."

"But doubling the rent without warning?"

"Like I said, we haven't increased rent in two years, and you won't find anywhere in the area for the rent we are asking."

"Well, I am googling as we speak, and there's a house in the next village that is bigger than this for nine hundred euro."

"But that is not the same area."

"It's five miles up the road. We'd be okay with that."

"But what about your parents?" she blurted out.

"Excuse me?"

"Okay then, we'll match that. We'll reduce it to nine hundred, but it starts from next month."

Ireland's economy was growing rapidly again, rents were rising, and our landlady had obviously decided she wanted in on the action. It seemed she also thought she had us over a barrel because she knew I had elderly parents and, hey, if we could pay three months in advance without being asked, then we must be okay for a near double increase, right?

I needed time to think. "Obviously this is a bit of a shock. I'll get back to you later."

I stared outside. The rain was pouring over the gutter, creating a pounding waterfall against my office window. I hadn't left the house in the ten days since we had been back.

I could hear Izzy in her room, packing—within a few weeks her room would be empty. I wouldn't have her chatter and company to lift the depression the Irish weather caused. The rain got heavier. I squirted vitamin D spray onto my tongue. "Please be instant and make me happy."

It didn't work.

Looking at the weather app on my phone, I saw that it was a pleasant twenty degrees Celsius in Italy. I wished we were back there. I spent my winters now tied to my desk, basking in the artificial glow of my computer screen. My eyes flashed to the window: gray skies, rain… I could do this in Italy. The same question came into my head that Ronan had asked all those years ago and that had planted the seed to move abroad: "Why are we here?"

I went in and sat on Izzy's bed. "How much would an apartment share be in a decent area in London per month?"

"About a thousand."

I was having jelly thoughts.

Next, I went to Luca's room. He was staring out at the overflowing gutters, distracted from his studies. "I miss Italy," he said, sighing.

He had just started his second year of secondary school after a five-year stint of homeschooling. He had enjoyed the first year and made good friends, but he wasn't enjoying school. He found it too restrictive. When something interested him, he liked to give it his full focus for hours, days, or even months. He didn't like jumping from subject to subject. The curriculum was already focused on how to pass exams that would be taking place in nearly two years' time: tricks and methods on how to get extra marks, with the students senselessly learning from pages of material to pass an exam rather than just absorbing the information because they found it interesting. These and more were all the reasons we had homeschooled him before.

"Luca, do you think you would be happier if you went back to homeschooling?"

"Yeah, for sure."

"How about you did homeschooling in Italy?"

"Hell yeah! That would be amazing."

That proved he wasn't tied to a country, never mind four walls.

"When are we going?"

"Leave it with me. I need to talk to Dad."

With that, I heard Ronan come in the front door. Steps heavy, carrying a bag of coal on his shoulders, he stomped through the sitting room, drowned by the rain, and dumped the sack outside the back door.

"This bloody country is becoming an uninhabitable island." He went inside to dry himself off and change his clothes.

I made myself a hot honey-and-lemon drink. My energy was fading fast.

"Wendy called," I shouted in to him from the kitchen.

"Yeah?"

"She wants to raise the rent."

"By how much?"

"Double, but I got her down to nine hundred."

"*What?* Is she joking?" He was back in the kitchen, towel-drying his hair. "So after Christmas we'll be paying nearly double?"

"Here's what I'm thinking…Why don't we tell her to stuff this place up her arse and move to Italy after Christmas? All our work is online… Izzy told me about moving to London… I don't want her moving to some hovel in a bad part of town, so with the money we save on rent here we could help her afford a better place in London. Luca is happy to do homeschooling again and…well, the weather is better?"

He stopped drying his hair. "You want us to move to Italy after Christmas? You do realize that's only three months? Don't you think we'd be putting ourselves under a lot of pressure? There's so much to sort out and think about: Where will we stay when we go over? There's all our furniture here—do we bring it with us, sell it, or store it? Then there's the dogs: we need to think of vaccines and passports they need, and then there's—"

"Yeah, I know we haven't had time since we got back to make a solid plan of action, but we can work on a plan between now and Christmas. Lucia will be happy to rent us one of her holiday apartments until we find somewhere. I know it's moving our plans forwards five months, but we can do it, I think." I was on a short fuse; I felt ill and my head was throbbing. I needed sunshine more than ever.

"Our plan was to go over for the summer, Rosie. You're not just moving our plans; you are moving our whole lives."

Scratching at the back door made us look up. Asha, our big, black, long-haired German shepherd, was standing at the door, staring in, saturated. As soon as I released the door handle, the door banged open, forced by the driving rain and wind. Asha stepped into the kitchen and shook her long coat, spraying us and the entire kitchen in dog-hair-ridden rainwater.

"Ooouuuu," I said as I grabbed Ronan's towel to shield me and he got the full blast.

"Oh, bloody hell, Asha." He looked at me and, while wiping sticky dog hair from his face, said, "Let's do it."

All my energy was gone. I crawled back to bed and slept for an hour but woke feeling panicked. I needed to call Wendy back. I made the call in the office, where Ronan was working on the photos of a beautiful sun-bleached wedding taken only a few weeks previously on what now felt like a different planet.

"Hi, Wendy, I've spoken to Ronan and we appreciate you haven't raised the rent in the two years we've been here, but as you can imagine, a doubling of rent is a bit of a shock. So we're considering our options and we may need to move on elsewhere after Christmas, after our three-month advance runs out."

"Three months' advance payment was never the agreement. You took that upon yourself to do. I'll need the full amount for November and December."

My short fuse had run out and the detonator had been reached.

"So you want me to pay you an equivalent of an additional two months' rent before Christmas at short notice?"

"Yes, that is the requirement."

"So if we move out this month, I take it you will refund my advance payments?"

"Well, I'm sure there will be no need for that."

"I'm asking you, if we move out by November, will you refund me the so-called unauthorized payments I have paid you?"

"Well yes."

"Fine."

"But you would need to be out by the 31st of October. If it goes over even by a day, I'm afraid I will require the full month's rent for November at the new rate."

"Don't you worry. We will be gone by the 31st of October."

If it was an old-fashioned phone I would have slammed down the receiver.

Ronan was sitting at his desk opposite me, gobsmacked. "Are you serious?"

"She's relying on our weakness. She thinks she has us over a barrel. I'm not feeding into her greed. We moved here in the space of three days, so why not? We can do it."

I was fuming. I lay down on the bed again. My head was spinning, but I needed to put a plan in place.

I had just committed to packing up our lives and moving country within three weeks. And at the same time, our daughter was moving to another country and our son was quitting regular school. This time

I would tell my parents we were leaving for good. Two years before, they'd sold their cabin and holiday plot and bought themselves a little cottage close by and near where my brother Jim lived with his wife, Ingrid, so they were now settled and more stable.

Ronan followed me into the room. "Rosie, you know the way we have both been sick and not out of bed in the last ten days and not listened to any news? Well, there's a hurricane starting to hit Ireland… Hurricane Brian."

"Hurricane Brian? What type of name is that for a hurricane? And this is Ireland. We don't get hurricanes."

"We do now apparently."

I looked at my weather app again—it was twenty degrees Celsius and sunny in La Dogana. "All the more reason to leave then. We can do this. What's holding us? Why are we here?"

There was that question again.

Ronan answered accordingly—"Okay"—and went outside for a cigarette.

Chapter 19

LYING THERE, HEADS STILL STUFFY FROM THE FLU, WE BROKE down a plan. The promise of Italy brought some energy to my aching joints. We had left most of our clutter—big furniture—in the last house, so we didn't have that much stuff. We'd bring whatever we could fit in the camper van, store any remaining stuff at my parents' house, and come back in the spring to collect it.

The dogs would need their vaccines updated and pet passports. We needed packing boxes to store stuff in. Clothes would be packed in suitcases and brought back by plane each time we returned for a visit.

For anything we couldn't bring, we'd take photos and sell it online in the next two weeks. At dinner we told the kids.

"We're thinking of speeding up our plans and moving to Italy sooner. Like very soon, before the winter…by November."

"You're moving to Italy that soon? I thought the plan was for next year? Where will I go?" Izzy dropped her fork from her mouth.

"Well, you are moving to London. We assumed that was a long-term decision?"

"Yes, but I still want us to have a home, somewhere I can come back to, for Christmas and birthdays and…when I miss you. Like, I want a bedroom and a house to think of as home." Her eyes filled with tears.

"Of course we'll still have a home, and of course you'll have a bedroom with all your stuff in it to come back to whenever you want or need. It just won't be here, it will be in Italy. We're going to go over and stay at La Dogana and then find a long-term rental with at least three bedrooms, so you'll have your own space and we'll have all our familiar bits and pieces. It will feel homely in no time.

"Home is where the four of us are. So when we visit you in London it will feel like we're home, and when we're all back in Ireland at the same time we will be home, but our base will now be Italy."

"But we will still be keeping this place as our base, right?"

"We could, but we'd prefer to let this place go and use the money to help you find a better place to stay in London than a sofa," I said.

"It's just weird not having somewhere to imagine you guys in. All the familiarity will be gone."

"We'll have a new home in Italy in no time, and after a visit or two you'll be thinking of it as home; don't worry."

The shock had subsided as Izzy came around to the advantages of the idea. "My friend Amy does have a spare room in her house, as her housemate is moving back to Australia, but it's nine hundred euro a month."

"In that lovely Edwardian house near Nothing Hill you stayed in?"
She nodded.

"Perfect. Call her and tell her you'll take it. We'll give you the additional four hundred per month you need to make it happen." This cleared up any misconception she had of the move to Italy being a bad idea.

"I'll go call her now, just so she doesn't give it to someone else. Don't clean up my plate; I'm not finished eating yet." ·

After a phone call with happy screeching from both ends of the line, it was set. Izzy could move in on the 7th of November, which meant we would be gone before her. Racing our adult child out of the nest was one way to avoid empty-nest syndrome.

"Luca, how about you finish school at the end of October midterm?"

"I've a better idea," he answered. "How about I finish school this week and help pack?"

That made sense.

"Okay, that's that decided; your last day of school will be tomorrow if you want."

"What did Nanny and Grandad think about this?" asked Izzy, taking her place at the table in much better humor.

"I haven't told them yet." I put down my fork.

This time I couldn't pretend that we were just going on a long holiday. I needed to tell my parents that we were leaving Ireland and leaving for good. The fact that they were that bit older now made it even more difficult. Would they feel I was abandoning them? *Was* I abandoning them? I justified it by telling myself they still had each other, and who knew what the future held? I had spent my twenties and early thirties nursing and watching out for Ronan and Eileen during the drinking years. Was it a selfish thing that I wanted part of my adult years to be carefree and to follow a lifelong dream?

My parents were healthy and living in a nice little house, with my brother close by, after all. These were the arguments going through my head, keeping me awake most of the night. We had so little time; I would have to tell them the next morning.

"Do you want me to come with you?" Ronan asked, seeing the dread on my face as I readied myself to visit my parents.

"No. I'll be fine. You focus on the vet stuff."

The familiar smell of sausages and rashers sizzling told me Mam had made breakfast in time for my arrival. I stood outside for a while, savoring the smell of my version of home. Rashers don't exist in Italy, and the sausages are not the same.

After chatting about Izzy going to London and preparations for the approaching Hurricane Brian, I finally got around to what I had come to say on my third cup of tea.

"Mam, Dad, listen; we're thinking of going to Italy for the winter." Why couldn't I tell them the truth? Spit it out, woman, screamed my brain. "Well, actually not just for winter but to live."

The room went quiet.

"Do it!" they both said in unison. "You'd be mad not to," said Dad. "If we were younger we'd do it, get out of this miserable hole of a country. Don't know why you didn't do it years ago."

"Emm, well, we nearly did, but then Eileen died."

"Hmm," Dad said, rearranging himself in the seat. He still couldn't talk about her. "You don't need to stick around for us, We're grand. We're not completely useless, you know," he joked. "You go

and build the life for yourself you always wanted to live in the sun.
We really don't know what the feck you are doing here; you've had
us confused."

"Sure, we might follow you over, you never know," chimed in
Mam.

And so it was that easy. I was released from the guilt that I had
been carrying for years, not just days. The guilt of someday having to
choose between abandoning my parents or abandoning my lifelong
dream of living abroad.

The thought of leaving my elderly parents was the most difficult
part of moving abroad, but at the end of the day they just wanted me
to be happy, the same way I wanted my kids to be happy, wherever
happiness led them. I don't know why I had never seen it that way
before.

The next morning we were up early and feeling better. We brought
the dogs to the vet. Looney puked on my lap after seven minutes in
the car, as usual, and we bought packing boxes on the way home.

We put two boxes in the center of the sitting room floor as the
"Take with us" boxes, and then two boxes in each room—"To store"
and "Give away." And we began. Large garbage bags were filled with
clothes we wouldn't need in Italy. Lots of coats, heavy sweaters, and
most of Ronan's secondhand jeans collection. He went through a
phase of dropping into charity shops each week and always came back
with a pair of jeans—"They were only two euro!" "These were only
five euro and still have the labels on them."

"Yes, Ronan, but they are four sizes too big for you."

"I like baggy jeans, and it's nothing a belt won't fix."

I called a halt to his charity-shop, jean-buying days after I counted twenty-six pairs in his wardrobe, and now they filled two black bags without him even knowing they were gone.

I boxed my favorite mugs, plates, and cutlery in a "Take with us" box, along with a lamp, clock, some ornaments, family photos, and some precious books. Just things of sentimental value that had been with us from day one: paints and brushes, notebooks of ideas, my tarot cards. I felt like I was doing that thing "If you were to be stranded on a desert island for a year, what would you take with you?" Or "If your house was on fire, what would you grab?"

We had this; we would be packed up in no time. I took photos of the large furniture we couldn't take with us, like our old kitchen-style range and our claw-footed bath from our last house. These had been stored in the garden of our rental since our last move. They sold quickly, and I watched them being loaded into the van as another part of our history moved on.

I still had to deal with clients, so the office was the last to be packed up. We were very organized for the first three days, and then Hurricane Brian arrived, like a big, clumsy bully after a few bad pints, full of wind, thrashing his arms around, uprooting trees, flooding roads, and knocking out our electricity—which meant no hot showers, no heating, and no cooker. We thought the power would be back on in a day or two, but then the water went also.

We got by cooking on the gas cooker in the camper van and living on takeaways and sponge baths.

The electricity came back with six days left until D-day: Departure Day. Wendy texted to say she wanted to come to do a "house inspection" on Sunday, in three days' time. The rain and wind were easing, and so were the last of our flu symptoms.

As most of the country was without electricity, no one had seen our for-sale ads. I finally put up my "out of office" auto-reply and packed up my computer and office files. We called a charity furniture shop to come take the big stuff. There was one piece I did want to put in storage: the writing bureau. I remembered my brother-in-law buying it; he'd often used it to illustrate his disapproval of my hippyish ways and to emphasize that money is an important part of parenting.

"Like that writing bureau you wanted. It's important to better yourself in life so you can buy the things you want. My kids will be the best at everything and want for nothing. If they wanted something like that, I would buy it for them."

I also remembered them arguing bitterly over it during their separation. Eileen had "won," and it followed her down to the country, where it took up a new residence as a junk mail holder in the corner of her bedroom. I now had it in the sitting room, directly outside our bedroom door, waiting for the day I'd get a chance to use it like it was supposed to be used.

Every time I passed it, I thought of her. Every time I passed it, I thought of how she finally broke and told me about the horrible fights they had and how he had broken our grandmother's beloved statue. I thought of all the anger it had experienced in their home together and all the sadness it had seen her go through, alone in her bedroom. It had experienced her death. I had painted it with white chalk paint to give it new life, but still it made me ache. Standing looking at it, I realized it was time to let it go—time to let it do good, time for it to be sold for charity to a new loving home that would not know its past. I didn't want to carry to Italy the wave of sadness that it brought; it was time for us both to move on.

Sunday was upon us, the first dry day in weeks. I really could have done without a visit from Wendy—we were at that point of moving house when all the last bits are piled in the middle of the floor. No matter how many car runs we did to Jim's and my parents' houses, we just seemed to have more stuff. How did we have so much stuff? The furniture was in three piles in the front garden—charity collection, dump, and decent stuff (for anyone who wanted it; otherwise it would go to the dump). I was clearing out under the stairs when Wendy and her husband walked into the sitting room, the front door wide open.

I was sweating, grubby, and in clothes I intended to throw out after this was over.

"Hello?"

"Oh hi. You're early, very early. Three hours early in fact." A lot could be done in three hours when you're under pressure.

Her chin was nearly on the floor. "The place is a mess."

"Ehh, we are moving and packing? I told you we would still be packing and it wouldn't be a good day to visit. I told you we would have things in the middle of the floor."

"Yes, but when you said you were packing and you would have things in the middle of the floor, I was expecting a couple of suitcases, not this."

"Wendy, four people have been living here full time for three years; Do you really think all our lives would fit into a couple of suitcases? It may be a holiday home for you, but it was a real home for us."

"But the skirting boards are dusty; they haven't been cleaned." She pointed to the location where the writing desk had stood for three years up until thirty minutes ago. "And there are marks on the walls," she added, pointing to where our paintings had hung up to an hour ago.

She really had become an expert at igniting my shortest fuse.

"*Really?*" I rarely got so annoyed. "In fairness, Wendy, you gave us notice to leave three weeks ago. In that time we have been recovering from flu, and in case you didn't notice, the whole country was whacked by a hurricane leaving us without electricity or water for nine days. In between all that, we have been trying to pack twenty-four years of our lives into boxes and a camper van ready for a three-day trip across to another country, as we can no longer afford to live in this one thanks to you. Unfortunately, I have not had time to redecorate, and please do not worry, your bloody skirting boards will be dusted before we go. Now if you don't mind, and if you are finished here, I have a lot to do."

They mooched around the house. We had cleaned as we emptied each room. So Izzy's room was perfect, our en suite and the kitchen were perfect, and, other than our bed still having its linen on, our bedroom was back to the way we had found it when we moved in.

It was the sitting room, front garden, and shed that were in a heap, which any sane person would recognize as a messy "we are moving" heap that would be soon fixed. I knew they were just looking for an excuse not to give us back our deposit. I didn't care; they could keep it. I never wanted to speak to these people again. A newfound greed was growing in Ireland, and it had forced us into a situation that we were battling to turn into a positive.

Chapter 20

OUR FERRY TO THE UK WAS LEAVING AT SIX THIRTY THE FOLLOW-
ing morning. My chest felt like I was wearing a bra that was three sizes
too small. The house still looked in a heap. Jim arrived and took my
precious Buddha statue, which Ronan bought me for our fifteenth
wedding anniversary, and the ironwood garden chair we loved so
much. They were too heavy for us to take to Italy.

I had ten plastic, stackable boxes filled to capacity with photos
and memories, things that needed to be decluttered and organized,
but I'd just never had the time, so we brought them around to my
parents' house and stacked them in the corner of their spare room.
By evening I had the corner of their conservatory packed full of cardboard boxes and black plastic refuse bags full of things we didn't need
but didn't want to throw out in their attic.

Even after all that, there was still stuff in our house; it just seemed
to be reproducing. Several times throughout the day I found myself
on the verge of crying "What the hell am I doing?" and I would go to

the bathroom and throw water in my face. I felt sick. Jim was calling; he had made dinner for us.

"We can't come. There is still too much to do," I said, exasperated.

I was crumbling, possibly on the verge of having a mental break-down, and he could hear it.

Within ten minutes Jim and Ingrid were at our door. They issued me orders to go shower, and within an hour they had the remaining stuff organized into piles. Jim would store the remaining stuff in his garage until it was homed, and Ingrid and Izzy would come the next day and finish the cleaning, not forgetting the skirting boards. "Now come and eat."

As soon as I arrived at his house, I heard the soundtrack of *The Godfather* playing. A giant "Arrivederci" sign, made by my niece, hung over the dining table. My parents and nieces and nephew were all there for a surprise going-away party. Jim had made an Italian feast of starters and spaghetti and meatballs, even though he himself was not a fan of pasta.

I spent most of the meal fighting back tears among a lot of laugh-ter as I watched my family come together for the last time. Izzy sat between her nan and granddad so she could have both of them close; soon she'd be gone too. Their three different laughs together sounded like a perfect piece of music that I knew I wouldn't hear again for a long time.

After dinner, while the rest of the crowd were busy playing cha-rades, I sauntered out to the kitchen to where Jim was preparing dessert alone.

"When you come to Italy, I'll book you a cookery class where you'll learn how to make real pasta; you'll like it after that. Your bruschetta was spot on."

"Eileen taught me how to make that. Do you remember her Christmas morning breakfasts we all had to go to? Where she'd have rakes of 'hors *de* d'oeuvres,' as she called them, perfectly laid out even though she'd spent the night putting together the kids' Santa toys while that arsehole slept? I didn't appreciate it fully at the time, but after having kids myself, I don't know how she did it."

"She would have enjoyed this, the whole Italian theme," I said as I reminisced, catching her eye in a family photo hanging on the wall.

"Ha! If she was alive we would have been making tapas and paella and had a bullfight in the back garden. You were going to Spain, not Italy, remember?"

"You knew about that?"

"Of course! We all knew about it! Eileen was as bad as you at keeping secrets. Everyone was surprised you came back to Ireland after your camper van trip. We were all nearly placing bets as to when you'd call and say you had bought a house abroad. You ruined all the free holidays we were all secretly planning."

"Even Mam and Dad?"

"Yes, especially them. They weren't too pushed about the idea of Spain, but when you said you were in Italy, we had to put up with them reminiscing for days about their first trip there, in the fifties, when they were nineteen, with Joan and Joe. You know the story: how they knew they were in love as soon as they threw the three coins in the Trevi Fountain, and how they stayed in separate dorms in convents for the whole trip, blah, blah."

"But all that guilt I felt for nothing. I should have…" I faded off. Jim didn't know what I was talking about, but I knew now more than ever: Italy was where we were supposed to be. It was our destiny.

My parents left the party first. Mam and I squeezed each other, both fighting tears. My dad left quickly, without saying goodbye. I patted him on the head as he passed, and he nodded. We both got it; neither of us says goodbye, or else the floodgates open. As everyone went to the door to wave them off, I went into the back garden and sobbed. What the hell was I doing?

Saying farewell to my nieces and nephew was a little easier, as they were all old enough to travel by themselves and promised to be over soon.

Ingrid refused to get upset.

"I know you pair," she said, hugging me. "The novelty will wear off and you'll be back in a few months, or maybe six at the most; that's why I'm okay about this," she said, reassuring herself.

Even though I felt Italy was our destiny, I couldn't help being shaken by what she said. She was right; Ronan and I were prone to making big, life-changing decisions at the drop of a hat, and we had no problem backing out of them just as quick, without any embarrassment, and that's why her parting words terrified me. What if she was right? What if we hated it after a few months, didn't fit in, and felt we had made the biggest mistake of our lives? What would we do? What Ingrid hadn't taken into account was that we couldn't return even if we wished to. Besides wanting to move to a better climate, the fact of the matter was that we could no longer afford to live in our home country. Returning was not going to be an option.

Jim and Ingrid would be around in the morning to help us get going and wave us off, while Izzy was going to stay at their house until she left for London, as she had no bed left in ours. She joked that there was no way she was getting up at five o'clock to wave us off. We all knew it was best to say arrivederci tonight so we could just get on with things robotically in the morning without all the emotion.

So the last person we needed to say goodbye to that night was the last person we wanted to say goodbye to: Izzy. We somehow did it. We were all moving on to better things, bigger, more fulfilled lives, but from that moment on, our family would be forever separated in different countries. I warned my boys I was going to cry as I got into the car. But I didn't just cry; I again sobbed: "What the hell am I doing?"

I lay in bed exhausted, but I couldn't sleep. I got up twice and vomited; my usual jelly belly was a solid mass. I would have been proud if it had been from sessions at the gym and not pure tension. Ronan slept, which was good, as he was going to be the one doing three full days of driving to get us from Ireland to Italy. The house was still not ready for us to leave. One more full day at it and I would be happy; one more full day to prepare myself mentally and I would be okay. That's what I believed.

Everything rushed around my head. My biggest concern was still the dogs; this trip was going to be a nightmare with them.

In the dark of the night I suddenly decided we didn't have to leave that day. I could change our tickets and we'd go in two days' time. Needing something to focus on, to be in control again, I began planning everything I needed to do to make the change. With the thought of not having to go in the morning, the tightly wound muscle in my stomach relaxed a little.

"Ronan? Are you awake? Are you awake, Ronan?" I whispered loudly, interrupting his snores.

"I am now. What time is it?"

"It's four, but I just had a great thought: we don't have to go today. I can change the tickets to two days' time, and we can—"

"Rosie, that's not happening. We are going today."

"But another day will give us time to finish clearing the house."

"Another day of us cleaning and fussing will not change anything. We are leaving today; now go to sleep."

And with that he was back in the land of Nod. His decisiveness was comforting.

I had been controlling everything, but in the last twenty-four hours I had withered. Jim, Izzy, and Ingrid were stepping in and taking control of clearing and cleaning, and Ronan was taking control of the schedule. The tension eased a little more. I rested but couldn't sleep. At four thirty I heard Jim outside, loading his pickup with the last of the stuff for storage in his garage.

Relieved that I didn't have to try to force myself to sleep anymore, I was up and dressed within minutes. I found Ingrid standing in the kitchen with the kettle on. "God, you guys are early."

They were full of energy and had brought hot breakfast rolls, tea bags, coffee, and milk, as our cupboards were now bare. Ronan was up and also surprisingly full of energy. As soon as we opened the van door to put in our duvet, Asha jumped into the back and wouldn't budge. She knew we were going somewhere big, and there was no way she was agreeing to be left behind this time.

Luca was up and singing in the shower. I'd never heard him sing before. He was happy, everyone was happy. It brushed off on me, the tension replaced by bubbling excitement.

After a final check around the now empty house, we gave Jim and Ingrid a last hug goodbye and piled into the front seats. Luca handed Looney to me. I had my wet wipes ready, a backpack with snacks, water, and a change of clothes for when she inevitably puked on me. My mother's going-away present was also in the front—a bag of old towels, in preparation, and disinfectant spray. Ronan revved the twenty-year-old engine more than was needed, but with each rev we all laughed a little louder. It finally hit us: we were moving to Italy.

Chapter 21

WITH WAVES AND BEEPS GOODBYE, WE DROVE OFF INTO THE sunrise. Looney didn't just get past the first seven minutes; she made it all the way to the port without a single puke. I took it as a good omen. Driving onto the ferry, we reached the part of the journey I was most dreading: leaving the dogs in the van, surrounded by unfamiliar sounds and sensations, for a full three hours alone while we went up on deck. Passengers were not permitted to stay or go back to the car until it was time to disembark.

We waited until the last minute, and then, leaving them water and treats, we went upstairs to the upper decks, where Ronan and Luca quickly fell asleep for nearly the whole journey. I was wracked with concern about the dogs and couldn't get back to the van quick enough when we were allowed. I could hear them barking as we approached; they were telling us off but were delighted to see us all the same. They didn't seem to have been as scared as I thought; all that angst and lack of sleep for nothing.

As soon as we were out of the port in Wales, we found a small park to pull into and gave the dogs a walk. New smells and their first time in a new country, the first of four on our three-day drive to their new home in Italy.

The journey across Wales and England to our first resting post was an eight-hour drive, but it felt even longer due to the exhaustion we still carried from the previous three weeks of mayhem, chaos, disaster, and recovery. However, it gave us and the dogs time to adjust; Looney sat on my lap, with her front paws on the dash, looking straight ahead between naps on my and Luca's laps. She was loving it, and mercifully, she remained pukeless. Asha stayed quiet, watching the scenery go by. We soon got to know when a stop was needed for a coffee or a dog pee, which usually synced well; another good omen. We eventually reached Folkestone, on the other side of the UK, where we were booked into a hotel near the mouth of the Channel Tunnel.

Other than the tiredness, the trip was much easier than I had expected. As we approached the hotel, I felt my stress levels rise again. Asha is the size of a small donkey and looks like a very large black wolf; she doesn't do well with other dogs or cats. I always said she could pull me over when on the lead if she wanted to, and David, our racist dog sitter, was proof of my theory. What if there were other dogs in the reception area? What if she started a fight? She hadn't been properly socialized as a pup.

I'd been working out a plan for weeks. "Okay, let's run through the hotel plan again: we find a quiet place to park; Ronan, you take Asha for a walk; Luca, you take Looney. I'll go check in, get the key, check if the coast is clear, and then come get you."

"She'll be fine. Relax, or the dogs will sense your anxiety," Ronan said, sick of hearing my dog plan.

"Stop playing it so cool, Ronan. Be on guard." I was beginning to freak out with my overthinking.

"Your room is on the ground floor. Just follow the corridor behind the desk to the left, and your room, 145, is on the right," said the receptionist. On the check-in desk there was a welcome sign and a dog bowl with dog biscuits. How cool. I felt a little more relaxed; they must have been used to all sorts of dogs staying, and perhaps they'd had a vicious black wolf before and wouldn't blink twice when Asha walked through.

"Oh my God," said the receptionist, looking towards the door. I swung around and saw Ronan had forgotten the plan and was walking into the foyer with Asha.

"Is that your dog?"

In my head, now that the receptionist had seen Asha and probably decided she was unacceptable based on her size and appearance, I was already trying to figure out how we could stay the night in the packed camper van.

"She's beautiful."

I stopped sweating. Of course she'd have to be a dog lover to work in a dog-friendly hotel, and to be fair, Asha is gorgeous. "Thanks." I grabbed the key from her, before she changed her mind, and looked down the corridor. All clear, so I waved the boys on to follow me. We were halfway to our room when I spotted a Great Dane down the hallway, coming towards us. It was too late to warn Ronan.

I was ahead at the hotel room door, frantically trying to open it, but the more I tried, the more trembly my hands got. Asha spotted him, her ears went up, and she jerked Ronan forwards and gave a muf-fled bark, probably confused, as this was not her territory. Ronan was in control, but I could see he didn't know what was going to happen next. She spotted me and did a double take, confused as to where I was disappearing to, just as the Great Dane strode past her. No one was watching Looney, who went straight for the Great Dane's ankle. She missed but yapped after him, warning him not to come back again or he'd have to deal with her.

We ordered dinner and brought it to our room. Both Ronan and Luca had ribs, and the dogs feasted on the bones on the bathroom floor.

After a great night's sleep, we were checked out and on the road by seven o'clock, with Looney in position and looking very in control with her paws on the dashboard, clearly pleased with her successful showdown the night before.

"How long does this take?" Ronan asked, talking about the next challenge on the itinerary—the Channel Tunnel crossing. He had done no research as usual; that was my department.

"One hour and thirty-five minutes."

I wished he hadn't asked, as I was trying not to think about being in a tube twenty leagues under the sea with all the weight of the water above pushing down. The idea of the tunnel had never appealed to me much. When I heard about it being built, I said not in a million years would you get me in there.

I was distracted from my claustrophobia by how organized and painless the whole process of checking in and driving onto the train was. The trains run like clockwork, with up to four departures every hour, and within minutes of driving on we were stationary but moving. Ronan decided to go for a walk to explore. I'm not sure what he was expecting to find in the series of identical train carriages featuring one long car park.

Luca and I were chatting for what seemed to be a very short time, twenty minutes, and then I saw we were above ground. Maybe we hadn't gone under the sea yet but had just gone through a regular rail tunnel to the edge of the sea. But then I noticed the signs gliding by were in French. Of course, when I had looked at our arrival time, I had not taken into consideration that France was an hour ahead. So the travel time was thirty-five minutes, not an hour and thirty-five. Ronan didn't know that. There were announcements to prepare to disembark, and Ronan was still on a walkabout. I began to sweat. The train stopped, cars and trucks started to drive off, and just in time, Ronan jumped back into the driving seat. "Bloody hell, that time went quick. I was right at the end of the train. It's so long."

"Were the carriages any different from this one?"

"No!"

We drove towards Lyon. Unlike on our last trip, we now had GPS on our phones and could see where there was traffic congestion so we could take a different route. On previous road trips, I had guided Ronan through the Massif Central, Provence, and small villages on side roads, all under the guise of their being the most direct routes to where we wanted to go, which they were not. With GPS on his phone, there was no way to hide the most direct route: the most boring motorway in France, a monotonous stretch of road where the only things breaking up the apartment fields were the regular gas station stop-off centers and toll booths.

On one such trip back through France to Ireland, we had driven through a small town where most of the houses had put furniture outside for a special furniture-disposal day. We couldn't believe our luck, although the kids thought quite the opposite and sat mortified as we filled what space remained in the van with fantastic wooden chairs and a coat rack, later to be restored and painted back in Ireland. We vowed we would return to France for an antique market tour if we ever got our own place again and had an empty van and no moaning teenagers.

On this trip there would be no diversions or leisurely antique browsing. We were on a mission to get our dogs to Italy, so the boring motorway route it was.

We stopped overnight at a dog-friendly hotel just beyond Lyon, and as I dozed off with my boys and dogs sleeping around me, I noticed my stomach had returned to its jelly-belly, pre-tension state.

The next morning, we had a leisurely breakfast before heading for the Mont Blanc Tunnel, which runs under the mountain connecting France to Italy. Again, going through a mountain, the weight of rock and snow crushing down on top of us, was not on my claustrophobic to-do list. It didn't help that when I thought of Mont Blanc, I thought of Mr. Travers, a much-loved physics teacher who had been killed in an avalanche on this very mountain during my school years.

As we ascended higher towards the blue-white glaciers of Mont Blanc, the scenery changed to alpine evergreen. I wound down the window, and my lungs expanded as quickly as a small balloon attached to a helium tank at the unexpected inhalation of fresh, sharp air.

"Wow, this place is amazing," said Luca, pointing out the ski chalets and wooden chapels perched on the surrounding mountains.

We were soon in the queue for the toll booth at the ominous mouth of the tunnel. I tried not to think of it gobbling us up as I held the leaflet that included escape instructions in the event of an emergency. Thankfully, we were spat out on the other side without incident, and we drove over a borderline on the road. We had made it to Italy.

We wound our way down the pine-clad valley to a rest stop in Aosta, where we had a picnic of panini and pizza for lunch, sitting on a car park bench, sunning ourselves in our T-shirts, surrounded by snow-capped peaks.

The plan was to drive for another three or four hours, then find somewhere to stay before doing the last four-hour drive to La Dogana the following day. We had forgotten to bring music with us, so as the Bruno Mars CD that had been left in the player started its 475th rotation, I snapped, promptly ejected it, and threw it in the back. To this day, Bruno Mars's "Just the Way You Are" sticks in all our heads on repeat for days once triggered.

It was All Saints' Day, a national holiday in Italy, so the roads were quieter than usual. We cruised along in our reliable workhorse, leaving the Alps behind, down ear-popping highways, past fast-flowing rivers and distant, ancient-walled towns to more industry-lined roads. Passing Turin and tempting turnoffs to Milan, we reached the outskirts of Bologna before sunset.

We had left France five hours before, and now we were just three hours away from our new life in Italy.

"Will I find somewhere to stay in the next town?" I asked Ronan.

"How about we push on and go for it?" he said, snacking on picnic remnants that had kept both of us from getting hungry.

"Tonight? Another three hours?"

"Yeah, I can sleep tomorrow," he said, winking at me. Luca was asleep, and so was Looney.

"Home it is then."

I can't say the last three hours were easy; my ass had gone numb and my back ached from sitting in the same position. Asha must have felt the same, as she was getting very uneasy, but Ronan got us there. Excited and elated, we pulled into the familiar driveway of La Dogana. Luca jolted awake at the bump in the path where we had met the sausage thief what seemed like a lifetime ago.

"What are we doing here?" Luca said, confused, expecting to see a hotel in Bologna.

"We're home," I screeched, making Asha and Looney bark excitedly. We pulled up outside our "old" apartment, which we had left just weeks ago.

Chapter 22

THE NEXT DAY, WE WENT TO A LOCAL ESTATE AGENT. LUCIA HAD called ahead for us, as there was an architect she knew in the same office building who could speak English.

"Hello. You must be the friends of Lucia," said the black-haired, bearded man opening the door and shaking our hands. "I am Michele."

"Mick Kelly?" asked Ronan.

"Sí," he said, smiling.

"That is a very Irish name."

Michele looked puzzled. "Really? It is a very Italian name also."

"I'm sure there are a few Mick Kelly and Sons in the building trade in Ireland," Ronan continued. I didn't bother explaining Ronan's humor. I knew I would just add to the confusion.

"Please take a seat in the office," Michele said, changing the subject and ushering us in.

I had written out what we wanted to say in Italian. Mick Kelly, as he had now been re-baptized, was patient with my chugging-along effort at pronunciation, but he obviously hadn't understood a word.

"It is okay for you to use English; please do."

So we explained, in English, that we were looking for a three-bedroom house with a fenced garden somewhere around the lake and that it must have good Wi-Fi.

"Okay, leave it with me for a few days, and I will ask around the neighborhood. In Italy it is sometimes the best way. People are left houses and they don't think about renting them. So there may be an empty house I know that will be suitable."

The following day he texted me: Meet me at the entrance of the agriturismo on Friday at 2pm. I have an option to show you.

I made sandwiches and packed fruit for the drive. He hadn't stated which town the house was in; if it was on the far side of the lake, we could be gone a couple of hours, and Luca was constantly hungry these days.

At 2:00 p.m. we were in the car and starting to follow Mick Kelly's car. At 2:01 p.m. we were driving through electric gates at the end of the road from La Dogana. We drove through a garden to a large villa.

"This can't be it, surely? Did we mention a budget to him?" Ronan said in disbelief.

"It's probably divided up into several apartments—let's not get too excited yet," I said, as the guys were freaking out about how great it was. "And let's not show we like it; otherwise they might up the price," I said, hissing.

Mick Kelly greeted a short, gnome-like man with a shock of white hair pushing a wheelbarrow. I recognized him from somewhere but couldn't place him.

"This is Giovanni, the owner of this property," said Mick Kelly, introducing us. "It is currently vacant. Please follow him and have a look inside."

Giovanni didn't speak a word of English but had a massive smile. He led us up twenty steps to the first floor, a spacious terrace outside the entrance facing the lake. He enthusiastically ushered us through the front door into a square lounge room with a big fireplace. There were doors on every wall, one leading to the small kitchen, one to the hallway leading to the bathroom and main bedroom, and the other wall had doorways to two other bedrooms on either side of the fireplace. From the kitchen there was a doorway into a second apartment with a bigger kitchen but only two bedrooms. We could have the choice of either.

While I was not overly enthusiastic about the decor or the old, clunky Tuscan furniture, the stunning view, location, and gardens compensated. "The dogs will love this," said Ronan, walking around to the fenced fields in the back.

"Ronan, stop smiling so much. We still don't know how much it is."

I took on the role of negotiator, as I knew Ronan was squealing like a small piglet inside and I couldn't trust him to contain himself. "It's good, Mick Kelly, but what price is it?"

"He wants six hundred euro per month."

"If he makes it five hundred we'll take it today," said Ronan, interrupting. "But we also need him to get a new fridge and install a washing machine for that price," I quickly added.

Mick Kelly translated. Giovanni's smile dropped immediately. He said a lot of Italian words, with his hands going up and down.

"He says €550 per month, including the washing machine and fridge."

"Deal!" said Ronan. Giovanni was delighted, his wide smile returning in seconds, and a booming laugh to go with it. "*Andiamo in cantina*" ("We go to the cantina"), he bellowed as we shook on it, and he led the way down the stairs to the door below the lounge room window. Inside, in the low light, we saw barrels with taps along the wall; like lots of houses in Italy, this one had a cantina where the owner made and stored his own wine. He filled plastic cups full of wine and handed one to me, and then tried Ronan and Luca, who politely refused.

Giovanni went to a small fridge in the corner and pulled out four bottles of bitters, a non-alcoholic drink that tastes like bitter oranges and handed them out, keeping one for himself.

"In Italy we must celebrate a deal with something to drink," explained Mick Kelly.

"Am I the only one having wine?"

"I am refusing, as I am working and driving. Giovanni, like many winemakers, does not drink alcohol. It is too tempting to drink it all the time when you have a cantina."

"I know the feeling," chipped in Ronan, making me snort with unexpected laughter.

Giovanni and Mick Kelly distracted themselves, talking together for a moment.

"I know where we have seen him before," said Luca about

Giovanni. "It's him! The main guy putting the grapes in that big mincing machine."

Oh. I was holding the wine from our grape-picking experience. An image of spidery legs and the swarms of bugs in the mincing machine flashed through my mind.

"*Bevilo. Dimmi se pensi che sia buono!*" bellowed Giovanni encouragingly.

"He wants you to drink it and tell him if you think it is good wine," translated Mick Kelly, who then stepped outside to take a call.

Giovanni was watching closely. I took a small, polite sip, "Ummm, *buono.*"

"*Sì?*" he was so excited to have my approval. "*Bevi, bevi!*" ("Drink, drink"), instructed Giovanni with delight, watching my every sip.

"A nice red, is it?" asked Ronan, desperately trying not to laugh, a task Luca had failed miserably at.

"A nice red, with undertones of earwig and a distinct buttery spider flavor, I would say." I met eyes with Giovanni, who was looking ecstatic at my approval. "But who cares. We are standing in the cellar of our new home in Italy. *Salute!*" I tapped plastic cups with our new landlord and knocked back the insect wine. It wasn't that bad.

Chapter 23

WE DIDN'T REALIZE WE WERE LIVING IN A HALLWAY UNTIL Christmas. "Where will we put the Christmas tree?" I said, looking around; every wall had at least one doorway. We had already had difficulty finding what wall to mount the TV on, and had decided the small space between the big fireplace and Luca's door was the best place.

So we'd all sit facing Luca's door every evening; this was particularly problematic when we were watching a horror movie and Luca would come out of his room unexpectedly, making me nearly jump through the roof; the sight of us all staring at his door in the darkened room, with just the light of the TV on our faces, accompanied by horror-movie music, made him jump nearly as high.

"Beside Luca's door," suggested Ronan.

"But there's no space beside his door."

"I mean here," Ronan said, parking the tree directly in front of Luca's door.

"How do I get into my room?"

"Oh, just duck around it."

"You mean duck under the TV and then squeeze around the back of the tree?"

"Just be careful you don't knock it over," I added, thinking of the precious ornaments I had carted with us all the way from Ireland, rather than of my son's eyes being poked out by pine needles.

Our first Christmas was definitely quieter than our usual; in Ireland we'd have had fifteen family members over for a big slap-up lunch that Ronan and I would spend months planning and the morning prepping.

On New Year's Eve we went out on the balcony and watched the fireworks reflected in the lake as they popped in the sky, coming from all the towns dotted around the lakeshore.

We soon learned that January to March were the coldest months in Italy, and we also learned that the house we were renting had no insulation. Having a bedroom that had walls exposed on three sides made it a sauna in summer and freezing in winter. We'd go to bed adding two layers to the amount we'd worn during the day, plus two duvets, and we still felt freezing.

"Under the Tuscan sun my ass. Why is it so cold?" I asked.

"Ahh, it is not usually this cold," explained Lucia, who was really suffering: she would wear an overcoat and shiver in September when we were still in short sleeves. "By mid-March it will be better."

Sure enough, as if God had flicked on the thermostat on the 15th of March, it got warmer, and kittens began to appear.

Italy is riddled with cats, which isn't a bad thing, as I love cats. I once stood at a train station in Tuscany and watched a well-dressed woman cross the tracks, open a bag, and empty several tins of cat food into bowls along a wall. She tapped the tin and cats came running from everywhere. In Ravello I had watched cats feast on pasta left out for them like it was wild salmon. In Calabria I happened across an alleyway with an old wooden table and some chairs around it with "*Gatto Ghetto*" graffitied on the crumbling wall. A clowder of beautiful cats sat sunbathing on the table and groomed themselves on the chairs and steps after cleaning off the food left for them by locals.

But not everyone wants stray cats hanging around, and neutering didn't seem a priority.

"Every year, at least one box of kittens is left on my doorstep. People know I will look after them, so it is an easier solution than taking care of it themselves," said Lucia, holding a box when I dropped Luca off to help her with the gardening. "Especially the black ones. Nobody wants them, as they are considered unlucky in Italy."

"It's the opposite in Ireland; black cats are considered lucky."

I looked inside the box and four sage-green eyes peered up at me; I was instantly in love.

"Can we have one?" Izzy asked like an excited six-year-old. She was back with us until another opportunity opened up for her. She knew I'd always wanted a black cat, and I had said that once we settled somewhere I wanted a cat.

"How about we take both?" I answered, not wanting to split up a family.

"What about the dogs?"

"Asha will just be over-excited, so if we introduce them slowly, and let them get used to each other, she will be all right; she'll know they're part of our family."

And so Moonface and Spooky joined our family. Looney didn't know what they were, but she wagged her tail frantically as Spooky rubbed her head up under her chin. The second day, I walked in from the kitchen to find Looney rolled onto her back, looking as startled as me, with both cats attached to her nipples. I called our vet, Maria, who we had on speed dial. "It is okay; it can sometimes happen, especially when young animals are taken from their mother too soon. Another species can feed them; it is not a problem."

"But she's never had pups. Will she produce milk?"

"Yes, she probably is already if they are staying attached," said Maria.

Moonface lost interest after a couple of days, but Spooky kept being nursed by Looney, her adopted Irish mother of French descent, for a month. I never got used to the sight.

We'd first discovered Maria after a sleepless night, with Looney continuously sneezing and pawing at her snout. I searched for an English-speaking vet and found her just a town away. Arriving at her surgery, I suddenly felt tall. I am five foot two. I've never felt tall in my life. Maria was less than five foot, smiley, and welcoming. "I think Looney has snuffed a seed up her nose. She will need to be sedated for me to examine further."

Now, in Ireland I was used to a vet either keeping the pet in overnight or giving me an appointment for the following day. Either way, it was a surgical procedure and would cost quite a lot. But not here in Italy; after telling us she would have to sedate her, I found myself holding a drip. It was happening right then and there, and we were part of the assisting team it seemed. Ronan was excited; I was not. Since having kids, I've never been good at these things. I'm squeamish as hell. Ronan looked after all the cuts, bruises, tiny bells inserted into ears, broken bones, laundry chemicals in eyes, glass eating—all the things having kids involves.

So I handed the drip to Ronan and backed off. I watched through a squint. Looney was dopey. Maria got tweezers with a light on the top and proceeded up Looney's nostril. "Ah yes, there it is," she said, pulling out the mucus-covered seed with long barbs. "Yes, these seeds you must be careful of. We have many seeds in Italy that dogs inhale and get stuck in their skin. Particularly these; they burrow into the skin."

She also pulled out two small rotting teeth, which we thought had been bothering Looney.

We had been with her nearly an hour. I went to pay. The sedation medicine cost thirty euro. The total bill was forty. "Are you sure?"

"Yes; I am sorry the medicine costs so much."

We were back with Maria within weeks, this time with Asha. We noticed a cut she couldn't reach at the top of her tail. There were flies around her. It wasn't pleasant. Off we went to Maria, who had her assistant vet with her that day, a slight woman, even shorter than Maria. I felt like a giant. Do you have to be a small woman to be a vet in Italy? Their love for animals was apparent, and Asha's size was no hassle to them.

While Asha was asleep, Maria returned and gave her the best Brazilian ever. She should have been a beautician. I gagged as she cleaned the infected wound. Luckily we had caught it early; otherwise it could have become very serious, she said, and she began to tell us how the flies could have laid larvae and… "Stop!" I shouted. Why did one of the few English-speaking Italians I know have to talk exclusively about things that made me want to throw up?

She gave us a prescription for painkillers and an antibiotic and said something about humans being cheaper, but I didn't quite understand. While we were there, she gave Asha a full checkup of her ears, teeth, and eyes. All good. The bill was only fifty euro; the sedation cost forty. Again, she was charging us only ten euro for an hour of her time. Our local chemist didn't have the antibiotic, but he looked it up on the computer. "It's a big dog, yes?"

"Yes."

"There is a human form of this antibiotic; it is the exact same, but under a different name. I can give you that? You need two boxes. The animal form of the medicine is forty-nine euro per box, but the human form is seven euro per box. The Italian government subsidizes medicine for humans, but not for animals."

That explained what Maria had been saying about humans being cheaper. That was the day Asha became classed as a human on the pharmacist's records.

Chapter 24

THE SUMMER TICKED BY, WITH WEDDINGS EACH WEEK KEEPING us busy and our bedroom turned from an ice box to a sauna.

Business was good. Being in Italy made things a lot easier, such as visiting new venues and having potential clients over for viewings. And, of course, we didn't have to travel back and forth from Ireland for each wedding lugging bags of camera gear.

Living in Italy was cheaper than in Ireland. We'd been working hard, and by the end of the summer we had been able to double our savings, squirreling away money when we could.

Izzy came over to stay for a month or perhaps more. She was getting by with acting jobs, mostly in indie films, which paid okay and got her through the lull to the next job. She spent the gaps in between with us, taping herself for auditions, with me as her reading partner.

Her new English agent seemed to have a lot of faith in her ability and was putting her forward for lead roles in big productions.

She had gone for four or five parts and gotten down to the final two for each but had not landed anything yet. Each time she got a rejection, she got a little more disillusioned, but she stayed determined. However, she did start to hint at thinking of an alternative career.

"What could I work at here in Italy if acting doesn't take off? I'm not giving up yet. I just think it would be a good idea for me to start thinking of a backup career."

"Why not go back to studying? You were always interested in the environment."

"Or languages; I like languages. I could study Italian and French, perhaps, and maybe get a job as a translator?"

By that evening, she had researched an Open University degree and requested more information. "Right; if I don't get a decent acting role by January, I am doing this."

The rejections continued to role in.

Then, as if by magic, she got a part in an American series that was being filmed in London. It wasn't a lead role, but it was something, and it would be a constant for a while, with a possibility of future series if the pilot went well. She was to start working on the series after Christmas and film for six months.

"Why not do the language degree also? As a backup? I mean, it's not a lead role, so you'll probably have a lot of time to study while sitting around on set."

With the money they were offering, which wasn't bad at all—the same as what I earned annually—it would keep her going for a year and pay for her university course.

"Yeah, you are right. I will!"

Luca had chosen an art course he wanted to do in Florence the following year, and he was busy putting his portfolio together and learning Italian in preparation. Both my kids would be starting their third-level education the same year and were becoming a little more Italianized. At least someone in the family would be able to speak Italian; my own efforts were disastrous. I still couldn't string a sentence together. Probably because all the people I talked to spoke English.

My brother Jim and Ingrid, together with my nieces, had booked a trip to come over to us in September. As soon as my parents heard this news, they decided to tag along to celebrate their sixtieth anniversary in the country they'd first traveled to together. On hearing that my parents were coming over, my other two brothers decided to come too, from New York and Northern Ireland. The event gained momentum. I booked all of them into La Dogana for the week, except my parents, who would stay with us.

We found out we could hire wheelchairs in Italy, so I got one for my mam, as her bad hip and arthritic spine didn't allow her to walk very far. Lucia and I planned a big Italian surprise dinner where both our families would come together. It was the end of season, so we got out all the tables and chairs, covered in white linen and dressed with silver candelabras and olive leaves along the center, with all the leftover pillar candles and tea lights.

I booked my favorite wedding singer, Francesco. He could go from being Pavarotti to Elvis with his booming tenor voice, but his specialty was Mario Lanza, my mam and dad's favorite.

My mam dropped her walking stick and danced with my dad under the moonlight as they joined in the chorus of "Three Coins in the Fountain." Francesco serenaded them both for hours into the night with songs that resurfaced memories of their first trip to Italy, over half a century before.

I was having my big Italian "Mamma mia" night, and it was more perfect than the one I'd dreamed of as Heaven nearly forty years previous.

"Honestly, this is the best night of my life," my mam said as we sat together for a moment, watching my brothers dance with Lucia and her parents—our newly adopted Italian family extension.

"There's only one person missing," I said softly, acknowledging what was in both our minds.

"She's not missing, she's here. There she is," Mam nodded at an exquisite moth dancing in the candlelight beside us. "Whenever I see a butterfly, I feel she's around. It's like she had butterflies in her soul."

For a moment, the dancing scene before me turned back into my kitchen in Ireland, with Eileen and Victor dancing the tango.

Dad and Mam were brimming with energy the next day at breakfast. "Holy God," said Dad, returning from his walk among the olive trees. "Rosie, if you ever buy a place here, will you make sure it has room for your ma and me?"

"Would you move here?"

"In a heartbeat. There's no way you're coming back to Ireland, is there? I mean, why would you, when you have all this?" Mam said, gazing out over the lake while sipping her tea on the terrace. "If you had a place without steps and where we could still have our independence, we'd come over for sure, especially if you could arrange Francesco to sing outside my window every night."

It was sad to see them leave, but what Mam had said about coming to live in Italy had given me a boost. Perhaps it was time to start looking for somewhere to buy; perhaps we could afford to get somewhere with our savings and a small loan. The thought wheels had been set in motion.

Jim stayed on a week longer than everyone else. Lucia had offered to pay him to do some wood sculptures for her in the kids' playground. He and I are alike; we're both Pisces—dreamers, planners, arty and crafty. From the time I was three, he bought me plastic dinosaurs as Christmas and birthday gifts and taught me their names and how they lived. Decades before *Jurassic Park* made dinosaurs trendy, I could spurt out facts about the Tyrannosaurus rex, triceratops, and pterodactyl, all thanks to Jim. He's an amazing artist and wood sculptor, but he has never done it seriously, just late at night after he's finished his more mundane job of forging metal into gates and railings.

We were driving to Passignano for a sundowner drink on the lakeshore when he asked if we would ever buy a place here.

"Possibly. Perhaps in two or three years. Just a small place, preferably somewhere here in Passignano."

Renting had been great, but I missed being able to put my mark on a property; I missed nurturing a garden, painting a wall, designing a room.

"How much do houses cost here? For instance, how much would that place be?" We were passing the Sighing House, with the aging "*vendesi*" sign, sitting, waiting patiently for a new owner to adopt it. It looked prettier than ever with the setting sun highlighting its warm-colored stonework, its face shyly hiding behind the giant magnolia trees on each side of the front gate.

"I've looked up houses on the internet, and they start at about three hundred thousand euro around here for anything decent. But I've never seen that one online. I have no idea how much it would be. It looks like it needs a lot of work, but I'd love to see inside it."

Over our drink, I googled the estate agent and found the house. There were no pictures of the interior. The price was not mentioned, but there was an inquiry form. I filled it in while Ronan and Jim talked about fishing.

The following day I got an email from Laura, who worked at the estate agent, explaining that the villa needed major renovations, including of the fixtures, electrics, and the water system, which need to be completely redone.

In the past it was used for three families, so there is much space. There is also a passage under the railroad that leads from the property to the lake. My advice is to go look at the property from the outside so you can better understand the position and also the state of the house. I also include links to other properties which might be more suitable.

The other links she sent were of lovely properties, ready to move into, some with pools, and all starting at two hundred and fifty thousand euro. I didn't want to make an appointment to see any of them. I already felt we were wasting her time by requesting this one viewing, but we needed to start somewhere, even if we found that it was not possible for us to buy for another year or two. We needed to start gauging what we could expect to get for our money, being realistic rather than sitting, scrolling through properties online and dreaming.

I responded to say I was familiar with the location of the property, as we currently rented a house close by.

> It does look like there is a lot of work to be done, but we would still like to have a look. How much is it?

She didn't answer my question about the price but asked if I had looked at the photos she sent and were we sure we still wanted to see it and not some of the other properties she sent links to.

An appointment was made for four o'clock on Monday, the 30th of September, and I told the lads over lunch. "I wrote to that estate agent to get a price for that house in Passignano. She didn't give me a price, but we have an appointment to see that house on Monday, just for a laugh, just to have a nosey, to see what the inside is like."

Chapter 25

WE PARKED AT THE SUPERMARKET AND WALKED ACROSS TO THE house. In the overgrown garden stood a woman in her twenties with wide eyes, big glasses, and wavy brown bobbed hair.

"I'm Laura. Pleased to meet you." She shook our hands warmly and we waded through the long grass to the back door—she didn't have a key for the front door; she fumbled through a big bunch of keys, trying to find the right one.

"I have only been working at the agency for a few months, so I haven't shown this house before."

"Has it been on the market for a long time?"

"It has been with us for three years, but it has been abandoned for ten years. There were four families living here previously." She opened the shutter but held her breath and hesitated to go in. A giant spider sat guarding the inner door.

"Wow!" said Jim, ever the nature lover, and he took out his phone to take a picture while Laura and I froze in horror. He scooped up the eight-legged house guardian and placed it in a broken terra-cotta pot. We all continued inside with caution, in case we'd just broken up a family.

All the shutters were closed, so it took a while for our eyes to adjust. We scooted around the downstairs, giving each other frights, avoiding cobwebs, and making spooky noises.

Even Laura joined in. It seemed an endless maze of rooms, but it felt cozy. There was still scattered old furniture, books piled high with encrusted horror-movie-style dust, and trinkets and ornaments that were now meaningless without their rightful owners. On the top floor, a pigeon flew out through a hole in the roof. The walls under the natural skylight were drenched from the previous day's rain, and black mold had spread in interesting mushroom shapes across the entire wall.

"It's quite artistic," said Luca, standing by my side. "If you stare at it long enough, I'm sure you'll see the face of Jesus."

"No thanks, I don't want to stay too long. I'm afraid something is going to land on me." I hurried back down the hallway to catch up with the others.

Ronan opened the balcony shutters on the top floor, flooding the room and hallway with light. That's when I noticed the tiled floor, inlaid with a decorative, geometrically designed border.

"They are original, from the 1920s," said Laura enthusiastically. "Only high-class houses had these tiles; they were expensive. Most houses had only the terra-cotta tiles, like the ones in the kitchen downstairs. These tiles are impossible to get now."

They wouldn't have been my first choice, but the story behind them made me like them.

From one of the three balconies we could see the lake between the evergreen trees, just a field away. The garden's grand, mature trees towered over an overgrown courtyard, with the sweet scent of the fermenting fruit lying thick under an old apple tree—which was just crying out for a swing to be hung from its branches—drifting up to reach us.

Laura and I sauntered back to the garden. "What is the price?" I asked out of pure curiosity, as it still had not been mentioned.

"Two hundred and forty thousand. But," she quickly added, "it is negotiable."

"How negotiable?"

"Very negotiable."

I could hear the guys laughing down the end of the garden. I went to walk towards them through the waist-high grass, and something scurried ahead of me, moving the grass like a scene from *Jurassic Park*.

"Snake!" shouted Jim.

"One just went over my foot," roared back Ronan.

The ground suddenly felt soft and bumpy under my feet. It moved. I felt like I was standing on Medusa's head and couldn't get out of the long grass quick enough towards the gate. The lads were out of breath and laughing like kids as they made their way back up the garden in big, clumsy leaps.

"It's a great house, but too big for us, and there's too much work to be done I think, but thanks for showing us around," I said to Laura. She understood and promised to send me details on other properties that might be of interest.

It was Jim's last evening, so he and I had a few drinks on the terrace after dinner. The conversation was all about the house: how there was so much stuff left in it; the potential it had in the right hands; the great location; the garden; the work that would need to be done. After a few more drinks, we were having a heated debate over what color to paint the shutters. Ronan, who had been the sensible, sober one for years, left us to it and headed off to bed saying, "There's no way we are buying that house—forget it."

… But I couldn't.

PART II

Chapter 26

THE DAY AFTER MY LAST WEDDING EVERY YEAR, I DO A BIG CLEAR-out. It's not a conscious decision; it just happens.

The last work event signals the end of my physical work year and always coincides with the end of summer, so it's time to prepare for the cozy season ahead, and after fulfilling other people's dreams all summer, it's time to do a little self-care and check in on my wish lists and my new year's goals to see which ones have not yet been done—usually most of them—and then I try to commit to getting at least one more completed before the year is done.

Autumn is also my time for watching house and garden makeover shows. I've found a new one on an English channel that captivates me. A couple with two young kids have sold up and bought a cha-teau in France. It's not just them; as the series progresses it follows a whole rake of people who have bought castles and manor houses in France and renovated them with no previous experience. They do little, detailed things like cut up wallpaper shapes and stick them to the walls; they shop for doorknobs and shine up copper pans to hang in their kitchen, smiling, laughing, and ignoring the fact that their roof is leaking and they have no heating. Ronan stays to watch an episode with me.

Some have only a budget of ten thousand euro and are doing perfectly well while living in their new home. They laugh and have a great time. We laugh as one guy literally doesn't know how to change a light bulb.

"We could do that." My mind drifts back to my dream since childhood of buying a house in the sun, next to water, and renovating it with treasures found at antique markets. The Sighing House calls to me. It's perfect.

Ronan knows me too well; he knows where my mind is. He hesitates but says it anyway: "It is a beautiful house."

Leaving the cobwebs and snakes aside, we both knew it would be an amazing house.

"Look at them," I say, pointing at the TV. "They have never renovated before. We have. Okay, so we vowed 'never again,' but look how happy they are. We were happy renovating. It was disastrous at times—well, most of the time—but when we got it right it was so satisfying."

Ronan, watching a guy fix a floor tile, says, "We could do that."

"I can't stop thinking about that house."

"Neither can I," he admits. "But look, let's not get carried away with ourselves, let's think about this more rationally than other decisions we've made in the past. Let's work out how much we can spend and—"

"One hundred and twenty thousand," I interrupt. "I've already worked it out. I wasn't thinking of that house, but was just looking at what we could afford for any house. We have eighty thousand euro saved by now from my online businesses, and I know we can get a loan of fifty thousand. So that would give us enough to buy the house for one hundred and twenty thousand, leaving ten thousand to cover fees."

"But what about the renovation costs?"

"We could take on double the number of weddings for next summer and work our socks off?"

"Yeah, or perhaps we look for somewhere that doesn't need so much work? We don't need a three-story house, Rosie. How about we look at some houses that are more turnkey?"

"Sure, that's an option." I agree, but my sights are set on the Sighing House.

So we've decided to get serious about buying. It would be more practical to wait until after next year's wedding season to see how our finances are, but our income has been very predictable for the last ten years, and we were never ones to wait around. I'm already on the *immobilari* website searching for houses for sale in the area.

I find a new entry, in view of the lake, with some grounds around it, and that is currently lived in, so it has a good roof and windows. It's smaller than the other and has four bedrooms. It's on sale for one hundred and twenty thousand euro.

I send off an inquiry for a viewing and, while doing so, send a text message to Laura; she has been in touch regularly, sending links to other properties.

We're interested in having a second viewing of the house in
Passignano.

She responds:

Not the cute one with the pool I sent you yesterday?

It's cute all right, but it's also €460k.

No, not the one with the lavender pathways and pool, the
one in Passignano with the cobwebs and snakes please.

The appointment is made for the end of the following week, the
day her boss is available; she probably doesn't feel experienced enough
to deal with crazies like us.

We arrange an appointment for Wednesday to see the other, more
sensible house.

Wednesday arrives and we meet the new estate agent in a hotel car
park and follow her to the house. It's out the other side of the town, more
isolated. We pass through a tunnel under the motorway and take a left
up a track that runs alongside but about ten meters below the motorway.

A couple in their seventies greet us, smiling along with their
daughter, who is in her early twenties and has special needs. They
show us the carefully thought-out and cared-for vegetable garden
and the terrace covered in wisteria, which is beautiful. The daughter leads the way, showing us around the house and enthusiastically
joining in on the sales pitch. It's a solid house for sure, just in need of

modernization and lighter colors. She shows us her bedroom, and I look out the window with its nice lake view. Suddenly, a train whizzes past below, about five meters away.

"Oh, the trains you get used to; they finish at ten o'clock, and they are electric, so they are not noisy," explains the estate agent. I can see they are all disappointed by the timing of the train. They know it's probably a game changer.

But it's not the train that puts me off so much; it's the motorway to the front. I'd never be able to relax with the thought of a truck crashing through the barrier and landing on the house. The estate agent texts me later that she thinks they would drop to ninety thousand for a quick sale, but I don't even bother telling Ronan. It isn't the price; the location is wrong for both of us. I feel a pang of sadness that I can't give the family some hope, but doing house viewings is planting ideas in my head. On the TV that evening there's another episode of the house makeover show, the happy people gluing beads on jars while the roof of their castle in France is falling in. I take an old notebook off my shelf, open to a blank page, and make a note for my future self: *Buy a good glue gun.*

I casually flick through the pages; it's a very old notebook of mine, a pre-Ronan one full of travel ideas and dreams built with not a care in the world to stop them from happening. Just as I put it down, it falls open on a page with an old, familiar dream written in purple ink: "To restore a beautiful house in an exotic country near a lake or a river and fill it with interesting things from antique markets." Beside it is a sketch of a house with shutters and lavender, a central door shaded by two big trees and a lake beside it.

Chapter 27

WE ARE A LITTLE EARLY FOR OUR SECOND VIEWING OF THE Sighing House. As I look at it now, the front garden is quite big, so the house isn't as close to the road as I first thought, it's set back about ten meters. The front fence is directly on the road, with no path, and on a bend, but we could probably live with that.

The grass has been cut, which means I can get to the end of the garden and see the secret tunnel and the shed this time. The scutch grass is still a little long, but is flattened over the bumpy ground. Perhaps the bumps are the dens of the scurrying things I saw on our last visit. I'm glad I'm wearing my boots.

Luca has stayed at the top of the garden but walks halfway down to meet us on our return.

"There's a little old woman coming in the gate," he reports. "Probably a nosy neighbor."

We walk slowly up the garden, hoping the estate agent will arrive before we reach the top. But no luck. There she is, standing in the middle of the courtyard. "*Buongiorno.*"

"*Buongiorno*," she replies, and she begins to gabble away in Italian with lots of hand gestures. She's under five foot, thin, crumpled, wrinkled, with witch-like features and a twinkle in her eye. She reminds me of a thin version of Beatrix Potter's Mrs. Tiggy-Winkle.

"*Scusi, non parlo italiano.*"

"*Aww, sí. Francese?*"

"*No, Irlandese. Non parlo francese, no.*"

"Aww." She looks disappointed but decides to talk to us in Italian anyway, only slower. I understand some words. *Zia*, *casa*, Alzheimer's.

I'm using all sorts of apps and online methods to try to learn Italian, but I still can't string a sentence together. I understand around one in every ten words, which leads me to completely misunderstand what is being asked or said most of the time.

"I think she is saying her aunt used to live here and she has Alzheimer's," I explain to Ronan. "Or she may have said she herself has Alzheimer's and she is looking for her aunt's house?"

"Her aunt has Alzheimer's? But she's about eighty herself, so would her aunt still be alive? It must be her," says Ronan loudly, smiling and nodding, as she doesn't understand a word we are saying.

We stare at her, trying to work out her hand gestures as she continues to bombard us with Italian.

Laura arrives with Mario, the head estate agent. He is short and round and acts very official, shaking my hand and doing an elaborate welcome. Salesman talk is the same all over the world, it seems.

I introduce him to Ronan and Luca. "And this is," I pause as I don't know what to say, but then realize that I am wasting my time anyway, as neither Mario nor the little old lady speaks a word of English.

Mario shakes her hand and greets her formally. "She's not with us," I say as I hiss at Laura. "We don't know her. I think she is just a nosy neighbor and I think she said she has Alzheimer's."

Mario talks with the little old dear, and I can see Laura is struggling to switch into English mode and listen to both what Mario is saying in Italian and what I am saying in English, but she gets the last of what I said.

"Yes, she has Alzheimer's," she says, nodding gravely.

They all walk towards the house, including the little old dear, who is still talking a mile a minute.

"Oh, that's sad. Should we help her find her way home before we start?" I ask.

But neither Mario nor Laura seems to be listening to my concerns. The two of them are ahead of us and are focused on what the elderly woman is saying.

"Oh, she's coming in with us, it seems," says Ronan as we look at each other, amused. We both shrug and just follow.

She stops at the persimmon tree in the courtyard and reaches up to take a piece of the fruit. Mario holds the branch down for her so she can take a piece, and he takes one himself. They both stand, necks jutting out away from their clothes and feet, munching into the large orange fruit, which has the consistency of a water balloon, nodding and grunting their approval at the sweetness. Laura fiddles with the key in the door lock—the front door this time.

As we enter the house through the main door for the first time, it looks more beautiful with its central staircase, and it feels strangely familiar. A wave of nostalgia I can't quite place washes over me.

Mario goes from room to room opening the shutters with grand, sweeping gestures. However, some stay welded shut, swollen from weathering, refusing to budge, while one creaks and falls forwards off its hinges.

While Mario fills our ears with sales talk, the little old lady just wanders around from room to room in wonderment. Thankfully, Lucia—who I'd invited along—finally arrives. "Sorry I'm late."

I do the introductions, and we follow Mario upstairs as he continues his grandiose sales talk, translated by Laura. Lucia immediately starts to argue in Italian.

By the time we get to the third room upstairs, Lucia proclaims loudly, "I don't like him—he is talking crap."

"Lucia, keep your voice down," I say.

"Ah, he can't f-ing understand."

The wandering woman drifts past the door. "Lucia, can you explain to Laura that we don't know this woman; she just wandered in and joined us." Lucia mutters to Laura.

Laura answers back in English, "She is one of the owners."

Lucia walks off to open a balcony door, leaving me alone with Laura. "Ooohhh, I see! We were not introduced. What is her name?"

"Uncle Francesca."

I'm about to correct her English but then decide it might be rude. Mario is by Lucia's side. "*E qui la bella vista del lago.*" I understand he's saying "And here is the beautiful lake view."

Lucia exclaims something in Italian along the lines of "But you can't see the lake; there are f-ing trees in the way."

Uncle Francesca says something that I later find out is "That is why the last person said they wouldn't buy it."

Did Mario just shush her?

"Who has Alzheimer's?" I ask Laura.

"The aunt."

"The aunt of Francesca?"

"Yezzzz. She is one of the three owners, and Francesca is taking care of the sale of the house for her."

Everyone wanders in different directions. Ronan and I are left alone on the second floor, looking at the trees blocking the lake view. We walk around, touching the doorframes that have been shaped with a 1920s art deco design.

We're getting a feel for the space, the rooms, the structure. "We could all have a floor each," Ronan jokes.

"You know, we could? It's not a bad idea. Izzy could have her own apartment; Luca could have his. We'd have the general living space, and we could set up a B&B in the other apartment to bring in an income."

Uncle Francesca brings out an enamel chamber pot from the house and starts trying to reach the fruit. Mario reaches for the higher fruit and helps her fill the potty and some ceramic jelly molds she has taken from the kitchen. Hmmm, she can take the chamber pot, but I hope she leaves the molds behind.

I'm smitten but don't want to seem too enthusiastic. I think Ronan is rapidly warming to it too. He takes a walk down the garden with Lucia to show her the secret tunnel while I stay talking with Laura.

Mario approaches and starts to reiterate the benefits within the grounds: Two wells; yes, they look like death traps for our cats—they'll be promptly covered up for sure. There's existing permission for another house of two thousand square meters; a three-story house with twenty-one rooms should be enough for the three of us and possibly three future generations.

"We do like it, but with the asking price of two hundred and forty thousand, it's not in our range unfortunately."

"Well, what would you offer?"

"One hundred and twenty?" I say in my best Italian.

"Oh no, it has two wells! The planning permission for a two-thousand-square-meter house is worth more than that."

Ronan is back from his walk and overhears the last part of our conversation.

"They can keep the site for the New York skyscraper, we'll just take the house," he says.

I nod. Why am I nodding? Oh yeah, I'm just cheering him on in this unplanned game. It's just a bit of fun.

I add in English—which Laura translates—"We viewed a similar house two days ago and they are willing to accept ninety thousand, and it has a new roof and windows. There is at least one hundred and fifty thousand worth of work to be done here. We're not interested in the planning, so let them think about it."

The estate agent goes back to Uncle Francesca, who is swatting a wasp from her face and running around the tree but then is distracted by a plump persimmon. Laura is talking to me but I'm not listening, as my stomach is rumbling and I'm too busy thinking about what to have for dinner, so I try to find a gap in the conversation to say goodbye.

Mario returns. "They will accept one hundred and fifty thousand."

"No, we can't do that. Thanks anyway."

"*Arrivederci.*" We wave goodbye to Uncle Francesca and to Lucia, who is already in her own car.

"I can't believe they would drop to one hundred and fifty thousand, but it's too big a project," says Ronan as we drive away.

"And it's too big a house for us, but it would be an amazing space for someone who wanted a place to host creative groups or meditation retreats in Italy."

We stop at the supermarket. I'm starving, but we have nothing in, so we need dinner ingredients, and I'm out of wine. Ronan shops for the practicals while I head to the wine aisle. My phone buzzes; it's a text from Laura.

On Tuesday come to our office at eleven o'clock to sign the sale agreement.

I go back over to Ronan at the fruit and veg section. "Do we need bananas?" he asks, holding a bunch in his hand.

"Ehhh, I think we've just bought a house?"

"Huh?"

"I think they have accepted our offer on that house?"

"Did we put in an offer?"

"It seems so."

"For how much?"

"I think I said one hundred and twenty thousand?"

"For just the house or the house and the field with planning permission?"

"I have no idea, but it seems we're signing for it on Tuesday?"

"It's a great house for that price. A steal! But what would we do with such a big place?"

"Host creative groups who want a retreat in Italy perhaps?"

"Did you say we needed bananas?"

I go back to the wine aisle and buy a bottle of a top-shelf red, unsure if it is to celebrate or to block out the confusion. Have we just decided to buy a massive renovation project, plus start a new business, in the space of time it takes to decide if we need bananas or not?

Apparently we've bought a house *and* bananas. It's exciting, but there's also a creeping fear that there is quicksand ahead.

Chapter 28

WE ARRIVE AT THE ESTATE AGENT'S OFFICE IN ASSISI.

The day before, we met with Mick Kelly, who has not only fabulous golden eyes but also a wonderful soft voice. Not as in sleazy smooth, but soft and calming. He's like an Italian Jesus Christ; you feel you could trust him with anything.

He explained to us the house-buying process in Italy. We will sign an official offer to purchase; it is called the "Term for Irrevocability of the Offer," which sounds very serious. That document will be presented to the owners, and they will sign it if they agree to the offer.

Once it's signed and accepted, they can't sell the house to someone else or change the price, and we can't back out without losing the retaining payment, which is usually a small sum of, say, five hundred or a thousand euro. Then documents are created by a notary and we will sign a preliminary agreement (*compromesso*) and pay a deposit. The owners then can't back out of the sale without paying us double the deposit, and we can't back out without losing the deposit. Then checks are done on the title deeds, a *geometra* gets involved, a final deed is drawn up, we sign it, pay the balance, and voilà: we own a house in Italy.

Laura emails us the deeds, which outline the boundary of the property and the house layout.

We send these ahead to Mick Kelly, who has given us one hundred percent approval of the price we are paying and agrees that about one hundred and fifty thousand over time will result in a fantastic house. "How much will the roof cost to redo, for example?" I ask.

"About twenty thousand," he says. I don't flinch; that sounds reasonable.

We hadn't really planned on finding a house so early in our preliminary, pre-search stage—that is, before we had even figured out how much we could afford and how we were going to pay for it. But here we are, going to an estate agent to sign something about something to do with buying a house with a lot of potential to those with imagination. Unfortunately, we both have been cursed with plenty of imagination; there's no yin-yang grounding partner in this relationship. Two yangs are dangerous.

We walk down the center aisle of the office, lined with five or six agents at their desks, to a glass-partitioned back office. I am not imagining it; they are all definitely staring at us with awe and big smiles. I am having my red-carpet moment. Any minute now I am expecting them to give us a standing ovation, saying, "*Bravi, bravi* for buying the unsellable house. You are so brave (or possibly stupid), but *brava* anyway for taking it off our hands, you mad Irish."

At the large conference table there's Mario, the head estate agent; Laura, the assistant, who is also acting as translator; and us sitting opposite. As Mario starts talking, a woman comes in and joins our side of the table. There's no introduction; we have no idea who she is. Maybe she's another owner or maybe she's here to take notes; at this stage we are used to strange women wandering into the process.

First, we establish that we want to include the field with planning in the sale. I now fancy the idea of perhaps building a house someday or at least just having a big garden with no possibility of someone else coming in and building an abattoir or a home for unwanted dogs because they bark too much.

Mario is all salesman-like. There is a four-page, standard—but very detailed—form produced by the estate agency that needs to be completed. We have an English version. Mario starts to ask us questions, and Laura begins filling it out with our answers. Name, date of birth, country of residency. I can answer all these questions so far; we are doing well. When he's finished, Mario hands me the Italian version to check the details and to sign on the dotted line. Where it states "We commit to buy the property in Passignano for the price of…," one hundred and thirty thousand is the amount written.

"This is incorrect," I say, and Laura translates. "We never offered one hundred and thirty; it was one hundred and twenty."

"No, it was one hundred and thirty," he says, translated by Laura.

"No, it was definitely one hundred and twenty. I know it was one hundred and twenty, as I don't know how to say one hundred and thirty in Italian, so I wouldn't have said it."

"But with the field and the planning and the wells, the property is worth much more than this," he says. "One hundred and thirty thousand is more than reasonable."

"The property is only worth what someone is willing to pay for it. We understand that it is a great property, but we told you we are only prepared to offer one hundred and twenty," states Ronan.

"Yes, I agree," Laura says. "It has great potential, but there is a lot of work."

She's lovely and honest and forgets she is there in a work and translation capacity. We're now talking about the potential and what we can do with it, such as retreats, vegetable gardens, and Christmas lighting.

Mario interrupts, his voice getting louder. He thinks Laura has been translating what he said and doesn't realize that we have just been chatting about putting a claw-footed bath in the main bathroom.

Laura either translates what we said or makes something up about the price staying at one hundred and twenty thousand.

Mario's voice gets louder and he gesticulates wildly with his hands. Red blotches appear on Laura's neck, and I feel bad for her, as I know she is caught in the middle. Mario is talking a mile a minute. We have no idea what he's saying, but his hands are flying all over the place and he's getting more and more animated. Every now and then he directs his litany at us, forgetting that we don't understand a word. I just sit smiling at him. What else can I do? I have learned that Italians can be dramatic; they use an excess number of words to express something that could be said in one sentence. They could be saying "The weather is nice today, I think we'll go for a picnic" and it sounds like they are having a massive argument. The opposite also applies: they could be saying "I will kill you and all your family" but it sounds like an undiscovered melody.

Mario stands up suddenly, drops or throws his pen on the table, and walks out of the room.

"What's happening?" Ronan mutters to me.

"I don't know. Did he drop or throw the pen on the table? If he dropped it, then perhaps he's taking a toilet break. If he threw it, then perhaps he's doing it for dramatic effect?"

"What is he doing?" I ask Laura.

"I don't know," she says, looking past our heads at him.

We watch him as he stomps into the middle of the front office, and then he starts to slow as he gets closer to the front door.

Not understanding Italian while negotiating a house actually seems to be working in our favor. If this were all in English, the huffing and puffing and drama from Mario would have probably had the effect he wanted. We would have argued back and then perhaps met in the middle. I know we would have caved. However, right now, we don't know if he's using an old-school sales technique, throwing a pretend tantrum at our preposterous offer, or if he ate a questionable lasagna the night before.

This technique—upping the agreed price and then storming off when it's rejected—may have had others calling him back from halfway down the office, but now he has reached the front door and stands outside, glancing towards us to see if anyone is coming, like a toddler checking if his tantrum has worked on his parent. He seems at a loss and starts to pick at the plants in the window box. The mystery woman has been on a call. Hanging up, she looks out, sees him still outside, sighs, and goes out to him.

"Who is she? One of the owners?" I ask Laura.

"That is Mario's wife. She owns this business with him." Laura is still looking a bit rattled. I'm afraid she's going to get the blame for not persuading us and that she'll lose her job.

"I'm sorry you are stuck in the middle, but I have a solution. I will call Mick Kelly and get him to negotiate on our behalf."

Before Mario gets back to the room, I have Mick Kelly on the phone and have explained that there is a "misunderstanding" regarding the price. I ask if he can talk to the upset Mario. I hand the phone to Mario, who rants for a full five minutes to Mick and then hands the phone back to me.

"He said the price agreed with the owners is one hundred and thirty thousand."

"But we didn't offer one hundred and thirty thousand, and we told him our limit was one hundred and twenty thousand. One hundred and thirty thousand was never mentioned, and we are not prepared to up it. Ten thousand is half a roof. Do you think they won't sell if we don't increase the offer?"

"I think we try to stick with one hundred and twenty and see what happens," advises Mick Kelly.

I hand the phone back to Mario. We can hear the soothing tones of Mick's voice responding to Mario. I hear Mick mention the road, the train track, the ten years, the roof. Soon Mario is saying, "*Sì...sì.*" He listens to Mick's reasoning while drawing little invisible shapes on the table with his fingernail.

Then he laughs. Mick sounds animated, but still in his soothing, Jesus Christ way. "*Sì, sì, sì,*" says Mario. They are now talking like old buddies. If Mick were here, Mario would be slapping him on the back.

Mario hangs up and hands me back the phone. The change in his humor is nothing short of miraculous. He says a few things to his wife and she leaves the room. He then explains to Laura, and they both stand up. He is smiling and laughing now as he leans over the table to shake our hands.

"It is agreed," Laura says triumphantly.

"What is?"

"The price for one hundred and twenty thousand."

"For the house and the land?"

"Yes! Mario's wife will call the six owners, get them to agree, and then do up the new agreement, which you will sign on Friday in your architect's office after his appointment to see the house."

We shake hands, and Mario stops just short of cracking open the champagne.

Six owners? I thought there were three?

Chapter 29

WE ARE BACK IN THE SIGHING HOUSE WITH MARIO, AND ALSO Mick Kelly this time. We want him to tell us we're not crazy and to get a better sense of what has to be done. He's impressed by the central staircase; in most Italian houses that are divided into separate living spaces, the stairs are on the exterior. He likes the detail of the architrave around the doors, and he dismisses the cracks in the stonework; the house has stood for a hundred years already. The roof will need to be completely replaced, not just repaired.

Some furniture has been left behind. There's a beautiful wrought-iron bed with an amber inset. It needs some TLC, but having grown up in a DIY house, and after watching so many reruns of shows about making do and patching up French castles, I can see the potential under the dust. About twenty saucer champagne glasses in a glass-front, sixties-style unit sit under a dusty bottle of champagne. There's a mishmash of veneered, bulky, antique-style furniture, a marble table and chairs, and a lot of cheap furniture that was popular in the sixties and seventies. One room still has books and papers piled on a drawer unit. And then there's the scary room—a walk-in attic with no light source. We see outlines of objects: a bath and what looks like an old gramophone stand. My inner pirate is triggered, and I'm bursting at the thought of the antique treasures that could be lying in the piles of cobwebbed shapes. I've already decided it will be Ronan the Brave who will be sent on that mission, while I stand at the door and supervise with unhelpful instructions.

I have a few questions for Mario: Is the house connected to the gas main, as I've heard the alternative can be very expensive? And is it on the water and sewerage mains as well (which Italians call "dark water")? He makes a phone call. "I have spoken with the geometra of the family. He knows the history of the house well and he says yes, there is public water and dark water, and the methane gas line runs under the road to the house, so there will be no problem connecting."

Geometra is a profession unique to Italy. They are like engineers for houses. They check all the plans and draw up new ones. This house had its own one, linked to the family somehow, and Mario has him on speed dial.

At Mick's office we are handed the agreement to sign, the price for the property now correct at one hundred and twenty thousand euro, but as I read down, I see Mario has kindly given himself a twelve-hundred-euro raise. I have done my research and know that estate agents' fees are paid by the buyer and are usually 3 percent of the sale price. "This isn't correct; it's too much. It should be 3 percent, no?" I say.

Mick Kelly translates.

Mario launches into hand-gesture-and-speed-talking mode, but I understand him: "There's a lot of work to be done with these owners; I had to renegotiate the price down again from one hundred and thirty to one hundred and twenty; there are expenses," and so forth. I actually don't mind paying him the little extra, as I know he'll have to convince all the owners to accept a payment far lower than the asking price; I just didn't want him to think I hadn't noticed.

Mick Kelly looks at me. "Do you want to negotiate his price down? It's up to you."

"No, let's just get on with this. I have a feeling he is going to earn it."

In Mick Kelly's office I learn that, in Italy, you must sign your full name, and it must be legible. So if you have a doctor's scrawl-style signature like mine, you need to develop a new one instantly. I revert to the one I practiced as a kid when I copied my hero celebrity Miss Piggy's signature from *The Muppets Annual*. However, this time I do it without the love heart instead of the tittle over the "i."

Ten days later I am at the supermarket and get a call from Laura. "Good news! All the owners have signed the document agreeing to the offer price."

"That is great news."

"So today you need to come to the office to sign the document to acknowledge their signatures."

"But your office is an hour away and I have gelato in my shopping trolley. I'll come tomorrow."

"Unfortunately, that is not possible. It needs to be done within ten days, and today is the tenth day. You need to come today to sign that you agree."

"What is it exactly that we need to sign? A document to say we accept that they accept the offer that we offered?"

"Yes, that is correct."

"How about I write a statement and email it to you to say I acknowledge that they acknowledge the offer that we offered?"

She checks with the boss. "Yes, that will do."

I send it as soon as I get back while eating the gelato. Who said buying a house in Italy is difficult?

The next step is to elect a notary. This is another profession unique to Italy: they are scrupulous people who work on behalf of both sides of a property deal. Lucia says they spend longer studying and are more qualified than judges.

We find Elizabetta through Mick Kelly. "She is very, very good." He has me at the second "very."

As soon as I meet her, I like her, even though she doesn't smile once. In her midthirties, blond, tanned, tall, and thin, she wears a Rolex, which makes me feel she must be earning well, so she must be good at her job; the watch company's marketing has been successful. Ronan and I rename her "Betty" for quick reference between us.

We have an initial meeting with her to discuss the possibility of her overseeing the sale and what her fee will be. I don't get an answer about the fee other than "It depends." In other countries, lawyers' fees can vary a lot, and you can be charged for every phone call or email they make on your behalf. I have no clue what the system is in Italy, so I'm worried, but I later discover that a notary is a public job and is subject to fixed fees depending on the size of the house. A meeting is set for the following week to get the house purchase started.

Chapter 30

THINGS ARE MOVING ALONG NICELY. MARIO, LAURA, RONAN, and I arrive at Betty's office the following week. Uncle Francesca is there first with a file of papers in front of her. We do our Italian kiss-kiss greetings with everyone. Laura acts as a translator between us all, although Betty does speak some English.

She has already received the documents, spoken with the geometra before our meeting, and gotten the permission needed from the owners to check the documents with the town hall.

"There are buildings to be destroyed," Betty announces. Italians use this word a lot when talking in English. "I was working in the garden all day and now I am destroyed," "I had three meetings today, I can't come over, I am destroyed." Every time I hear someone describe themselves as destroyed, an image flashes in my mind of a superhero being brought to their knees, deprived of their energy source, like with Superman and kryptonite. Now, as my notary says buildings need to be destroyed, I picture a spacecraft dropping bombs in the garden as we speak.

There are three outbuildings in the garden, and there's some confusion about whether all have been built with the permissions needed. So Betty will check which buildings need to be destroyed. She flicks through the plans and descriptions.

"*Allora*" (a great word which means "so"), "there are nine courtyards, four houses, a vineyard, and three outbuildings, two of which may need to be destroyed." That word again. Cue evil laugh.

"What? Sorry, could you go back to the four houses and nine courtyards. I didn't realize I was buying the whole village?"

Laura is quick to step in to explain. "The house is divided into four separate units." She flashes some Italian at Betty, and they both laugh a little.

"Units, not house buildings," Betty says as she corrects herself, smiling for the first time. She likes my joke about buying the village, which wasn't meant as a joke.

"Will I have to pay separate tax and utilities for all of them?"

The answer is yes. Betty looks at me with sympathy, crinkling her brow.

"But I don't want that."

They all start discussing stuff in Italian, all talking at once and answering and nodding. The Italians have an amazing knack for listening and talking at the same time, or at least for pretending to listen while talking over each other at the same time.

Finally Laura says, "The family geometra will need to submit paperwork to get the house recognized as two units rather than four separate units. It can be considered two units for the sale. One is not possible. After the sale, your architect can submit it to be considered as one unit, one house. It is then possible. Then you pay only one set of utilities. Okay?"

I sort of get it, but don't.

"And what about the nine courtyards? And vineyard?"

"Look." Betty pushes the aerial-view drawing in front of me. The fenced garden has been subdivided into nine different shapes, each with an assigned registry number. One is probably about three meters long and one meter wide, and in the middle of all the others.

"Why is the garden divided like this?" I ask.

Laura shrugs. "It is Italy. Often with inheritance, things like this happen; each child is entitled to claim an equal amount, no matter what is written in the will. This is why we have property law people like Elizabetta who spend their career figuring out inheritance property complications."

And this is probably one of the reasons so many beautiful houses lie abandoned all over Italy.

"We need to ensure that all plots are listed during the sale," explains Betty in Italian.

I understand and explain it to Ronan. "Basically, it's her job to ensure we are the owners of all the plots, because otherwise the person who owns that small central plot could come along, fence it off, and be perfectly entitled to leave their savage Rottweiler there."

"She said all that and you understood?" He's looking impressed.

"Sort of."

"What about the vineyard?" I ask.

"Perhaps there was a vineyard on the property at some point," says Laura.

My expectation of owning the village shrinks back down to reality.

Betty asks Uncle Francesca for something, who shuffles through her papers and hands a document over. Betty reads through it and the two chat, Betty all facts and seriousness, Uncle Francesca responding sweetly, smiling, with lots of prayer-like hand signals.

Laura translates. "Yes. Francesca has got the power-of-attorney document from the court to act on behalf of her aunt, who has Alzheimer's, but the notary has told her she needs to go back to get it specified with the areas her aunt owns. Otherwise it could cause problems when it comes to paying the other owners, as it looks like she owns the whole property."

Uncle Francesca's sweetness and "I know-a nothing" attitude while shuffling through papers is not going down well with Betty. She suddenly becomes a little-old-lady character out of a fairytale, and I don't mean a nice one; I mean one who, when challenged, flips and vents her wrath with a deep bellowing cackle. Laura and I jump a little at Uncle Francesca's sudden change of tone as she argues back, but this doesn't work either. Unfazed, Betty tells her firmly that she needs to go back and get the document changed.

I'm beginning to lose hope for a quick sale. From everything I've been told and read on social media groups, Italy's bureaucracy slows everything down, so with buildings needing to be blown up and court documents obtained, I can't imagine how long this is going to take… Months or years, perhaps.

On the way home we stop at the house and take a walk down the garden. In the center of the bottom boundary fence there is a large shed built with yellow cement bricks and covered in thick ivy. The shed seems to be divided into four rooms. This is one of the buildings that may need to be *destroyed*. We peer through the ivy and see cob-webbed shelves, old suitcases, and possibly a barrel.

We'll need to come back, better prepared to fight through the ivy. Behind the boundary fence there is a gully for rainwater runoff in the winter, and beyond that the ground rises up to the train track. In the bottom right section of the fence there's a gate to the gully and the secret tunnel under the train track. On the other side of the short concrete tunnel, an overgrown embankment leads onto the cycle way around Lake Trasimeno. We are the only house with a secret tunnel to the lake.

In front of the shed that needs to be *destroyed* there is an avenue of the kind of concrete posts used to hold up vines in old Italian vineyards. On the posts near the shed that needs to be *destroyed*, there are still three old, gnarled vines, badly in need of pruning before they collapse.

"Ah, here's our vineyard," I call out to Ronan, who is trying to get into the shed through the ivy.

All the other posts are bare. Hopefully we can save the remaining vines.

The estate agents have stopped by the house to meet the geometra, and Uncle Francesca is there to let them in. She's scurrying towards her car with a bag; she gives a little wave but quickly averts her eyes, looking guilty about something. We take the opportunity to look around inside again. Yes, we still want it, more than ever.

We enter through the grubby lean-to, which has a moldy, cracked Perspex roof, with the glass leaning too much for a lean-to. By the looks of it, it could well fall in on itself and self-destruct before we actually get to knock it down.

In the glass cabinet there are neat, clean dots in the beige dust. "Ah crap, she's taken the champagne glasses."

Uncle Francesca has the two ceramic jelly molds and some rosary beads on the table near the door, ready to go. As one of the owners, she's perfectly entitled to take what she wants; I just wish she'd cleared them out in the years previous instead of waiting until I'd seen and coveted them.

"Are you happy about the meeting today?" asks Laura.

"Yeah, we're just wondering how long the process is going to take."

She shrugs. "Because of Christmas, perhaps two months?" she says apologetically.

"Oh really? That quick?" My voice lifts with hope again. "Okay, so what is the next step? When do I pay the deposit?"

"You pay the deposit on the day of the *compromesso*. The notary will tell you the different amounts for each of the checks for the different owners, and then you give each of them a check on the day."

Back out in the garden, where Uncle Francesca is gathering more fruit from the persimmon tree, I ask, "Can Uncle Francesca tell me some of the history of the house?" Laura translates, and Uncle Francesca gives an animated, enthusiastic response.

"It is very interesting. She says she will write it down for you and get you pictures."

I'm intrigued.

Izzy is back for the Christmas holidays. We bring her up to see the house, just from the garden as we don't have a key, but Ronan tries the back door and it's unlocked. Izzy loves it; she thinks we're insane but knows we are in our happy place when we have a renovation project to do.

I text Laura on the way home to say the back door needs to be secured to save any miscreants like us from walking in and wandering around. She assures me she'll get Uncle Francesca on to it.

She also tells me that Uncle Francesca has an appointment at the court on the 5th of December to obtain the power of attorney for her aunt with Alzheimer's, so the offer to purchase can happen soon.

Chapter 31

HAPPY NEW YEAR! MY 2020 VISION FOR THIS YEAR'S GOALS
include the following:

- Buy the house in Passignano and renovate it beautifully.
- Be able to speak Italian by this time next year.
- Write a book.
- Move Mam and Dad over to Italy.

It will be a busy year, as we have lots more weddings booked, but
I have Aoife, my niece, coming over in April for the summer to help.
She and Luca are going to work at the bar for weddings, so it will be
a fun summer for them too.

On New Year's Eve, Lucia comes over for dinner, so I read her
tarot cards like I did the previous year; it's becoming an annual
tradition.

I am not very happy with the reading. There's a lot of negative stuff in it. I try to put a positive spin on it, but because I bought her tarot cards for her birthday and she has been learning, she can see for herself the future year ahead is not looking too rosy.

There are some positives, but the Tower, the Three of Swords, and the Nine of Swords are not good cards to draw.

"There is something devastating coming. It's time to gather resources and money in preparation for a frugal time. It's like you will be caught in a situation you can do nothing about, no matter which way you turn."

"Oh my God, Rosie, what is going to happen? That all looks terrible!"

"The World card is also here, which gives hope, so it's not all doom and gloom. And there's lots of love, so it looks like you'll get a boyfriend," I say, trying to lighten the mood, but she looks worried. "Remember, they are only cards. Let's read mine and see what's going to happen to me."

I shuffle the cards and lay them out in three rows of five: past, present, and future. Past and present tick along nicely, but as I turn over the future row, it looks grim. The Tower never shows up in my cards, but there it is, just like in Lucia's future. The Three of Swords and the Nine of Swords follow. My cards read of devastation, disaster, love turning its back and walking away from me, being trapped, and going it alone, but something good would emerge from it.

"Oh Lordy, what is going to happen to us?" I laugh.

"What does this mean?" Lucia asks, pointing to the combination.

"Well this shows love walking away; maybe something awful is going to happen with one of my weddings, or maybe Ronan is going to leave me? No, it can't be that, because that would be good news," I say, laughing, again trying to lighten the mood.

"I think we have broken 2020," Lucia says when leaving.

"Oh, don't worry; nothing could be that disastrous," I say, but I thought about the cards for hours after Lucia has gone. As both of our readings suggested businesses failing and devastation, and as I have half of my weddings booked at her agriturismo, La Dogana, it would have to be something to do with my weddings there. I try to dismiss it; they are only cards after all, but the thought stays.

The following week I wake to good news from Laura. "The geometra has arranged all the documents for the *catasto*," the land registry, "and the notary is doing the last updated *visure catastali*—the history of the properties structure and ownership—so we can proceed to the compromesso for the 23rd of January. Is that okay with you? At the time of the compromesso, we'll fix a closing date before the end of February."

"This house purchase has been a breeze. Excluding the Christmas break, it looks like it will take ten weeks from start to finish," I tell Karen and John over a New Year's dinner. Some English neighbors of theirs who'd bought a house twelve years previous are also at the table.

"So do you have to do the bag-of-money exchange?" asks the neighbor.

"Oh no, that all stopped a few years ago," interrupts John, knowing exactly what they're talking about.

"Bag of money?" I'm still oblivious.

"When we were buying our place, we were instructed to bring a bag of cash, so on the day of the final deed, I found myself in the bank with the two young lassies from the agency, with the bank manager loading one hundred and ten thousand euro into a paper bag, which was then handed over the counter to me and we drove to the notary's office. I was terrified that it was a setup and there was going to be a heist on the way. Anyway, the deeds were signed, the notary excused herself and left the room, and we, the estate agents, and the owner sat at the table counting out the money.

"They are very strict on that not happening anymore; now everything goes through the books. But ask about your checks; they may not accept them if they are not from an Italian bank."

The following morning I contact Betty, the notary, to tell me the amounts to write on the checks. There is a pause of three hours and then she writes back.

"The deposit payments need to be made by bank draft from an Italian bank."

That's a bit difficult, as I don't have an Italian account. "Can I make payments into a client account with you?"

I would much prefer this method, sending money to a law firm rather than to individuals. Another couple of hours go by as I wait for her reply.

"Yes, it is possible."

I'm glad I asked rather than just turning up on the day with my checkbook and being unable to continue.

She sends me the bank details of a client holding account, as well as her business bank details for her fee, which, with taxes and expenses, totals less than two thousand euro. This seems reasonable.

Later that week I get a call from Laura.

"Sorry, we need to change the meeting to Friday at eleven, as this is the only day the owners can be there, which is required by law."

"Will all the owners be there?"

"For the compromesso next week, only some of the owners will be there. I think six. For the final deed, all eight will be there."

"There are eight now? And six will be there?"

"Yes. See you there!"

"Oh, you and Mario are going to be there too?"

"Of course."

I try to think how all of the owners, the notary, the two of us, Lucia as our translator, the estate agents, and the geometra will fit in the small office of the notary.

My previous experience buying houses in Ireland involved the estate agent communicating between us and the seller, and a surveyor who took about ten minutes to look over the house and then wrote a vague report on their opinion of the attic insulation. There was no pomp or ceremony like in the movies, with a big key being handed over; instead, the keys were left in an envelope behind the reception desk of the estate agent's office for collection. Usually, when a house is bought in Ireland, the buyer and seller never meet.

I'm quickly learning things are different in Italy. Everyone is involved at every stage.

The day before the meeting Laura emails me:

The two owners in Milan will not be there tomorrow. They will sign by post. Attached is the bill for the brokerage commission of

our agency. You must pay it at the moment of the compromesso—
that is tomorrow.

There is no way I'm handing over the deposit until the deed is
done, excuse the pun. What if the estate agent disappears into the pale
blue yonder and Francesca and her merry men spend the deposit? So
it's agreed that, after the owners at the meeting have signed, Mario
will take the deed and drive to Milan to get the two other signatures
rather than do it by post. Then we will pay the deposit and the agency
fee. Now I feel Mario's starting to earn that extra bonus he added for
himself.

On the way to the signing meeting, I read a report about a new
virus in China that they think started from people eating bats. The
world needs to turn vegetarian, so I add, "Get back to being a vegetarian" to my goals for 2020.

The signing of the compromesso involves the notary reading out
the sale document, everyone agreeing and signing it, and a final deed
date being set.

We file into the office. There is Uncle Francesca at the end of
the table, and there are three middle-aged cousins, two of whom—
Stefana and Paolo—I figure out are sister and brother. Paolo speaks
a bit of English. The other guy, Riccardo, has heavy-lidded eyes, is
stocky, and looks like he had a late night out on the town and just
stopped by on his way home.

Mario and the geometra sit opposite us, with Betty at the top
of the table, and on our side of the table are Laura, Ronan, me, and
Lucia, who will be my interpreter.

So we are all ready. Betty begins to read the twenty-page document. She gets halfway through the second sentence and Uncle Francesca pipes up with a protest. I catch Paolo looking at the ceiling, muttering "Mamma mia." Betty's lips tighten. Uncle Francesca has a bunch of papers in her hand from her ever-growing file, and she's quite irate. Betty waits till Francesca blurts out everything that she has to say and then calmly says something back. But this sets Francesca off ranting again. Riccardo's phone rings loudly and he takes the call.

All of a sudden, Lucia, who is supposed to be here just to translate, shouts a litany at Francesca. The estate agent is nodding in agreement.

I whisper, "Lucia, what the hell is going on?"

"She's crazy; she thinks she knows better than the notary about getting the court document changed. No one knows more than the notary. That is why she studied for years. You don't argue with the notary; it is like arguing with a judge. You just do what they tell you to do. And that is what I told her."

There is a ping-pong of words between Betty and Uncle; I understand "*dopo*" (after), which calms Uncle, and she shuffles her papers back into the file.

Betty continues to read, and Riccardo continues his call. Twelve pages in and we have had no further interruptions, just a few fact-checks back and forth between the geometra and the notary. It's all going well until the part about the buildings that need to be destroyed.

It's a heated discussion; everyone not on our side of the table is ranting. I might as well join in. "*Scusi*," I shout. The room quietens. "*Momento*." I'm quickly running out of words I know in Italian.

"I need to know what is being said, so can you wait until Lucia has time to translate for me?"

"They must agree to destroy the buildings before you can buy it. They are arguing over how it will be paid for, as some of them don't own the sections of the land they are built on."

"Can I clarify which are the buildings that need to be destroyed?" I point to the plans where both outbuildings are labeled "*Fondo*." I quite like both of these crumbling red-brick buildings.

"It is not these. These are okay; they have the planning permissions. It is the one at the end of the garden and the attachment to the back."

I realize she's talking about the grubby, lean-to porch, which we intend to flatten as soon as we own the house, if it hasn't already fallen in on itself by then.

"That? Don't worry about it; we'll look after the destroying."

The notary and geometra are looking at me, bewildered. "*Che?*"

"That's *brutto*" ("ugly," another one of my words used up). "I'd have that down all by myself in an hour. We were going to get rid of it anyway. We'll take care of it."

"*Sì?*" Betty is smiling. I've just made her job easier, I think. "But what about the other?"

"It's Ronan's birthday next week; I'll buy him a sledgehammer." Lucia translates, sniggering.

"But you need a company to do it. They need to take the brick away and it's a lot of work."

"Ronan is a big guy. We are good at destroying things. If it speeds things up, we'll take the responsibility so we can move on and get this agreement done."

Everyone looks surprised as the notary explains what we've just agreed to.

"Okay then, if you are sure." Betty scribbles notes in the margin.

Nothing is hidden or private at the reading. The amounts everyone will receive are read out. The aunt with Alzheimer's, represented by Uncle Francesca, will get thirty-three percent; Uncle Fran will get thirty percent; and the remainder will be divided among the six cousins. The fee for the estate agent is also read out: forty-eight hundred from us, and three thousand from the sellers. Stefana and I catch each other's eye. I don't think either of us knew we were both paying Mario, who is shifting in his seat and not making eye contact.

By the time Betty is finished going through the document, two hours have passed. Just as she finishes, I say to the notary, "Can we note that it is sold as furnished?"

I have done my research: I know that if you don't state "furnished" in Italy, then they can remove not just beautiful dusty champagne glasses but everything that is not screwed to the wall, such as kitchens, light fittings, bulbs, and sometimes bathroom suites. I'm thinking of the wrought-iron bed, the marble table, and the sofas I now want to upholster. There are also some nice light fittings.

"Also, is it possible to get a key so we can get measurements for work to be done?" Again, I have read that this is sometimes possible when buying empty houses in Italy.

The notary asks the three cousins, who say, "*Sí, sí,*" and shrug their shoulders, but I notice Uncle Francesca looking flustered out the corner of my eye.

"Okay?" the notary asks Uncle directly.

"*Sì*," she says, her hands lifting off the table a little.

We're now going to take a break while the notary's secretary makes the amendments to the deed.

Uncle is up on her feet, taking her phone and explaining she needs to go to the pharmacy. She's out the door before we notice she's left her purse behind.

We chat with the cousins in pidgin English and miniature pidgin Italian. I ask them if they can tell me some of the history of the house.

"We used to visit when we were very small. I have not been there in perhaps fifty years. I don't know anything about it. Ask Francesca."

While the notary is still busy, Mario, Ronan, and the geometra go outside for a cigarette. Uncle Francesca returns with her phone in hand and makes an excuse that there was a queue in the chemist.

She sits and shuffles through her papers. Riccardo is looking at her, waiting for her to make eye contact; it's not working, so he says something to her. Silence falls in the room. I don't know what he has said, but the atmosphere has shifted. Within seconds their voices are raised at each other.

I don't know where to look, and I'm embarrassed for them, having a full-blown row here in front of strangers. Paolo is on his laptop, and his sister is looking at her nails; then she starts to scroll through Facebook. She laughs and then shows Paolo a short video of a cat falling off a shelf; I know because she leans across the table, avoiding Riccardo's finger pointed at Francesca above her head, and pushes the phone across the table to show me too.

"I have a cat like this!" she says loudly in Italian so that I can hear her above the raised voices. Neither of them seems at all bothered that their cousin is shouting at his seventy-eight-year-old aunt and that she is being left alone to fight back.

"What is happening?" I ask Laura. It seems to be the thing I ask most during this whole procedure.

"The cat missed the shelf and fell," says Laura, laughing. She doesn't seem bothered either.

"No, I mean about this." I gesture to the war of words that no one else seems to notice.

"They are arguing about a previous inheritance. He believes Francesca took more than she should have. It was in 1978 and their families have been arguing about this since then."

I want to break into the theme tune of *Frozen*: "Let It Go." Paolo and Stefana start to complain about being starving. This quietens Riccardo and Uncle Francesca; they all agree they are starving. If there's one thing Italians can agree on, it's food. Nothing interferes with their three-hour lunch breaks. It's nearly one o'clock, so I know things will start to speed up so that everyone can go for lunch.

Betty walks back into the room, and at last we get to sign the document and everyone starts to leave. Ronan is back. He's missed the row and gives Francesca a bone-crushing hug goodbye, and then we go into town for a quick lunch and pass by the house on the way back. Francesca's car is outside it.

"I hope she's not looting the place," I say.

Chapter 32

THE FOLLOWING SUNDAY, WE CAN'T RESIST STOPPING BY THE
house. I want to take measurements of the shutters, as I've seen lots
of secondhand ones for sale online, but windows in Italy seem to have
no standard sizes. Ronan tries the back door and it's still open.

I start measuring the windows with Luca's help, but something
doesn't feel right; something has changed, and I can't put my finger
on it. The house looks sadder, more derelict. I notice a broken tile on
the ground where Ronan stands in the doorway of the kitchen. I'm
not listening to what he's saying; instead I look at the bare surround.

"Was there a door here before?"

We both stand staring at an empty doorway, then walk through
to the next room, its door off its hinges and lying against the wall.

"That's odd. I think I would have noticed that before."

We go back down the hallway. "There's no door here either."

"There were doors, weren't there?"

"Oh! I took a walk-through video on my phone the last time we were here," I say, scrolling through my phone and eventually finding it. Yes. There were definitely doors here, and now they are gone.

Upstairs I find three empty doorways; not only are the doors gone, but the doorframes too. The lock on the second-floor apartment has been busted open. We go to the next level: more doors gone, plaster scattered on the floor where the frames have been prised from the walls. The three of us run from floor to floor, counting: nine doors gone and three more lined up to be taken. My eyes take in the bareness of one of the rooms. Not just the doors.

"What the hell? What? No!"

They've taken the marble table and chairs and the wrought-iron bed.

Has someone tested the back door and come in and helped themselves to the doors and the furniture? We look for clues.

On the sofa in the hall there are piles of old books that were not there before, romance novels mostly, and *Reader's Digest*s from the seventies, and there's a plastic sewing box with scraps of lace—Eileen had the same one for her home economics class. There are also two faded pictures from the wall and an old brass drinks trolley.

Luca notices a perfect, cross-shaped clean spot on the wall—a crucifix has been removed.

There's also a *Children of Fatima* book from the seventies on top of the romance novels, ready to be taken with the second load of doors. So we can guess the thief is religious and likes romance novels. The irony is not lost on me. We all agree it must have been Uncle Francesca with the help of her son, who she had mentioned fondly before.

I scribble a note with the help of Google translate. *"Francesca, the doors and missing furniture must be returned immediately, otherwise the sale is canceled. Rosie and Ronan."* I leave it on top of the books on the drinks stand.

Ronan is raging. "That's it. They can all shove their house up their ass. We're not buying this, even out of principle, I wouldn't buy it now."

I text Laura.

Sorry for texting on a Sunday. We are up in the house and someone has taken nine of the interior doors and doorframes. They are part of the character of the house and would be difficult to replace. I'm guessing it was Francesca, as she has piles of books ready to be taken, as well as other items. There is a bed and table and chairs gone too. Those were items I liked, and they were the reason I asked for the furniture to be included. Ronan is so upset about the doors he feels like pulling out of the sale. What should we do?

I had remained calm, but on the way home we all get angrier, so I send a second text to Laura.

We have thought about it and our upset has turned to anger. To replace those doors will cost thousands, as they are all different sizes. We agreed to buy the house as we saw it, and it was agreed on Friday that the furniture would remain. So we need all doors and the furniture replaced as agreed, otherwise we will not be proceeding with the purchase. I'm sorry for you to be in the middle of this, but you guys need to get onto Francesca before she does any more damage to the house. She, or whoever it is that is taking them, may be intending to return for more, as there were other doors taken off their hinges. Please get Mario to call Uncle Francesca and let me know if the crazy woman admits to taking them.

By the time we drive through our gate, fuming, a "ping" arrives from Laura.

Hi Rosie, thank you to have warned us. I'm so sorry for this fact. Mario has called Uncle Francesca to know how this is possible and who done it. She knows absolutely nothing. We have warned all the owners and tomorrow we'll know who did this and get you back all the doors, we understand your anger, please give us time until tomorrow, because today is Sunday and is difficult coordinate.

By dinnertime our anger has turned to sadness. We have all built up ideas around the house for our future aspirations in Italy. I had envisaged working in my *orto*, growing vegetables and bringing them into Ronan in our big kitchen, where he would have miraculously become a master chef as soon as he entered the Sighing House. He would conjure up amazing three-course Italian dinners inspired by different regions and my perfectly produced vegetables and herbs.

Luca had sketched out the layout of his room: where his drawing table would be, his computer and wardrobe. He had planned to be there by November, just before starting college in Florence. He already has the train timetable and had worked out his morning schedule to include a hot shower in his own bathroom and the five-minute walk to the train station.

Instead, it looks like Luca is doomed to the dribble shower with the sticky curtain, and we're doomed to keep eating our Irish-style beige dinners that don't take much effort and require as little time in the tiny kitchen as possible. Today's involved opening the door of the oven while standing in the sitting room doorway and sticking in a chicken to roast. In Ireland I would have at least added some stuffing or herbs, but this kitchen isn't inspiring my Italian cooking skills like I had expected when I dreamed of moving to Italy. Instead, it has managed to knock any pleasure out of cooking.

Ronan isn't eating his dinner, which means either he's very upset or my cooking skills have reached an all-time low.

"It's like offering to buy a car on Friday and then arriving to collect it on Monday and the owner says someone has stolen the engine but we're still expected to buy it."

"Let's just sleep on it," I say, scooping more Bisto gravy onto his chicken to encouraging him to eat. "Mario won't want to lose his commission. He'll get to the bottom of it."

We all find a way of distracting ourselves for the evening; mine is to do some work. I check my emails and find a long one from the two owners in Milan—a cousin and her mother—pleading with me not to back out of the sale. They've spoken to all the other parties involved and assure me that none of them are thieves and that we all must find a solution.

"How did she get your email address to write a pleading letter?" asks Ronan. "Good to know data-privacy laws are alive and well in Italy."

I can't focus on work, so instead I go to my room and take out my tarot cards. "Will the doors be returned?" I ask.

I get the Magician and the Sun—my interpretation is that the doors will "magically reappear."

I sleep soundly.

Chapter 33

THE FOLLOWING DAY I CALL LAURA TO TELL HER ABOUT THE EMAIL
from the Milan relatives.

"Ah yes, these two owners are very religious; they would not
lie. Unfortunately we have no news yet, Rosie. However, tomorrow
morning Mario and I and the geometra will come to the house in
Passignano. Are you available for a meeting?"

I'm now suspicious of the Milan relatives—with the religious
books and crucifix gone, maybe it was them? So I email them back a
guarded response:

> We are meeting with the estate agent tomorrow, but we will not
> be taking the keys until we have a solution—I can't see a solution,
> but perhaps with some of us together we might find one. We will
> talk to the agent tomorrow and he will update you.
>
> Hopefully we will find the doors somehow and we can get
> on with finishing the purchase.

The next day, a somber-looking Mario, Laura, the geometra, and Uncle Francesca are at the house. I asked Mick Kelly to come too, but he hasn't arrived on time. They are all very apologetic and want us to know this is not normal, reassuring us it was none of the owners.

We walk around the house together, slowly, looking at the spaces where the missing doors had been; maybe they were hoping the doors would miraculously reappear. The house looked sad before, but now it looks like a slum.

Mario announces that a police report must be made. Before Laura has finished translating what he said, Uncle Francesca suddenly makes an announcement that a neighbor saw the thieves on Sunday morning with a van.

We all then agree that it was definitely one of the owners— who else would turn up with a van and take what they could within twenty-four hours of our signing, when the house hasn't been touched for ten years?

Uncle Francesca isn't finished; from the neighbor's description, she believes she knows whodunit.

Ronan and I were previously convinced it was Uncle Francesca (in the kitchen with the crowbar), but she says she believes it was the devil cousin Riccardo getting his revenge on her for the long family dispute over the other inheritance and because she is getting a higher percentage of this house sale than he is.

But why the piles of romance novels in the living room? He was searching for secret documents about the last inheritance, she concludes. Of course!

So it looks like it was Cousin Riccardo in the library with the candlestick.

Cousin Riccardo was at the deposit meeting; we met him. And, yes, I did scowl at him a little when he took the call while Betty was reading, but a little scowl doesn't justify taking nine doors. He also didn't seem interested in the house in any way. He had never been to it, so what would drive him to break in and remove nine doors and some furniture?

Mick Kelly arrives and comes up with a solution. He knows an artisan carpenter who can make doors from old wood that will replicate the others. "I will get a quote from him to replace the doors and it will be deducted from the amount they pay at the final signing."

Mario is in complete agreement. Uncle Francesca avoids eye contact by fumbling through the lace in the sewing box. Leaving the house is different this time. It's like after giving birth; suddenly there are invisible threads connecting me to this previously unknown object, and I don't want to ever be away from it. And it doesn't want to be away from me. We have bonded. The sense of familiarity has also grown stronger, but I still can't put my finger on why I feel like I know the house, like I've always known this house.

We have lunch on the lakefront. With or without doors, I want the house, and I want Ronan to still want the house. After large plates of *tagliatelle cinghiale* and truffle risotto, Ronan and I start to see the funny side of the whole situation; how could we not, with Uncle Francesca's dramatic performances?

"It couldn't really have been her, could it? It's one thing grabbing the champagne glasses from under the rest of the family's noses, but doors? I just can't imagine her prising them off the walls with a crowbar and carrying them down the stairs. She could barely hold the chamber pot with the fruit the first day we met her."

"I still think she was involved. She must have had an accomplice," I say, enjoying my second glass of wine as life in Italy begins to feel less stressful again.

"Well, it couldn't have been any of the cousins at the meeting; they all hated her."

"The cousins in Milan then?… But they seem to have been ruled out by Laura on religious grounds."

"Oh, and religious people have never done anything wrong?" says Ronan, laughing. "There are still confession boxes, you know. They make the weekly subscription easy to renew. Look, whoever it was, we now have a backup solution; the carpenter can make replacement doors and we'll just deduct the cost at the time of the balance payment."

It's heartening to hear this from Ronan. At least now I know he's back on track and wants the house as much as I do. So I order another glass of wine while he has his coffee.

An email from Milan is waiting for us when we get home: the cousins are anxious for an update. The wine with lunch adds courageous fuel to my response:

> Don't worry, there are CCTV cameras in the town and we know
> the color of the van and the time it was there, so the police will
> find the number plate, I am sure, and hopefully find the doors.
> Also, my mother in Ireland is praying hard to Saint Anthony that

the lost doors will be found. She has a very strong connection with the Almighty, and is also very good at putting curses on those that do wrong.

My thinking is that if the fear of the police doesn't scare them into returning the doors, then the fear of God and an Irish witch cursing them might.

There is silence for the rest of the week. The following weekend, the famous Arezzo Fair is on. If there's a place to sell antique doors, this would be it. The Arezzo Antique Fair is one of my favorite places to be. On the first weekend of each month, all the streets of the old town are lined with antique sellers, displaying everything from books and buttons to chandeliers and massive wardrobes.

The Italians love their antique furniture. Dark wooden furniture that we couldn't give away in Ireland—such as my bookcase—carries a high price tag here. They tend not to throw things out. Furniture and clothes are made to last, so secondhand clothes shops are a rare find. But not in Arezzo, where there are a couple of vintage clothes shops worth a browse.

Truthfully, I'm not just dragging Ronan to the Arezzo Antique Fair to look for our doors. I'm also going with the aim of buying something for the house; anything at all, just something to make me feel it's still going to be ours.

Up the cobbled main street, we wander past vintage costume jewelry and silk scarfs, past glossy instructional posters for medical and geography classes, weighted on each end with a strip of wood. Past the chalices, tabernacles, and crosses, the books and ceramics.

The waft of chestnuts roasting in an open pit mingles with the aroma oozing out of the pizza shop window as we turn down towards the main square. Underneath the portico-lined walkway there are silver-ware, frames, war medals, copper pots, and surgical instruments from bygone, terrifying medical eras.

The medieval old town square, with its historic facades and wooden balconies, is the center for the big furniture: doors, carpen-ter's benches, red velvet cinema seats, wardrobes, wall paneling.

After an hour or two of browsing, I buy a set of art nouveau door handles before we stop off for a slice of pizza and my favorite orange-chocolate gelato.

"Well, no sign of our doors."

"They'll have to return them. They won't want nine thousand euro deducted for new doors. Can you imagine all the arguments that are going on between them at the moment? I mean, they can't all be in on it. I just can't figure out who would have done it."

"Well, the people in Milan wouldn't travel down this far with a van to nick doors, and Stefana and Paolo weren't bothered. They haven't been in the house since they were little."

"But Riccardo had the same dismissive attitude at the meeting," says Ronan.

"Maybe it's the aunt with Alzheimer's? Maybe she's super strong from years of rolling pasta, and she and Uncle Francesca clubbed together for their final heist of the family inheritance?"

"I think the ice cream has numbed your brain. Should we put bets on who did it?"

"At least we have door handles," I say while checking my phone.

"Oh, there's a text from Laura." I read aloud, "'Great news! All nine doors were taken back to the house. They are on the ground floor.'"

It's a miracle, I text back. Who did it?

She doesn't answer our question. She wants us to go see the doors with Uncle Francesca on Wednesday, but we refuse.

We'll go see the doors next week with Mario. If all is well, we will go to the notary and pay the deposit and the estate agent's fee on condition that the owners leave the keys with the notary and none of them have access to the house once we pay the deposit—just in case they take a liking to the windows also.

On the way home, Ronan is counting his fingers on the steering wheel. "Hang on—there are eight owners, right? Uncle Fran, the aunt with Alzheimer's, the two in Milan, Riccardo, Paolo, Stefana...that's seven. Who is the eighth? Maybe that's who the door thief is?"

"Ohhh, why didn't we realize that before? The missing owner. Legally, they need to be at the final signing, so we'll see them then, but I'm still sure Uncle Francesca had something to do with it."

We get back home and relax into our usual Sunday routine, reading the Sunday papers online.

"Two Chinese tourists visiting Italy have tested positive for that coronavirus," Ronan says, not lifting his head from the paper on his iPad. "Supposedly it's like a bad cold or flu and you just need to stay home and treat it like that."

I'm in the kitchen making coffee. "I'm not sure what the big deal is, but it's in the USA also, and they seem to be taking it seriously. I read an article in *USA Today* with the headline 'Rush Is On to Develop Vaccine for Coronavirus.' The article said there have been five cases in the USA. It seems a bit of overkill to be rushing to produce a vaccine for five cases, doesn't it? Do you think they're expecting it to get worse?"

"The Americans have vaccines for everything. It's how the pharmaceutical companies make their billions, so of course they're creating one."

We both drink our coffee and think nothing more of it.

Chapter 34

telling us what we already know:

> The doors have been found! They have been put in the house, and the main door has been locked, but since you can still enter from other points of the house. It would be better if you went to get the doors tomorrow to keep them safely. I talked with Aunt Francesca and she agrees too.

I read it aloud to Ronan.

"So they want us to go up, climb in the window, and take the doors away for safe keeping, in case her cousin has the urge to steal them again? What next?"

The email is hotly followed by a text from Laura:

> All the nine doors are in the house. For now it is better if you

leave the doors in the house because for the law you aren't the owner yet.

Where is everyone getting this idea that we want to bring nine hefty doors on a holiday?

We visit the house with Mario and Uncle Francesca, and the doors are all neatly stacked, with intact frames still attached. I learn that they are called Madonna doors—the doorframes attach to the wall, and the doors hang from them. I was going to insist on charging the owners to get the doors rehung, but we've completed much more difficult tasks in our years of house renovating, so it's not worth the hassle of another family argument.

As always, Uncle Francesca launches into a long story about the doors, which Laura translates for us as she speaks: it wasn't Cousin Riccardo, as she first thought. It was Cousin Vincent—well, the Italian equivalent of the name, which I am unsure how to spell, so we'll just call him Cousin Vinny.

It turned out that, like Cousin Riccardo, Cousin Vinny was out for revenge on Uncle Francesca over the 1978 family dispute.

Everyone is relieved the thief has been identified and will no doubt be subjected to Uncle Francesca's scorn.

We all travel immediately to Betty's office so we can, at last, pay the deposit. The more time we spend with Uncle Francesca, the more obvious the cause of the forty-five-year family dispute becomes. Uncle Francesca, the little, crumpled, four-foot-ten lady, has a real knack for causing arguments. At the office, Uncle Francesca argues again about the court document the notary had asked her to get; it's now the only thing holding up the finalizing of the sale. Betty tries to keep calm and explains again what Francesca needs to do to get the document, then finally tells her she will write the correct wording for her to bring to the judge. Uncle has no argument for this; she just shrugs and looks a bit disgruntled before moving on to her next topic—she wants to hold on to the keys so that she can shame Cousin Vinny into returning the missing furniture also. Mario ends up raising his voice at her and flailing his arms, making lots of hand gestures. Basically, he doesn't want to have to drive the hour from his office every time we need to have access in order to allow builders in, and it was agreed at the last meeting with the owners that we would get the keys upon payment of the deposit. I joke to Laura that they could give me Cousin Vinny's number and I would sort him out.

We are given the keys.

On the way home I get a text from Laura.

Uncle Francesca will follow up about the furniture, but here's Cousin Vinny's phone number just in case.

What was I supposed to do with the phone number of the thief? Send him disturbing texts in the middle of the night? Songs by the Doors perhaps?

Now all we're waiting for is the power-of-attorney letter with the correct wording from Uncle Francesca, then we can set a final date to sign over the house. March 10th is suggested, which would be after I get back from Ireland. It will be the first time the cousins are all in the same room, with the forty-five-year family dispute bubbling under the surface. I was going to bring cake to help sweeten the meeting, but on second thought, I'll bring popcorn and watch the show.

Chapter 35

WE HAVE BEEN IN ITALY FOR OVER A YEAR, BUT WE HAVEN'T really integrated into life here yet. I still wait until I'm back in Ireland to get my hair cut and go to the dentist, doctor, and beautician.

It's the end of February, and in a few days I'll take a trip back to Ireland to go to various appointments and to visit home. My parents call me four or five times a day to ask if it's safe for me to travel back because of the virus spreading in Italy.

"I haven't seen you since Christmas. I'm starting to think you are afraid of me coming?"

"No, not at all; we're just afraid you might not be allowed back. What if Ronan got sick, him being diabetic, and you couldn't get back to him?" answers Mam.

It's not just my parents; for once, people aren't telling me how lucky I am to be living in Italy. With its balmy climate and *dolce vita* lifestyle, Italy can do no wrong in the eyes of my family and friends. If I complain about my life not being as rosy as they imagine it to be,

I'm just being an unappreciative wench. For instance, when I moan about how cold the house is in winter, they say, "Well, at least you're cold surrounded by beautiful Italian scenery."

When I grumbled about having to do three days of twelve-hour weddings in one week in forty-two degree heat, a friend said, "Oh, it must be lovely flouncing around in the Italian sun." Because that's what everyone thinks wedding planners do: flounce around. They don't imagine us dealing with blocked toilets, drunk guests, missing grooms, psychotic mothers-in-law, and irate caterers.

If I broke my leg, I'm sure someone would say, "Well, at least it's in Italy you have a broken leg. Lucky you!"

But this time it's different: everyone I know in Ireland is telling me how bad the virus is in Italy, as if I haven't heard. It's where I live; don't they think I know what the situation is? Maybe it's a slow day for news in Ireland and they've done a big report on it, as the number of "thoughts and prayers" sent my way through social media is ridiculous. I keep having to explain that I live over five hundred kilometers away from where the outbreak is. And life is the same. We went out for a coffee and a spritz beside the lake last night; everything is okay.

I start to think I might cancel my trip to Ireland, as I don't want to have to explain myself every five seconds, and I imagine Dublin Airport will be a huge hassle for those arriving from Italy.

In the end, I decide to go, as Ronan needs his medication, which we still get from Ireland every eight weeks. A good friend is having a birthday party in Dublin that I don't want to miss, and it will be good to show my parents that everything is all right.

To help ease the messages from concerned friends, I type out a post for social media:

We are over 500 km away from the area where there is the "outbreak." Italians are very cautious about their health, and they are tracking and tracing all physical contacts of people who have had a positive test.

I end my post with:

I'm flying to Ireland tomorrow (if they let me in). I'm looking forward to seeing family and buying teabags and Bisto, but I am dreading the weather, as the ironic thing is, I nearly always come back to Italy with a cold or flu. So please do not worry. It is not Ebola. It is just a virus that a week in bed with some paracetamol will cure if you don't have underlying health issues.

While waiting to board at Rome airport, I create a meme of two pictures: one of zombies and one of a jolly crowd having an *aperitivo* in Lucca. Across the zombies I write, "What people think is happening in Italy," and across the happy people, "What is happening in Italy."

The flight is full; a few people are wearing masks. The Irish Olympic boxing team are on the flight. Their training session with other European Olympians in Assisi has been cut short because of the virus. That's odd, as the outbreak is miles away from Assisi, which is near where we live.

I arrive in Dublin Airport and breeze through; no temperature checks or questions about where we have traveled in Italy. As we are going through customs, there is a poster stand with a cute picture of a pig and a headline about swine flu. Does that still exist?

I check my phone; the meme seems to have gone viral. Italians are loving it.

It's bloody cold. I get the bus to my parents, and after dinner I blend in with their routine of watching the evening news. There are at least forty minutes of sensational coronavirus headlines, all about Italy. "With the death toll rising in Italy," begins the reporter.

What the hell? There has been one death in the last two days. And I thought the Italians were the dramatic ones? A virus expert comes on and tells everyone it's not that bad, but still the headlines stay sensational. The only other news is that there's just one girl in Ireland doing an apprenticeship in carpentry; the rest are lads. Ireland needs more apprentices. Nothing else seems to be happening in Ireland, or the world.

The following day I have a beautician's appointment. While I am having a coffee beforehand, every conversation I overhear is about the virus in Italy. The assistant at the cash register is talking to a customer who works in the chemist about masks selling out.

I play with the idea of standing up and announcing, "I arrived from Italy yesterday." The shop would be empty within thirty seconds, and I could eat all the cakes. At the health-food store I hear a woman telling the cashier that she's starting to stock up for when "it" comes.

Lying on the beautician's plinth, she talks about the awful Irish weather. I mention I'm over from Italy. She makes a joke about leaving the room. But then she does actually leave the room. She comes back to finish.

"The eyelash dye has taken well; there's no need to leave it for the full ten minutes as usual. The couple of minutes it's had already will do."

There's none of the usual upselling of moisturizer or face serums. I get the feeling she wants me to leave as soon as possible. I go to pay, and a bottle of sanitizer is on the counter.

"That's seventy euro," the cashier says as she scowls at me, squirting her hands with sanitizer in the most dramatic way possible. The waiting room is suddenly quiet, and the beautician smiles awkwardly. She knows that I know she told everyone.

On the way to the car park, I look in an estate agent's window. Nondescript houses are renting for between one thousand and fifteen hundred euro—for a two-hour commute to Dublin. Houses that are nothing special are priced at two hundred and forty thousand. I couldn't afford to live here even if I still wanted to. I think about the Sighing House in Italy by the lake: three floors of potential beauty for half the price.

I turn on the car radio. Every station is talking about the impending zombie apocalypse. It will arrive; the only question is when.

In the evening, my parents have the news on again. And again we are fed forty minutes of coronavirus. An expert tells people, if they do get the virus, to stay indoors, wash their hands, and avoid other members of the family. "And wash your laundry at sixty degree Celsius."

In other news, another storm is going to hit Ireland tomorrow. It's the third one in a month. The middle of Ireland is basically under water, there are homeless families sleeping on the streets in zero-degree weather, yet the news is more focused on the "rising" death toll among an aged, sick population of twelve towns on the northern border of Italy. There are twenty-one dead now.

I travel to Dublin for the party, and at the check-in the hotel receptionist asks where I'm visiting from.

"Ita… London."

"You are very welcome."

"Thank you."

The wind is rising; it's freezing. There are people sleeping in doorways. I want a Guinness. The party is in a pub in the heart of Dublin that sits practically in the shadow of the Guinness brewery, where my grandfather worked for years.

"What do you mean, you don't sell Guinness?"

"We sell craft beers here, not Guinness."

"But I haven't had a Guinness in over a year. I'm over from—" I stop myself.

I ask my friend, "Why can't he give me a Guinness? Is he joking?"

And my friend explains, "The Guinness company requires a pub to have a minimum number of draft taps if it wants to serve Guinness. So pubs tend to choose to be either a craft beer pub or a Guinness pub—they don't have enough bar space to be both."

I'm starting to feel sad. The Dublin that I love is becoming a shell of itself. I was one of "those" Irish people who—even though I sing like a cat that has been partially run over—imagine themselves in old age sitting by a fireside in a local pub, beautifully singing old Irish songs from their youth, leaving out the less fond remembrance of how the tunes were beaten into them by nuns. But this vision is crumbling quicker than the old walls in the Sighing House.

The following morning I have a nice breakfast at the Shelbourne Hotel, where my other grandfather used to work and where Hitler's brother also worked and married a woman called Brigid. They had a son and called him Patrick—Paddy Hitler. The only descendant of Hitler, he later changed his name and disappeared in America. This was my first breaking-news story as a young journalist.

The breakfast costs me thirty-two euro. So I eat enough for lunch as well. On the two-hour bus journey back to my parents' house, I count five people coughing and sneezing. None of them have hankies, and I'm watching as they get off the bus and put their hands on every headrest walking down the aisle. This wouldn't happen in Italy.

Italy might have the virus, but even at the best of times Italians are very careful of their health, never mind during a pandemic. I have no doubt they will deal with this better than most other countries. There's a thing they fear called *colpo d'aria*, which means "a blast of air." The closest Irish equivalent is "catching a draft" or "getting a chill," but *colpo d'aria* is more serious.

Only a few weeks previous, Lucia had stopped while jogging and blamed it on stomach sickness caused by *colpo d'aria*, and that wasn't the first time I heard her speak about it. She has previously said her joint pain was from not cooling off properly after working out and going straight into an air-conditioned supermarket where she got *colpo d'aria*. Like a lot of Italians, she hates air-conditioning—recycled cold air? No thanks. She won't let me put on the AC in the car, no matter how hot it is.

Italians wear their scarfs and overcoats until after Easter, even if it's twenty Celsius. Going out with wet hair is a near criminal offense. Every house has a thermometer that is regularly used to ensure no one is close to getting a fever in winter. If your temperature goes up in any way, a whole series of old wives' cures are used, from herbal teas to warm wine and the wearing of *il corno*, a charm that looks like a red pepper.

I collect Ronan's prescription from the chemist. The woman behind the counter is spraying disinfectant on pens at the counter and wiping them down like crazy.

"You can't be too careful," she jokes.

I say I'm there, and she shouts back to the pharmacist, who peeks up from behind the counter.

"How is Ronan?"

"Fine," I answer.

"He's not in Italy, is he?" Oh, here we go.

"Yes, he is."

The counter assistant steps quickly away from me and goes to fix the already neat shelves in the furthest corner. "Whereabouts? North or south?"

Everything from Rome up is considered Northern Italy, but if I say north it will have a catastrophic effect.

"Middle." I say.

"Are you going there?"

"Yes, I fly back on Monday, and I can't wait. Warm weather, good food."

He's looking at me like I've lost my mind. I'm so sick of this. I stare at him. "It's fine. There are eight thousand towns in Italy. Twelve are affected, up near the Swiss border. The Italians are very health conscious."

He steps forward with the prescription. He's not looking too healthy himself; he's pasty from lack of sun. He serves me as the assistant continues to straighten the straight boxes.

Chapter 36

THE NEXT APPOINTMENT I HAVE IS AT THE DENTIST, TO GET FIVE fillings renewed. I hate going to the dentist, so I announce, "Look, straight up, I am over from Italy. If you don't want to treat me, that is okay."

"Yes, we saw that on your chart and it raised a few eyebrows all right. Whereabouts in Italy?"

I tell her. She understands it's not in the red zone, and she's happy to proceed. Damn. She chats normally and makes me feel less like an outcast. She's so friendly I feel like crying.

"Do they have pitch and putt in Italy?" my dad asks from behind his paper as Mam sets the table.

"No, but the garden is big enough for you to build your own course."

"I'll bring my clubs so."

"Do you think you'll have the house finished by the 4th of May?" my mam asks over dinner.

"It would be a bit of a push getting it done by then, but we could try. But why that date, Mam?"

"That's the date I moved into Abbeyfield when I was three, and the date I left it seventy years later, when you and Ronan moved in, remember? So I want it to be the date I emigrate to Italy when I'm eighty-four."

I usher her to sit down and I finish up, as I can see her stooped back is bothering her from standing too long. "Well, we need to fix the roof first, and then we can focus on the downstairs rooms for you. If the builders are ready to start next week, then we could just about get it done on time. But I think September will be a better aim."

"No, let's aim for May. As long as Italy gets this thing under control, we'll be there."

I know damn well that with the virus thing growing, the house will probably not be ready for them in May, and arriving at the start of summer won't give them time to acclimatize to the heat. But to keep them optimistic I agree. September would be better, but even still I'm wondering if I'll be able to get them over by then. Will I even be able to get back to see them before then? There's talk of the pandemic lasting for years and that it's only a matter of time before it spreads around the world.

When it's time to leave, I kiss my parents on the tops of their heads while they're still sitting and say goodbye. The saturation of news during my every waking hour there has had its desired effect; I don't want to give them the virus if I have it, and I am freaked out about Italy. I want to get back as soon as possible, but as my lips leave their hair, I already miss them too much for words.

"See you in May," they shout, waving me off.

"Yes, start packing," I call back, but my heart is sinking. I don't know when I'm going to see my parents again.

At the bus stop there are two junkies. I don't think I've seen a junky in Italy. I'm sure they exist, but the drug problem is not so in your face there. Actually, come to think of it, other than at weddings, I think I've only seen one person drunk in Italy, when we were walking home from a wine festival one night.

There are three people properly hacking their guts up on the bus. I feel a bit ill. I want to get back to Italy, where I feel safe, back to normality, and to complete our house purchase, to start turning it into our cozy home.

Dublin Airport is eerily quiet: there are no queues, and just sprinkles of travelers here and there. I've been traveling back and forth between Italy and Ireland all year round, and I've never seen it like this.

"Wow, it's quiet. Is it because of the virus?" I ask the woman at the passport desk.

"It's always a bit quiet at this time of year, but yes, a lot of people have canceled travel because of it."

"I'm going back to Italy to get away from all the hype," I joke. She's not impressed.

"Well, you're going into the eye of the storm."

"It's not that bad," I say.

"Sixteen hundred cases? You don't think that's bad?" She sneers at me. It's like she's blaming Italy.

How dare she. I feel like ripping into her with facts. "Italy has tested over twenty-one thousand people to date, more than all the other European countries combined. No other country is taking the same precautions or extensive measures as Italy. The USA has tested about five hundred and doesn't know the source of contagion for three of their dead." I want to defend *my Italy* against the crap people are spewing about it here in *my Ireland.*

Everyone working in the airport looks miserable. Perhaps they have all applied for time off due to fear of the virus and none were given it.

I drink two pints of Guinness. I can't wait to get my parents over to live with me in Italy; then it will be just the Guinness that I miss. Plus the odd fried breakfast. I walk through the souvenir shops and look at the beautifully crafted Aran sweaters, bodhrans, and bog oak carvings; all the things I once loved about my culture I have grown to think of as diddily-dee crap and tourist tat.

Every time I come back, I feel more detached from Ireland and more a part of Italy. This time the feeling is stronger than ever. Here, I don't feel they care anymore, but I know that if I get sick in Italy I will be cared for. I'll always be a foreigner in Italy, never truly belonging, but Ireland has lost its charm; it's becoming a waterlogged rock in the Atlantic, one that's too expensive to live on. My love of my home culture is disappearing, and I feel a stab of sickness with the wave of regret and absolute sadness. Maybe the Aperol spritz will replace Guinness as my cultural drink of choice.

The plane only has about fifty people on it, and we arrive in Rome to a welcoming committee in what looks like full nuclear-prevention gear: red suits, masks, gloves—I'm expecting to see E.T. lying on a slab in an oxygen tent at any moment. They're here to direct us through a temperature screen, a portal where a radiation-suited woman is watching a screen like someone looking for Whac-a-Mole. I glance at the screen while walking past, and the shadow people on it are overlaid with a few red dots. I wonder what she needs to watch for, and what happens when they find it? Is a person with a high temperature tackled to the ground and cuffed, or are they brought into a nice room and given warm wine, a hot water bottle, and perhaps a *cornicello* charm?

I've booked the train back. I didn't want Ronan driving, as he hasn't had his diabetic tablets in three days and it can make him tired and foggy brained. But I don't mind, I like traveling by train. I often take the train into Florence or down to Rome and spend the journey looking into the gardens that back up to the track. Something I've noticed is that there are no flower gardens—flowers are kept to terraces; gardens are for vegetables. Each plot has rows of zucchini, artichokes, potatoes, cabbages, tomatoes, and lettuce, alongside peach, orange, apple, pear, cherry, and fig trees, and, of course, grapevines, all with different fruiting seasons.

I enjoy strolling through food markets and the supermarkets in Italy, which are full of the aromas of locally grown fruit and vegetables, wheels of aged cheeses, and joints of aged hams. Fresh fish is expensive in Umbria though, as it's landlocked. *Baccalà*—salted fish—is still a staple food here, originating as a way of preserving fish back in the time when pilgrims walked the roads to Assisi.

There are aisles of wine, all from Italian vineyards; Aussie or South African chardonnay is impossible to find. Processed and imported food is minimal.

I have no doubt Italy will get through this okay, as their wartime survival instincts are still strong—it is common to see old people with rickety legs from when they were children of the war, when they had to hide in the mountains with just nuts and weeds they could forage as food. In spring, in the woods near where I live, I often see foragers with bags full of wild asparagus they have just collected. The use of pesticides or weed killer seems to be frowned upon. They know how nutritious and delicious some weeds can be; they know their mushrooms, roots, and nuts.

On the train, an English woman in her late sixties sits opposite me. She tells me her daughter has asked her to come and stay to help mind her children, as she is a doctor in Florence and they say things are going to get busy with the new virus cases. She's considering moving here full time but is nervous she will be lonely as she gets older.

"Oh, don't worry," I say. They still love and respect their grandparents here in Italy. Many people still live in homes divided into apartments that are shared between three generations. In town centers you'll often find they have converted an empty shop into a place where the elderly can gather to read the paper, chat, play cards, have a coffee. Older people are loved and respected here."

It's true. Old people in Italy don't suffer from loneliness as much as in other countries. In every town you'll see groups of old gents playing cards outside coffee bars, while the women stick to the benches, balconies, and church steps for their chats.

By the time my train pulls in at the station it's ten thirty, and Ronan is there to meet me. I feel a swell of relief to be back with his meds and away from the chaos and mayhem. To be back with him, my rock. I'm in his arms and I don't want him to let go.

It's a forty-minute drive to our house, and the roads around the station are empty. Is it because of the earlier rain, or is it because it's late? Is it because of the virus? There are two old lads sitting outside a bar in overcoats and hats under the arch. There's no one else around and only a few cars on the motorway home.

"It's been like this for two days," says Ronan. "Things are becoming strange. They're getting quieter here, but in other parts of the world they are running out of toilet roll. Have you seen the news reports? Australia and the UK seem to think stocking up on toilet paper is the thing to do to keep the virus away."

"What are they doing—wrapping themselves in it like mummies? I haven't seen. The only news they report on in Ireland is about how bad it is in Italy."

"Lucia has invited us to lunch tomorrow to celebrate our getting the house, you being home, and whatever other excuse she could think of. She's missed you, I think."

At the mention of the house, I'm excited again. Only two more sleeps and it will be ours.

Lunch at Lucia's is delicious: she serves long strips of pasta she made that morning, tossed in a creamy sauce, and topped with shavings of truffles found in the surrounding hills. We chat about this year's weddings and her idea of doing up the barn when she gets a break in the autumn. When we say goodbye to Lucia, little do I know that this will be last time I hug my friend for a long time.

We had planned to go for pizza later, but Lucia tells us that there were two cases of the virus found in Chiusi, the train station town I was in two nights ago. On the way home, we hear the news on the radio: cases are rising and spreading, so I suggest, "Let's not go. Let's start to stay in a bit until we know more about this virus. I'll contact the notary tomorrow and check what can be done about the final signing, as there is no way the owners from Milan will be able to come down. Perhaps they can sign with a notary close to where they live. I'm sure there's a way."

The following day we do what in Ireland we call "a big shop." It should last us about ten days, with some supplies lasting a month; we'll only need to pop out for milk and one or two other perishables.

We bump into a Scottish friend of a friend who has lived here for thirty years. "I heard about your house; congratulations, and best of luck with the renovations. You have a big job there. I renovated mine about ten years ago. Wouldn't do that again, and mine is only a one-bedroom apartment. I can't imagine the amount of problems you're going to have. How much did they quote you for the roof? Let me guess, twenty thousand?"

"How did you know?"

"Because that's the price they give everyone," he says, laughing. "Wait until the work starts and then you'll see the prices change! Italians are terrible for not turning up, and they seem to constantly have national holidays. With this virus thing, you might never get it done." His negativity reminds me why he's a friend of a friend and not just a friend.

I buy seeds and compost—sunflowers, tomatoes, and lettuce— and plant them in pots on the terrace when I get home. "By the time the sunflowers bloom, things will be better," I tell myself. As I'm watering my freshly planted seeds, Lucia calls. "Have you heard the news? Conte has announced the quarantine measures are to be expanded to the entire country from tomorrow. There are nine thousand cases in Italy now. Maybe you should tell Izzy to come back in case the airports close?"

"She won't be able to; she's still working. But thanks for telling me. I'll go online and check what's happening."

I spend the rest of the evening hopping between my laptop screen and the international news channels.

Conte has requested Italians to avoid engaging in *furbizia*—craftiness to circumvent the lockdown rules. I note the word in my notebook. I like the sound of it but have no clue when I'll use it.

The hashtag *#IoRestoACasa* (I stay at home) is already trending. There are reports on international TV showing queues of people in Italy waiting to get into supermarkets with empty trolleys, and they hint at food shortages.

"Ronan, look at how they are showing Italy," I shout into the kitchen. "Journalism has gone to the dogs. If they did any research or even thought about it, they'd see the queues look long because everyone is keeping a meter apart and their trolleys are empty because they haven't gone into the supermarket yet. What a stupid report."

Ronan is reading reports too. He comes in solemnly. "Did you hear the courts are also closed except for urgent cases? That means Uncle Francesca won't be able to get the signing done. No one from out of town can travel here. We won't be getting the house tomorrow."

Chapter 37

ON THE 10TH OF MARCH, DAY ONE OF LOCKDOWN, I WAKE FIRST, as always. It's supposed to be the day that we sign the final deed and at last own our casa in Italy, complete with doors and everything. Instead, the whole of Italy is locked indoors, hiding from an invisible deadly virus that looks like the everlasting gobstopper from *Willy Wonka*.

The roads are quieter. The sun is shining. I can hear the birds singing; spring is in the air. I wait for my tea to turn the right shade of brown before I remove the teabag, gazing out the back kitchen window thinking, "It will only be for a few weeks; we can get through this." I notice something at the end of the back field—a squirt of a brown dog humping Asha.

"What the hell?" I run out with my dressing gown flying in the air, screaming at the four-legged Casanova. By the time I get close, he has dismounted and is wagging his tail. "You haven't let a dog near you in ten years. Why now? Are Italian dogs smooth barkers? So the dog next door hasn't been whining every evening, he's been serenading you, has he?" Asha is smiling from ear to ear; the damage has been done and she's very pleased with herself. They trot off to the woods together while I scream obscenities at them.

The vet lives two villages away. I'll need a police pass to get there. "Why pick the first day of a three-week quarantine to lose your virginity at this stage in your life? And not a condom in sight!" I chastise Asha when she returns for lunch.

I sit out on the terrace and research "morning-after pill for dogs."

A website I check daily shows the spread of the virus across a map of Italy, with red dots where the virus has reached and black dots where it's really bad. Poor Italy looks like a squashed ladybird. I will never look at polka dots the same way.

Then I do a final check of the national train network website, with a glimmer of hope that the Milan owners could make it down to do the signing on the basis of its being important business. The train company has posted a message that people can only travel for work or health with self-certification. Underneath, in the comments section, there's a question from a Vincenzo:

Can I travel to Naples to visit my family, which requires a bus and a train?

A can of worms opened and an onslaught of replies:

Only if you want to bring your mother or grandmother the gift of Corona. Stay at home sitting on the sofa.

Don't be so selfish, I haven't seen my parents for twenty years. You can last three weeks.

Follow the instructions fool.

Think of all the refugees who have not seen their families for three years. Don't be so selfish, you can wait three weeks without running back to your mama.

Vincenzo then replied:

I'm seventy. I just wanted to go to my daughter and get my glasses fixed.

Poor Vincenzo. Social media can be so cruel, but it does give me comfort to see how seriously the Italians are following the stay-at-home order.

After a few hours on the terrace, I'm feeling very hot. "Oh no, it's happening—I have a fever."

The fear makes me feel hotter.

I've become super aware of every sneeze or cough in the household; both Ronan and Luca know that I can pounce at any time during the day with the palm of my hand smacked onto their forehead. To be honest, unless they had a raging fever, I wouldn't know an "off" temperature if I felt it, but whacking them on the forehead gives me a sense of being motherly.

My paranoia seems to peak in the middle of the night, after I've indulged in too much wine and read scary headlines just before bed. Several times, I've woken up in the wee hours with a sudden urge to reach out and gently feel Ronan's forehead, but as I'm half asleep and feeling somewhat panicked, my coordination is off and I've ended up whacking my hand on his face in the dark and then groping my way to his forehead. He's very understanding, but I think he's getting a bit tired of it.

Now, sitting on the terrace, I'm sure I have been "corona'd." I hurry to the bathroom and root around in the medicine chest for the thermometer before catching sight of my face in the mirror. It's clear that I've made my annual mistake of sitting out for too long at the first appearance of the sun, resulting in a big red face. "Oh thank God. It's just bad sunburn."

I sit on the couch and watch an instructional video on the news advising viewers how to wash their hands. Up to this point, I'd thought I was quite professional at washing my hands, as I've been doing it by myself since I was about three years old, several times a day. However, now I wonder if I'm washing them long enough, for the full twenty seconds that's recommended. I haven't washed my hands in the last couple of hours.

"Lads, we need to wash our hands more. Let's do it now and sing 'Happy Birthday' twice." I'm up on my feet and at the bathroom sink, with the door open, and start to sing "Happy Birthday."

"That's too fast. You sound like an ice-cream van in a car chase," shouts Ronan. "Sing the first two verses of 'Come Out Ye Black and Tans.' That's just over twenty seconds. I've timed it."

"Jesus, I can't remember the words of that. I haven't sung it since school."

Ronan proceeds to teach me the words while peeling potatoes.

I'm not very good at learning songs and get stressed tripping over the words.

"Bloody hell, I'm never going to get this right. I think I'll just go back to singing 'Happy Birthday' more slowly, or perhaps the fast version three times."

"Why don't you just count to twenty?" says Luca, walking past to go out to the terrace.

I never thought of that. I follow him out.

A lizard scuttles across the wall; it's the first one I've seen this year, which means the ground is heating up. I hope warmer weather will kill off this virus and the growing paranoia I'm infected with.

Ingrid rings around dinnertime.

"I saw on the TV that the Italians have been keeping spirits up by singing and playing instruments from their balconies."

"Yes, it's quite scary."

"What do you mean? It's beautiful."

"Yes, they brought tears to my eyes and lumps to my throat, but something needs to be understood. Italy is the home of opera. Most kids learn a classical or traditional instrument from a young age. Wait until people start mimicking this in other parts of the world: garage bands competing with each other, drummers drumming to their own hard-metal beats, wannabes belting out their versions of Whitney Houston and Adele. It will be like living in a live version of *X-Factor* reject clips 24/7."

"So you think people should be warned to skip the toilet roll aisle at this point and stock up on the headache tablets, is that what you're saying?"

"Exactly!" I say, laughing.

"Anyway, any word on the house?"

"No, everything has been put on hold. The whole country is in lockdown, so the meeting has been postponed for three weeks."

"Oh, that doesn't sound good. Perhaps it's time you all come home until it clears up over there?"

I lie on the terrace sun lounger and think about the balcony singers. Italian kids' experience with music is different from the experiences of those in other parts of the world. Every town has its saint's festival day, and throughout the summer they have medieval and cultural festivals. In autumn, towns have a *sagra*, which is a festival of the local food and wine harvests. In all parades and local traditional festivals, music plays a big part.

Kids practice together regularly throughout the year for these annual festivals, and they continue to participate as adults with the same people they grew up with.

In Italian cities, many people live in apartments, and a lot of towns have districts that compete against each other during their local festivals, such as in Siena's Palio or Gubbio's Festival of the Candles, where three districts carry giant heavy wooden structures to the church on top of the hill—don't ask. It's fun to see, gets the adrenaline pumping for sure, and it all ends with them having a massive street party together.

Many members of these close-knit communities live in apartments near one another, so when, for instance, Marco whips out his trumpet on his balcony, Alessia in the apartment two blocks down knows when to join in with her tambourine, as she's familiar with his music and has probably played with him many times before. And so their impromptu flashmob works out.

Community spirit is very strong in Italy, but I still feel I'm on the outside of it.

Chapter 38

NOW THAT WE ARE DOING WEEKLY "BIG SHOPS," MY BRAIN, looking at the full fridge and full wine rack, seems to have switched to party mode. Normally I have a glass of wine when I close down my computer in the evening after doing eight hours of emails. But now, as my work inbox for wedding inquiries has tumbleweed blowing through it, I'm finished work in less than an hour, so I'm making nice lunches and having a glass of wine with them. Sure, why not? I'm not driving anywhere.

I check in on emails after lunch, more tumbleweed, so my work day is finished by four o'clock, and the celebratory closing-of-the-computer wine has moved forward three hours. Then I'll have one with dinner, which has become a huge feast of all our favorite stuff, followed by a nightcap. So now my month's supply of wine is already half gone and we're only on day four. Also, party brain has decided I should indulge in my month's supply of chocolate—to get over the shock of being quarantined, I think. I have two Bounty bars left.

I'm not sleeping well either. It's not because of the worries about the world; it's indigestion. I've never suffered from this before.

The Italians do this all the time—a proper sit-down lunch and a cooked dinner. It has taken me a year of living here to discover the secret of why they're not all obese with the amount of food they eat. The secret seems to be that they keep the carbs—the pastas and risottos—for lunchtime, and then for dinner they have fish or meat with vegetables. So the carbs get burnt off during the day. They also don't really do breakfast—just an espresso for most. So maybe they're unknowingly doing the 16:8 fasting thing we all hear is so good for us?

By week two of lockdown I've gone up two kilos, or it might be four—I don't want to look close enough at the scales to see if the little dashes stand for one or two kilos each.

While standing there on the scales, I have a premonition of my future grandkids looking through a family photo album:

"This is my great-great-great-grandma Ellen—she lived through the Irish Famine. She became the mother of ten children, who did great things throughout the world."

"This is my great-great-grandfather Jim—he lived through World War One. He became a soldier and won medals."

"This is my grandmother Rosie—she lived through the coronavirus pandemic... She became obese."

It's time for me to start getting active again, to turn the clothes horse back into the glorious treadmill it once was, and to get Luca to show me how to use his weights. I knew I wasn't going to end up with a *Cosmo* beach-ready body, but at least my knees wouldn't give way by the end of quarantine.

The following day I decide to start the day off right with an early-morning walk around the two fields behind the house. A grass laneway runs down the side of one of the fields. At the end there's a drop where oaks grow. We call this "the woods," even though it's only about four trees deep. Beyond that, there are the vineyards of the local winery—rolling hills with perfect rows of vines.

It becomes a pet walk rather than a dog walk, as I'm followed by our two black cats as well as Looney and Asha.

As it's early, I'm in my dressing gown—it's a long, cozy gray one with a loose hood. On the way down the steps I grab a large stick from the wood pile just in case the four-legged Casanova decides to visit. I walk down the lane towards the woods. The birds are singing (still) and the neighbor's hen is laying an egg. I've never seen this hen, but it clucks and "bok, bok, *bawks*" way too perfectly, so I imagine it's a cartoon hen—one-dimensional, cross-eyed, and running around in circles.

I haven't bothered with shoes. Looney decides she doesn't want to walk anymore, so I pick her up and tuck her under my arm. I cross the end of the field parallel to the woods and begin my walk back up the other grass lane, which faces onto the road. The road is always quiet on weekend mornings, but Mass has been canceled and the supermarket is not open yet, so today is extra quiet.

A car approaches and slows to a stop at the top of the lane. I see them looking towards me. I think it's Lucia, so I lift my hand to wave; the hand with the stick, as the other is busy carrying a little white dog. It's not Lucia, and the car pulls away so quickly that the tires squeal. Strange.

I get back to the house and get dressed. Without thinking, I change from my old PJs into a clean set. I look in the mirror and realize I haven't brushed my hair for two days. Ronan is still in bed, having just woken up.

"What is happening to me? I've worked from home for over ten years and have never done this. My brain has gone from party mode to 'let's just be a slob' mode. I'm a mess."

"I'm the same. I haven't shaved in over a week. It's because we know that no one will be calling in and we won't be going anywhere."

"Now I know why the car sped away. I must have looked like a mad hermit coming out from the woods: long gray hooded cap, bare feet, with a wolf and other crazed animals circling, waving my wooden staff at them."

"What are you talking about?"

"Or perhaps a biblical vision with the Lamb of God under my arm... They shouldn't have been out breaking the quarantine anyway. Maybe that will scare them into staying at home."

"Rosie, I don't know what you are raving about. Have a shower and a cup of tea; you'll feel better."

After lunch I sit outside with Luca, making a daisy angel, which is like a snow angel but in a patch of daisies. While lying in the grass looking up at the blue sky, I see a plane, and our conversation turns to where it's going and where it could have come from—this has never been a topic of interest before.

"Greta Thunberg must be less stressed now," I say, thinking of how I prepare to be sad every time I see her little face come on the TV. "Fewer planes in the air, less cruise ship pollution, fewer cars on the road, factories closed, all leading to less crap in the air and in our water systems. Birds, bees, and fish are breeding without human interference. Noise pollution is down. Nature has a chance to recover. She must be feeling a little bit happier now, right?"

Luca doesn't respond; he's looking down the road where a distant noise is getting closer. So we stand and wait for it to come into view. A van drives slowly from house to house, stopping outside each for a moment. Behind it is a car…no, wait, it's more than that—it's a police car with lights flashing and a megaphone. I find it hard to understand megaphone announcements in my own language, so a megaphone plus Italian, plus distance makes it very difficult to understand.

"What are they saying? Are they dropping stuff off at houses, or is it like the 'Bring out your dead' scene in *Monty Python and the Holy Grail*?"

They reach the house next door. The van slows, a police announcement is made, and the van moves on. Next they're at our house. But they don't just slow down at our gate; they stop and buzz to get in.

"Oh my God, they want us! They are looking for us! WTF?! Why our house? What have we done?"

Our driveway is about twenty meters long, and we have solid electric gates that can't be seen through and that can only be opened from inside the house. When someone buzzes to get in, the dogs go nuts, so a whole coordination thing has to take place—someone needs to run up the stairs into the house to open the gate; someone else needs to head to the gate; and we have to either get the dogs into the house or hold on to them so they don't run out onto the road and scare the crap out of whoever is there. I shout at Luca to go into the house to open the gate. The dogs' barking is drowning out the police car announcement. I stop halfway down the driveway, holding the collar of one mad dog, and watch suspiciously as the gate slowly opens.

There's the van, ready to drive in, but it's stopped. The driver has already gotten out and has his back doors open. The police car has stopped behind him. "Stay in your house," they bellow at me in Italian.

"Okay," I'm thinking, "so they want me to go back into my house?"

I can't make out what else they are saying. I just stay still. Meanwhile, the van guy has appeared from behind the van with a large cardboard box. He's a smiley chap. "I'll leave it here," he says in Italian, looking at my worried face, and he places the box inside the gate and then backs away into the van.

The gates start to close, and the police car moves on. Luca and I stare at the box. "What do you think it is?"

"I don't know, Mam, but they only dropped a box at our house, not an anyone else's."

I carry it up the drive; it's very light. We get a knife and open it carefully.

We're still listing things it might be. Protective gear?

Disinfectant?

Decorations for the street party we should have when this is all over?

It's a light shade. I ordered it two months ago for our bedroom in the new house and completely forgot about it.

I'm completely confused, but Luca figures it out. "The delivery van was slowing to try to find our house number. He had nothing to do with the police car; it was just a coincidence they were driving slowly up the road at the same time!"

Chapter 39

WEDDING BOOKINGS ARE DROPPING LIKE FLIES. EVERY DAY I wake up to a new postponement or cancellation. I haven't spoken to Lucia much since lockdown started, so I give her a call to break the news.

"Hey, how are you doing?" I say, trying to start off positive.

"Oh, I am cleaning. It's how all of us Italian women de-stress."

"I think I must be the only woman in Italy who hasn't cleaned her house from attic to cantina twenty times already. I haven't cleaned it once. My brain has gone through several stages during quarantine, sort of like Worzel Gummidge with his head changes. It started in party mode, then slob mode, and now it's in lazy-slob mode."

"What is Worst Rummage?"

"Worst Rummage? Oh, you mean Worzel Gummidge. He's just a scarecrow with a turnip head and a wooden girlfriend. Forget I mentioned him. I was going to save cleaning for week three, when we would all possibly be so bored that we'd find it interesting, but

I don't think I can wait that long. I better get some done today. It's a pity there's a lockdown, otherwise you could have come over here with some friends. My house would keep you de-stressed for weeks."

Cleaning is not really a priority for Luca or Ronan either.

We keep on top of the laundry and dishes, and Luca keeps his room in sparkling order, but we need a motive to get the rest tidied. Our motivation usually supplies when we know family are coming to stay or a friend is coming over for lunch or dinner. As soon as we know someone's coming, we go into overdrive and the place looks amazing within two hours.

Sometimes, when I notice the housework is getting a bit out of hand and I don't want to do the cleaning by myself, I'll say, "Oh, I got a text from Lizzy; she's going to be passing here around lunch-time and is going to drop by," or "Lizzy might drop in to borrow the strimmer tomorrow, so we'll all get up early and give the place a good clean, yeah?"

The house gets sparkled.

Lizzy always cancels, probably because Lizzy doesn't exist. I use her sparingly, only in emergencies. Neither of my menfolk has realized that Lizzy has never actually been to our house. Both of them think they've met Lizzy at different times when they were out with me alone: with Luca, I stopped in the supermarket to talk with someone I know through my business, and with Ronan I greeted a friend of a friend on the street. Both times they asked, "Was that Lizzy?"

Caught off guard, I just casually responded, "Yeah."

So Ronan thinks Lizzy is a tall woman in her thirties with an English accent, and Luca thinks Lizzy is a short Italian in her sixties.

I'm going to have to think of a different motivational strategy now, since family can't come to stay and friends can't call by, not even invisible friends like Lizzy. I miss her.

"Look, Lucia, I called to talk to you about this year's weddings. In the last three days they have all either canceled or requested to be postponed until next year."

"I guessed that would happen. All my summer holiday clients have canceled too. It is terrible; I don't know what we are going to do."

"I know; it's disastrous."

"Oh, Rosie, I have just realized: this is it. The tarot cards—this is the disaster they were predicting. Weddings walking away and things being out of our control and us locked in."

Entering our third week in quarantine with no end in sight, we have no weddings left for the summer, which means no income for me or Ronan. Luckily, we still have the nest egg saved, but that, together with a small loan I've been approved for, is just enough for the house. All the extra work we took on for the summer was to go towards the renovations.

The week doesn't get any better. In fact, it hits an all-time low, as nearly a thousand people die in Italy in two days, mostly in Lombardy. Army trucks transport coffins as funeral homes have long gone over their capacity. People can't be with their loved ones when they are dying, and funerals are banned.

I take a walk in the garden down the grass track that runs close to next door's garden. I realize I haven't heard my neighbor Giorgia's voice since this all started. Is she okay? Has she got the virus? Is she dead? I hear her son working in the garden, but I don't have enough confidence in my Italian to shout to ask if she is okay. I probably wouldn't understand his response. I feel helpless and lost in the country I love. The language barrier has cut me off from gossip, news reports—basic knowledge in this emergency.

Where is Giorgia? How many people in the area have the virus? What about the little old couple who we see walking to the supermarket holding hands, both at least ninety? What about the next-door neighbors, Maria and Giovanni, whom we met at the Sighing House? They took an interest in our garden and gave advice about grass cutting. I had looked forwards to getting to know them. What about Raffaele and Luciana, who own the restaurant and who both have their elderly mothers living with them? How are they coping? What about the punk lady in her late sixties with the pink hair and tattoos who owns the cafe in town?

I feel like we are free-falling down a black hole with no end in sight. What about my parents? When will I ever see them again? I am sobbing, walking and sobbing. I have rarely sobbed so hard, but I recognize it as grief. I grieve for the normal that was. I grieve for the sadness that covers Italy and is slowly expanding all over the world. I grieve for the loss of my communication skills after moving to a country where I don't know the language. I sob for Giorgia, for our neighbors, for the pink-haired woman with the tattoos, the old couple holding hands. And I sob because reality hits me; we are not going to be able to afford the Sighing House.

My sobbing takes me across the back field, and I slowly start to walk down the other side, trying to get a grip on myself. Then I hear it. I hold my breath... Yes, there it is again: it's Giorgia shouting at her son.

I turn and quickly retrace my steps along the back field and the track near her garden so that I can be sure. Yes, it is her, giving out that he's doing something wrong in the garden. My sobs turn to sobs of relief.

"*Andrà tutto bene.*"

I make a pledge to myself to make an extra effort to learn Italian during lockdown, and I sign up to three classes a week with a teacher online.

"Is that nuclear fallout?" asks Ronan the next morning, opening the bedroom shutters in his Eeyore-like "Nothing would surprise me at this stage" voice. He yawns.

Is that a typical response from someone who sees nuclear fallout? I look from the bed. I'm less pessimistic. "Noooo, it's…cherry blossoms being blown around?"

We're both at the window taking a closer look. "It's a blizzard. It's bloody snowing."

It doesn't stick, but seeing snow fall in this part of Italy in March—or in any month in fact—is unusual. The cold snap forces me to stay inside rather than loll around on the terrace.

On the Covid tracking map I check online daily, Italy looks like a ladybird, littered with black dots of contamination in the hot red zone. The top of Italy's little leg has become so infected that it might just dissolve and float out into the Mediterranean at this point.

Giovanni arrives at the house early. It's the first time he's been here since lockdown started. He's checking to see if the heating is working okay for us during the forecasted cold snap. He looks jolly and sticks out his foot—the new way to greet—even though I'm up on the ter-race and he is way over at the garage.

"How is your papa?"

"*Bene.*"

It's good to hear. His ninety-five-year-old father lives with his "little" brother, who is ninety-three and who in pre-Covid times could still be seen cycling around faster than I ever could.

"Any *contagione* in the town?"

"No, none here."

Relief floods through me. At least now I know that my new elderly neighbors and all the ancients I love to see while driving around are okay.

Chapter 40

BY WEEK FOUR I'VE BECOME A MASTER OF FRIDGE ROTATION. I wake in the morning and think about the meals we will have that day. Over my morning cuppa, I strategically move items around the fridge like chess pieces, arranging them by their best-before dates. The veggie drawer is checked. A lentil vegetable stew was made yesterday for dinner, with enough left over to freeze for two other days. Today we'll do chicken with a cream sauce, as both need to be used soon. Tomorrow we'll have roasted vegetables and tuna pasta, with my chickpea curry the next day and the frozen stew again the following day.

We have enough meals for another five days before we have to go out the gate again. We are now past day seventeen, so if we were carrying the virus when we started quarantine, it would have shown by now. I feel relieved, cocooned, safe, and none of us want to go outside our gate at all. We don't want to take any chances.

As we run out of items, they are noted on a shopping list stuck to the front of the fridge. Meal plans are done nearly two weeks in advance, so we know exactly what we need to buy on that one precarious trip to the supermarket. As a result, we spend a lot less on groceries and there is a lot less food waste. Greta Thunberg would definitely be smiling now if she were here.

I've also begun to dig deep into the back of the freezer, something I've been meaning to do but which I'd put on the long finger—the cats are being fed fish I have had in there for about five months, as I wouldn't fancy it for human consumption. But they think it's Christmas come early, and we're saving money on cat food. Although, it will probably cost me more in the long run when they refuse to go back to eating tinned food and expect to be fed shrimp and salmon every day.

I've become a doorman, as the pets don't like cold weather either. They'll cry or whine to get out, go out for five minutes, then cry, whine, bark, or meow to get back in. They do this individually at least twenty times a day—the constant up and down motion from a sitting position is toning my glutes nicely.

I saw a report that there are two-hour queues outside gun shops in some American states, which is a little concerning. What's that all about? After buying their 100 kilos of pasta and 850 toilet rolls, they stop off at the gun shop so that they can protect said pasta and toilet rolls from their neighbors who have also bought 100 kilos of pasta and 850 toilet rolls?

I bought a five-kilo bag of pasta here in Italy last September. It was on sale for only €2.40 and I thought, "Well, I'll get it in case of an emergency." I was thinking of perhaps a sudden-craving-style emergency that only a good ragù would satisfy, rather than a full-blown worldwide pandemic emergency.

After six months we still have four kilos of the bag of pasta left. These guys have watched way too many zombie apocalypse movies; if they get through half that much dried pasta in the next four weeks, they'll be throwing the remainder at their neighbors they'll be so sick of it.

I've been avoiding any discussion about the house with Ronan or my family, who call and ask every day when we'll be closing the deal. They just don't get what lockdown means in Italy compared to in other countries. Nothing is open, and we're not allowed to go anywhere beyond our gate other than the supermarket.

Over lunch, I feel it's time to have the conversation I have been avoiding. "The final wedding canceled today; well, they didn't cancel, but they postponed until next year." I pause; Ronan's not reacting. "This means we have no income this summer or for the rest of the year; you do realize that?"

"Yes, but most have been postponed, so we'll have lots of work next year to make up for it, don't worry."

"But the house? Have you thought about the house…?"

"Of course. I haven't been thinking of much else in the last few days. I know you have your heart set on it, we both do, but I think we're both thinking the same; I just didn't know how to say it to you. There'll be other houses next year, when we're back on our feet, or this one will still be on the market."

"It might still be on the market, but with that hole in the roof it's just going to deteriorate even worse and cost even more to fix up."

"How do we stand legally if we back out now? Do we lose the deposit?"

"No, I checked the agreement: the date for the deal to be closed expired yesterday, so we can get the full amount back. I'll email Betty in the morning and ask her to transfer the funds back to us. I'll say I'm worried the Italian bank could close down if the economy crashes and that our money would be lost. I won't say we're backing out of the sale. Not yet. I'll wait until this lockdown is over and then tell them. I don't want to add to everyone's misery, and to be honest, I'm still waiting on a miracle, hoping something will change in the next few weeks." I'm on the verge of tears and he knows it.

He comes over and gives me a hug.

"Come on; losing the house isn't the end of the world. We just have to put our dream on hold for a while."

I bury my face in his arm, fighting the urge to scream. I don't want to put my dreams on hold again, not again.

I need to do something to make myself feel better rather than going around feeling miserable, so I decide it's time to do something about the mess that looks back at me in the mirror. My roots are showing and the frizzy, dry ends of my hair need to go.

I've had two frozen shoulders for nearly twelve months, which means I can only lift my arms to Frankenstein's creature level. I can't put on my own coat, a bra is a struggle, and brushing my hair is a challenge. I haven't been able to touch the top of my head for nearly a full year, so doing a self-dye will be impossible. There's only one thing for it: call in Ronan's help.

"Just take an inch off of all the ends," I say. It's just the ends off my long hair, which takes ages to grow. Chop, chop, chop go the thick fabric scissors. I look to the floor and there are some very long clumps of hair.

"The middle was uneven so I had to take more off there."

"My hair goes in a U shape at the back…"

"Oh…you need to rephrase that: it *used* to go in a U shape," he says.

I should have known to stop there. Letting him give me a straight-across-but-a-bit-crooked bob was a bad enough idea, but letting him dye my hair is a worse decision. It's not one of those moments where you say, "Aw you missed your calling; you should have been a hairdresser." Far from it. There's more dye on my face, shoulders, neck, and Looney than on my hair. I take a photo and send it to Lucia. She nearly calls an ambulance; it looks like someone has tried to scalp and skin me alive.

After cleaning up the crime scene, I scrub my skin and begin to think, "Why am I doing this? Why am I so afraid of letting myself go gray?"

I come from a family of early grays, so I started dying my hair from twenty-six years old. I had played with the idea of going gray several times in recent years, as I hated piling a load of chemicals on my head every six weeks, especially after an article I read years ago, in one of these "really, really true story" magazines, about a woman who suddenly developed a reaction to hair dye and had a stroke. It wasn't a good thing to read while I was sitting in a hairdresser's getting my hair dyed, and after that it always came to mind during a dye job.

I have six weeks before my next dying session to think about it.

ROSIE MELEADY

I run the idea past my niece back in Ireland, "Maybe in a few years. It might make you look really old now...like forty-five or something."

I'm forty-seven.

I run it past Lucia, "What? *Nooo!* You look so young with your hair dyed. You look thirty-four."

"But I'm forty-seven. I have a twenty-three-year-old daughter; why do I want to look thirty-four?"

She didn't answer.

"Why can't I look forty-seven?"

She thought for a moment and then blurted out the real reason: "But Italian men love red hair!"

"I'm married twenty-four years. We're still doing okay. I'm not looking for an Italian man."

"Ah, but why limit yourself to one man?" She's so Italian.

I feel lucky and proud of the age I've achieved, so why am I trying to look like a younger form of myself? My grays are like my badge of honor for surviving this long. Many women haven't, including Eileen. She'll now forever be remembered as younger than me.

The more I think about it, the more I want to let my hair color grow out. So with my new Covid hairdo done, I decide to become a silverhead.

Chapter 41

WHEN THE MINISTER OF HEALTH ANNOUNCES THE EXTENSION of the lockdown for another two weeks, we're expecting it. I am secretly glad, as I'm still procrastinating on things I've always been meaning to get around to doing. One of these things is to clear all the boxes of clutter which I had packed up and shipped over from Ireland a few months before and that still have not been opened. I definitely don't want to move them with us to the next house, whenever that happens. So today is the day of great intentions.

"Right, Ronan, enough is enough; we need to start sorting these boxes and reducing the contents to perhaps one or two boxes rather than the current twelve."

"Just make a big bonfire and put them on it unopened. We haven't looked in them for years, so we're not missing anything."

"No way. There are precious memories in there."

"Like what?"

"Like this." I grab the large storage box full of pre-digital-age print photos.

"Ah yes. Well, not the photos, but the rest…"

"They're my memories. Let's just look at them first and then decide what to burn. Clear a space on the dinner table."

We both grab a handful of photos and start to go through them; soon the large pile from the box is just a large pile on the table.

"We need some sort of system; we need to categorize them. Let's start with a pre-us 'you' pile and pre-us 'me' pile, where photos of ourselves when we were kids, of our families, school, and old friends can go, and then we put all the photos of us together into this pile."

Soon there was a WTFIT sub-pile—a "Who the F**k Is That" pile with photos of people that we vaguely remember or who we met on a holiday and never stayed in touch with; in some we just don't know who the person is or why they've stayed among our treasured memories for so long, such as an Elvis impersonator on stage in a holiday resort.

There were one or two awkward moments of "Will I put the photo of this beautiful-looking person on the WTFIT pile?" when Ronan or I would say, "Ah no."

"Why, who is it?"

"Ah, just an old flame."

"So why do you want to keep the photo?"

"It brings back nice memories?"

"And the eight hundred seventy-six other photos of me and our kids don't have the same effect?"

Silence.

The WTFIT pile is put on the fire in a ritual burning. The beautiful people were saved. Inevitably, at least one of the WTFIT people will contact us in the next week, remind us of a fabulous time we had together, and ask if we still have the photo from when we met.

We also made a WTH pile—"Why the Hell (have we kept these photos?)"

These are of random sunsets, empty fields, an out-of-focus squirrel, and nondescript scenery. This pile includes photos we look really crap in, and one of a pigeon flying in front of Ronan's face.

Ronan looks through the "After Children" (AC) pile again, getting gooey-eyed over our babies.

I'm busy dividing the AC pile into houses one to five; it's easier to categorize by house than by year, as we have moved five times in twenty-five years.

"Here, let's have a game. I'll turn over a photo, and judging from the photo's background, the first to guess the house location, the room, and the occasion wins. The loser has to make dinner."

I turn over the first photo and slam the table, "Kitchen, Dublin, Easter nineteen-ninety-eight. Do I get a bonus point for naming the year?" I'm very competitive.

"I don't know, Rosie; you made up the rules just five minutes ago."

I win another five rounds.

"Guess you're making dinner."

"It's not fair. Most of those years are a blur to me."

"Well, that's what you get for drinking too much."

"What? You lose Photo Cluedo twenty years later? If only I'd known this was the consequence, I would have given up the drink sooner. I'll start making dinner. I'll leave you to this," he says, kissing me on the head on the way to the kitchen.

I make two more sub-piles labeled "Child No. 1" (pre–Child No. 2) and "Child No. 2" (without Child No. 1).

Child No. 1 (pre–Child No. 2)—these are photos of Izzy, and the pile is huge. So many great birthday cakes, holidays, and carefully chosen outfits.

Child No. 2 (without Child No. 1)—this is Luca's pile. There are five photos. I was the last of five kids, and there are two photos of me when I was a baby and tons of Eileen, who was the first child. For years I thought the photos of her were of me, because that's what my parents told me. Obviously they were feeling some guilt for forgetting to record any of my childhood.

With five kids, I completely understand that the novelty of "firsts" can wear off, but I only had two kids.

"Ronan, come here for a second."

He comes to the doorway, potato in one hand, peeler in the other.

"Why have we only five photos of Luca?" I whisper urgently, not wanting our son to hear my guilt from his bedroom.

"Because we then switched to digital photography. I'm sure we have lots on the computers. We'll sort through digitals another day."

"Oh phew. We should print some of him."

"To add to the forgotten box?"

"No, to hang on the wall of the new house, whenever we get one. We've never been somewhere permanent enough to do that. Let's pick some photos and do a wall of photos."

"Let's get a wall first, and then we'll do that during the winter."

I placed the large WTF pile in the fireplace for a ritual burning—except the pigeon one; it made me smile, so I keep it.

Just as I finish, Ronan calls, "Dinner! Will you set the table, Rosie?"

There are over twenty piles on the table. So what now? I carefully pick up each pile, put them back into the box, and carry it back into the cupboard from whence it came.

"Did you hear the UN secretary-general is calling for an immediate global ceasefire around the world so we can focus on the fight against Covid? Already two long-term feuds have halted?" says Luca over dinner.

"That was a couple of weeks ago, I think," says Ronan. "Conte made a similar appeal on US television last week. In the meantime, Trump is still calling it the 'China Virus.'"

"I think it should be called the Hippy Virus," I say, making both the lads laugh.

"Think about it: it's changing people's lives even if they don't get infected; it's turning us all into hippies. When have leaders ever called on warring parties across the world to lay down their weapons in support of the bigger battle against something we can't even see?"

"Yeah, and nearly the whole world has slowed to a stoned pace," laughs Luca.

"Actually, you might have a point, Rosie. Governments are giving people a basic income. Hospitals are being built at rapid speed, and medical equipment and scrubs are being made by companies that were once focused on luxury consumer goods. Temporary homes have been provided for the homeless. People are volunteering where they can. It's quite amazing what governments can do when there's a sudden urgency. Long-term social problems have been dealt with."

"It's grounded air traffic and stopped mass tourism, reducing carbon emissions and waste. That's very hippy, isn't it? You both should know, as you are both bloody hippies anyway. 'The world has time to heal'—I think you said that the other day, Mam?"

"I think the most hippy thing that is happening," I say, topping up my wine glass, "is that people who have never gardened before are growing vegetables, people who have never baked are making bread, and people who have never cooked are quickly learning because they can't go out to eat."

"And lots of people I know are starting to paint and play instruments that they haven't played since they were kids. Chloe has even started playing ukulele."

"And lots of people are doing yoga and meditation who have never done it before."

"Material wealth, celebrity status, and influencers are less important than shop assistants, garbage collectors, and health workers, who are the new heroes."

"And women are discovering the joys of being braless and not having to wear makeup every day," I say, finishing my last bite. "You see. Need I say more? Everyone is being infected by the Hippy Virus. I tell you, one thing's for sure: what this lockdown has taught me is how to enjoy the simple things in life again. When this is all over, and wherever we end up, I'm becoming a homesteader, We're going to become self-sufficient, and I'm getting off this hamster wheel of business. Women had the right idea in the old days: stay at home making stuff and enjoying life. That's what I'm going to do."

Chapter 42

I WAKE UP FEELING EXHAUSTED. I SLEPT WELL, BUT I DON'T WANT to get out of bed. I know why: it's grocery-shopping day. Going to the supermarket now is such an ordeal. You'd think I'd enjoy it, considering it's the only time we can leave the house. But no, this week it feels like a thing of dread, like a dental appointment without an anesthetic.

I wanted to go during the first week of lockdown, as I was curious to see how the Italians would cope; they have never been ones for queueing. The second week I really didn't want to go, as I felt two people going doubled our chances of bringing the virus into our home. Everyone had started to wear masks, and it felt a bit surreal. And the third week I felt we were on a clear run: we hadn't contracted the virus, so I didn't want to take any chances.

By the time we go on our sixth shopping trip, I'm having a tantrum. A full-on argument inside my own head with myself. I don't want to go. I don't want to play this shopping game anymore. It's boring. It's no fun. It's everything horrible.

I look in the fridge, freezer, and on the shelves—we have nothing suitable for dinner. But in saying that, our cupboards are still full.

"How can we have full cupboards but nothing to eat?" my tantrum brain asks. "That's ridiculous. Of course we have food; let's see what there is. I'm sure we won't have to go out for another few days if we are inventive," says my I-want-to-stay-at-home brain.

I start to search…

Because the kitchen is so small, we need to invent cupboard space above the range and under the table. It's limited, so things are piled on top of each other, and it's easy for things to be pushed into forgotten moth corners, like the variety of items bought for recipes that were either never made or made once and never attempted again: chocolate drops, almond crème, coconut chips, blanched almonds, black olive pâté. Also bags of flour and pasta.

I also have makeshift shelves made from plastic grape crates in the hallway where I keep my staples, which I always have plenty of "in case of emergency." There's rice and tins of tomatoes and chickpeas. I could make chickpea curry again, but we had it last night and we'll have the leftovers for lunch today. I'm already close to hating my favorite comfort dinner. Three times in forty-eight hours would make me never want to eat it again.

There's a tin of dog food, a brand we know the dogs don't like, but we keep it "in case of emergency." They'll eat it if they're really hungry.

There's a jar of baby food… When did we have a baby in the house? I find a bottle of sweet wine and some out-of-date cans of Guinness—"Best before May 2018." Were we even in the house then? There are cute tins of flavored tea leaves I was gifted for

Christmas two years ago. I don't want to throw them out; I would use them if I were desperate, perhaps. There's also a huge range of different coffees. Ronan likes his coffee and is always trying different ones that he ends up not really liking, but he keeps them "in case of emergency."

There's a huge amount of quinoa from when Izzy was here, but I still can't cook it correctly. Then there are things that we bought by accident thinking they were something else, such as bulgur wheat, which we mistook for quinoa. We don't want to throw it out; we could use it "in case of emergency," I'm sure. There are other foods we bought when intolerant friends came to visit—gluten-free pasta, long-lasting gluten-free crackers—and items relatives bought when staying with us but that they left behind without using, such as the two cartons of minestrone soup. We don't like minestrone soup, but we don't want to throw them out—it's good food, after all, and we can use it "in case of emergency."

In the fridge we have several bags of different grated cheeses, and in the freezer there are three bags of frozen broccoli that have welded themselves with glacier ice to the back wall. We originally had five bags of broccoli, as Ronan seems to think it's a good emergency food to have, so he buys a bag on every shopping trip, even though none of us really like broccoli.

I've also got lots of vitamin supplements on a top shelf, which I buy and then forgot to take, so now their lids have a coating of dust held in place by a film of grease. Maybe I could live on them for a few days?

I feel exhausted. I am listless and list-less. I go to bed for a lie down. The shopping can wait until tomorrow. I soon realize I'm not resting; I'm sulking. WTF, have I turned into a three-year-old?

I don't want to go to the shop, full stop.

Is the worst pandemic to hit mankind in over a hundred years not the emergency the kitchen cupboards have been yearning for? Would it not be good to be free of all this stuff waiting to be used? Like the toys in *Toy Story 2*?

I put together a menu for tonight's dinner:

Starters: Black olive pâté on gluten-free crackers.

First Course: Bulgur wheat and quinoa in a rich minestrone soup.

Second Course: Pasta with a profusion of florets of broccoli in an eclectic cheese sauce with just a hint of baby food.

Dessert: Rice pudding with—probably—out-of-date chocolate chips and Christmas cake decorations, accompanied by a sweet wine and gone-off Guinness, and followed by an opulent coffee and a tea-tasting session.

I need to grow up, stop having a tantrum, and go to the supermarket. After a shower, I face the first challenge: finding a hair dryer. I normally let my hair just dry naturally; having the coronavirus in Italy is one thing, but going out with wet hair is probably more risky in the eyes of Italians.

The second challenge is to find clothes that are not piled in a creasy mess, as I haven't ironed anything. The third challenge is to find a bra. I haven't worn one since my last outing to the shop, over a week ago, and it has been pushed back to the back of a drawer or lost somewhere. The fourth challenge is to get my gloves and mask. We only have gloves in one size: XL. I grab the shopping bags and get our two carefully prepared lists.

We need our passports and self-certificates with us whenever we leave the house. The certs need to be printed out from a government site and completed with details of where you left from, what time you left at and where you are going. It's a pain in the ass but with police checkpoints on nearly every corner they are necessary.

Keys, wallet, phones, and we're off. Except we're not. The car hasn't been used in a week, and it has an old battery, which is now flat. So it's put on a charge. We both go back into the house and let our adrenaline subside over a cup of tea.

We decide to give it another shot before lunch. If you miss the early-morning slot, it's best to wait until one o'clock, when Italians go for their ritual lunches.

So we try again. Only one person from each family is allowed into the shop, but Ronan needs to stay in the car to keep the car battery charged.

As I'm approaching the store, I see another woman getting out of her car and heading towards a trolley bay. It's hot and sunny, and there are already six people in the queue, so I speed up.

The other woman sees me and clearly thinks the same: we're now both doing fast trots to our chosen trolley bay.

I have my XL gloves on, but rubber gloves get sweaty, and the hand part has now stretched to the first knuckle on every finger, leaving flappy bits on the ends. I get to the trolley bay before her, and I insert the euro coin into the trolley release. One of my flappy bits gets stuck in the slot, but I keep going, wrangling the trolley out of the bay. I pull my mask up with the other flappy hand and maneuver the trolley out with my elbows so as not to lose time. My phone starts ringing. The woman is gaining on me. I'm closer, but I have the disadvantage of a trapped finger, and I don't want to sprint to the queue as it would look too obvious, so I decide to skip. I haven't skipped along in forty years, but hey, I'm skipping.

I get to the ticket dispenser just before the other woman and grab my number: twenty-seven—yes! Masked and sunglassed, neither of us can read each other's expression. My phone buzzes again, my flappy bit is still trapped, and my dust mask has moved up my face to midway under my sunglasses and is sticking in my eye. It's twenty-two degrees Celsius and I'm wearing a wool jumper, as it's the first hot day we've had and I hadn't really thought my wardrobe choice through. I finally get my glove released without losing a rubber finger. I pull the mask down to get some air and to save an eye. This in turn yanks my hair, as the elastic is entwined around the hairs on the back of my head. My phone is ringing again, and the queue is moving surprisingly quickly. I open the phone cover to see that it's Mam. I try to answer, but of course, since I have rubber gloves on, the phone won't take my thumbprint ID, nor will the slide-to-answer function work.

"*Ventisette*"—oh, that's me. We have to hand-sanitize our gloves before going into the shop.

First stop is the veg aisle. They've got great walnuts here, perfect for banana-and-walnut bread. I bag them, weigh them, take the label, and stick it on the bag, but now my flappy bit is stuck on the label and the bag. I try to release it with the other hand, but now I have flappy bits on both sides stuck on the label. I stand, shaking a bag of clacking nuts attached to my flappy bits, sunglasses falling back onto my nose.

I pull my hand away to push my glasses up while thinking, "Don't touch face." The bag rips and nuts fly all over the place. I give up: we don't need nuts that much, or any other veg that requires labeling. By the time I reach the wine and chocolate aisle, I've had enough. My phone rings again. I can see on the screen that it's Mam again. My anxiety is rising: something must be wrong. I pay for the shopping and exit as quickly as possible. I see Ronan in the car park revving the getaway car. My phone rings again. Oh, bloody hell. I start to load the shopping into the back. Ronan gets out to help, not thinking about the flat battery.

"*Noo!* Stay in," I shout, closing the door. My flappy bit gets caught in the handle.

"Go, go, go, keep the engine running."

He automatically jumps back in, starts the dying engine, and drives off with my flappy bit still attached. It stretches about a foot, surprisingly, and then pings off my hand. I try to steer the trolley back to the bay with my elbow and my covered hand, which now has ponds of sweat gathered at the top of each flappy bit, while Ronan cruises the car park and comes back for me. I pick up the coin with my uncovered hand. Contamination breach. Crap. I've fallen at the last hurdle.

We have hand sanitizer in the car, so I douse myself and my phone with it. I call my mother. At this point I have missed six calls in the space of thirty minutes.

"What's wrong?"

"What's wrong?" she responds.

"What? You called me six times."

"I called you six times because you didn't answer, so I was worried something was wrong."

"Nothing's wrong."

"Nothing is wrong here either!"

I thought by the age of forty-eight I wouldn't need to tell my mother whenever I left the house, especially since I live in another country.

Bloody hell, that was so stressful. While himself unpacks, I call Izzy in London and wonder why she isn't answering. So I call her a second time and she answers, saying, "What's wrong?"

Chapter 43

I SAW LUCIA FROM A DISTANCE AS WE DROVE BACK FROM THE supermarket. She was talking to a friend of hers on the road but keeping a distance.

I wonder whether Italy will ever get back to the kissing greeting again. It must be strange for them. It would be sad if it didn't return, as it's part of their warmth and culture. It's hard to imagine going back to the old normal. When I was watching TV the other night, there was a crowded street scene, and I felt myself panicking a little, thinking, "They are too close together! What are they thinking? They're not social distancing."

A social-distancing rule is a godsend to someone like me in Italy. After a year of being here, I still don't get how to do the hello-kissing thing. Do I kiss everyone I meet, or do I shake hands with some but kiss the ones who appeal more to me?

I am an all-or-nothing type of person, so either I hug you for at least thirty seconds or I stand back and nod a hello. Italy requires a happy medium, an air kiss with a semi-hug to anyone you meet who you semi-know. I never know which cheek to go for first. Many times I have hit noses or slammed my lips into another person's accidentally while I go for the wrong cheek.

Ronan, on the other hand, doesn't hold back; he'll full-on give a bone-crushing hug to anyone I introduce him to.

I used to try and stop him, but now I just leave him to it. It's particularly amusing to watch when it's small-framed women friends. I can see them blink as his six-foot-two frame approaches, first expecting him to go for a gentleman-style handshake, but then their faces change: "Oh, he's going to kiss me like in an Italian greeting. Fair enough," they think. But no. Then I can no longer see their faces; they're buried somewhere below his armpit. I know what they are going through; it's a fine line between comfort and the fear that a rib will snap as the air is squeezed out of their lungs. If I think it's going on too long, I will use the safety phrase "George, can I pet the rabbits?"

He releases, I can hear them gasp for air, a look of shock on their faces, but they smile as they try to wiggle their ribs back into place. People do like Ronan, but I think most people will have the same sense of relief that I do about social distancing when they meet him again.

I want to be able to chat with friends here in Italy like Lucia does with her friend on the road. Understanding Italian would have been a real help during lockdown—we could understand what the hell is going on in the news—but I also want to know Italian because I miss chatting. I feel I have lost my personality. I want to be able to joke and understand innuendos and banter with Italians, or perhaps that's just an Irish thing? Whatever it is, it is part of who I am, and to feel less alien here and to really *live* in Italy, I am determined to be able to speak Italian before the lockdown is over.

I know a lot of words in Italian; I just don't have confidence when using them, as my pronunciation is still crap. I can't get it into my head that "a" is pronounced "ah" and not "ay," but "e" is pronounced "ay," while "i" is pronounced "ee." And it's quite a dangerous language if your pronunciation is off.

In practically every conversation with Lucia, when I make an effort to speak Italian she bursts out laughing. "I think I know what you mean, but you just said a word for penis," or "You can't say it like that; you just said something about your vagina."

This is particularly the case when talking about a recipe, growing vegetables, or doing grocery shopping, as every fruit and vegetable seems to have a pun or innuendo attached to it.

The most common of these words is probably "*patata*," which is commonly used as a nickname for a female's private anatomy. Saying "*Dammi la patata*"—give me the potato—can be taken two different ways. If you are having peas with your potatoes, you need to be aware that the word for pea, *pisello*, is a childish word for penis. So if you are not careful, you could be saying "Give me your vagina" and "Would you like penis with that?"

Discussing fennel and figs is also a minefield.

Another problem is pronouncing double consonants. A common one is "*penne.*" If not pronounced correctly, it means penis. This is why you see penis-shaped pasta in tacky gift shops in Italy, as most tourists in restaurants ask for penis pasta. Similarly, "*anni*," which means "years," if said too quickly can means "anus." Ronan, who has decided to communicate with hand gestures rather than learn Italian, merrily wished everyone a "Happy Anus" last New Year. Maybe that's why 2020 was such a crap year?

But it works both ways. Lucia, who corrects me on my perverted Italian, decided to create a hen house during lockdown; she's delighted with her new hobby and last night sent me pics of her hugging her chicks with a message: I will be called Queen of Chickens!

I texted her back: That sounds like you're leading a nation of cowards. Better to use the adult name.

Ah, okay, I see... she replied. Okay then, I will be Queen of Cocks.

On day thirty-two, lockdown is extended for another three weeks. Things are starting to look better for Italy, but it's getting worse in other countries.

By Easter, I get a surge of desperation every now and then, wondering when it will be over, when I'll be able to work properly again? When will airlines be operational again? When will I see Izzy again?

I'm scared that I'm not going to see my parents for a long time. I'm scared I'm not going to be able to hug Izzy for a long time.

These are my quiet fears, but I'm going to have to voice one fear to Ronan and turn it into a decision. I've been looking online, and there is nothing that comes close to the Sighing House in value and size. Yes, we could possibly buy a two-bedroom apartment further out of town for the same price, but the house has the potential to generate an income, to pay for itself. It would be such a great investment. But we can't buy it; if we don't have the money this year to repair the roof and windows, it's just going to crumble more and become a ruin. It's just not practical.

One of the Milan owners sent me a deferment form to sign. This extends the date of our commitment to buy. I haven't told them yet that we're not buying. I said my printer is out of ink but I'll get it back ASAP.

I read my tarot cards, and they say a long-term dream will come through and a family celebration is in the future. Something is telling me not to let go of the dream just yet. So I will stay positive until this whole crappy situation is over.

After dinner, we drive up past the house. I want to see if the magnolia tree is in bloom, but it's not. Perhaps we missed it, or perhaps it doesn't flower anymore. The grass is long, but otherwise the house is still just sitting there, patiently waiting for life to be breathed back into it. My heart aches. I want to go hug the house like it's a person so it can comfort me that everything is going to be okay. I want to sit in it and feel its stability and a sense of being grounded, but we can't; due to Covid regulations, we're not supposed to even be in this town.

When we get home, I have a long, leisurely chat with Izzy—that always makes me feel better. She will start filming her series again in September. She has also sorted out her bank account at long last. She hadn't received her pin codes for online banking, and her local ATM has been broken since the start of lockdown in London, so while she can use her bank card to buy food at the grocery store and stuff online, she hasn't been able to get cash out, nor has she had any way to check her balance to see if she has been paid for the first five episodes they filmed pre-lockdown. She eventually got through to the bank and ordered new pin codes to be posted to her.

I lie in the hammock, and high up in the blue a swallow flies over me, the first to return. My heart lifts a little.

The following day, I realize going to see the house was not a good idea. I'm feeling frustrated. I want our house. I want to go back to the old plan. I want fabric shops to be open so I can get upholstery material. I want garden centers to be open so we can start on our garden. I want DIY shops to be open so we can start to decorate. We had planned to do a road trip of antique markets in France. I want the world to be open again.

This all feels surreal sometimes. Yesterday, a woman in Rome was stopped and fined while trying to take a turtle for a walk. Police said it was not considered a valid reason to leave the house.

Chapter 44

DELIVERIES AND THE POSTAL SERVICE IN ITALY ARE SLOW AT THE best of times, but since lockdown, Amazon has ceased delivering to Italy, and other deliveries tend to arrive at a snail's pace. I received a delivery yesterday and had no clue what it was. This was the second time a mystery package arrived. It was something I had tried to order for Christmas, for Luca, but the Japanese company proudly announced they had sold their stock of fifty thousand items, and so I pre-ordered it for his birthday, in February. The delivery was only three months too late—two posable drawing mannequins, to help him with his art-work. The Facebook ad looked fabulous. They were more bendy and adaptable than the wooden mannequins you get in art shops.

They arrived neatly packaged. The first thing that struck me was that they were tiny, about three inches high. The second thing was the packaging. For the male mannequin, a caricature of a James Bond–style character had been printed on the front of the box, to illus-trate the drawings you could achieve. The female mannequin's box had a scantily clad, Manga-style character showing off her skimpily knickered crotch and bosoms busting out of a bikini that must have shrunk down three sizes in the pool. Not only that, but there was a step-by-step guide inside (in Japanese) for how to re-create such a drawing. It appeared I had bought my son a guide to drawing hentai porn. I wonder how the fifty thousand parents who bought these as pre-wrapped stocking fillers for their much-younger, aspiring-artist children explained Santa's mindset.

I think of other things I ordered before and during lockdown that have yet to arrive; some clothes that will probably be out of season by the time they get here; toilet brushes from a Kickstarter campaign I supported—I ordered five for some reason. I think I was thinking ahead for unique Christmas gifts, but I should just admit that this was during the early lockdown days when my head was in party mode and I was lashing into the wine supply. Late-night online orders with drink consumed are never a good idea. Then there were the gorgeous light shades for the hall, the antique doorbell, and the cushion covers for the sofa we don't have yet…for the sitting room we are not going to have. I'm preparing myself for the drip-feed of intense sadness when they each arrive.

I was telling Izzy about our delivery, and by coincidence she had just gotten some deliveries too. She needs to pack up her small apartment as soon as her lease ends in the summer, so she ordered what she thought were a small roll of bubble wrap and a few boxes. The roll of bubble wrap turned out to be five feet high. Not only that, the internet connection was a bit iffy the day she was ordering, so she pressed the cart button several times.

So far she has received three rolls of five-foot bubble wrap and five bales of large cardboard boxes, with ten boxes in each bale. She's not sure how many more are on the way. There's no way of returning them during lockdown, and her tiny living room is now full of bubble wrap and cardboard. Perhaps she can amuse herself by building a cardboard fort? Or she can build a replacement apartment, one very well insulated and weatherproofed with bubble wrap?

Everyone I've talked to this week seems to have a similar story. Nothing has to be signed for during lockdown, and with such a huge backlog of parcels, delivery services are not being very diligent. Karen in Tuscany ordered books and DVDs a couple of weeks ago and got a "Delivered" notice. Someone in Naples is now enjoying her Covid entertainment selection.

When I told Izzy's story to Louise, a friend who is a wedding hairstylist in Rome, she interrupted, "Oh! You've just reminded me of something I ordered at the start of lockdown… I wonder where my dollie head has gone?"

"What's a dollie head?"

"It's a 'head' with real hair that a stylist can practice on, I ordered one to save myself from going nuts and to try a few new styles during quarantine. I'd completely forgotten about it."

I know that by the time we were finished our phone call she had again forgotten about her missing dollie head. So it will probably arrive around Christmas, or, like Karen's stuff, it will go to the wrong address. Either way, someone is going to get a mystery delivery with a bodiless head inside. Cue the theme tune to *The Godfather*.

Another thing I decided during lockdown was that by the end of it I would have completed something artistic, something to hang on the wall to remind us of the struggle we went through to finally get the Sighing House. When I am ninety, I want to be able to point to it hanging in the same dusty place it was first hung and say to my off-spring, "Do you see that hanging on the wall? I created that during the Lockdown of 2020." And for generations no one will really want the artistic mess created by Grandma Rosie during COVID-19, but they won't want to throw it out either. So I ordered a cross-stitch embroidery kit. It arrived, and it's huge; it will take three pandemics for me to finish it, but I started it anyway, getting a strange comfort from the fact that I will forever add to the clutter of future generations.

Getting back from a walk, I decide to work on it. I flip down my glasses from on top of my head and begin to sew. I "acquired" reading glasses about four years ago. They are mild—so mild I'm often three pages into reading a book before I feel the strain and remind myself I need to put them on. Every year my optician sends me a reminder to come get a checkup, but I never go. However, doing up-close stitch work, I now realize that I really need to get a stronger prescription. Today, especially, I'm finding it very difficult to see the location of the next stitch, but I persevere. Ronan is having lunch at the table.

"When this is all over, I really need to go to the optician and get my prescription renewed. This is killing my eyes," I say.

He's very sympathetic. As a photographer, having to wear glasses was a pain in the ass for him for years, so much so that he got laser eye surgery. I struggle through a section of the embroidery pattern. My needle threader drops and I bend to pick it up. My glasses fall to the ground. They don't break, but I realize that I haven't been wearing my reading glasses but my sunglasses. I don't know which is more ridiculous, the fact that I've been trying to embroider for a full hour while wearing sunglasses, or the fact that I've had a full face-to-face conversation with my husband *inside* the house about my failing eyesight while wearing sunglasses, without him noticing.

We will be making an appointment at the optician after lockdown, for sure, but not for me: for him.

We usually bring Looney to the doggy-grooming parlor at this time of year for a makeover. She's looking raggedy and needs a manicure. So I start to search "how to groom your dog" on YouTube, getting as far as "how to" before Google decides to preempt with a list of fifteen options.

The first three search predictions are: "how to survive a zombie apocalypse," "how to survive the apocalypse," and "how to survive a nuclear attack," all pretty damn intense searches. However, by the time we get to the fourth entry on the list, things have lightened to a degree. After we've all learned how to survive damnation, the next important things seem to be "how to lose belly fat," "how to cook chickpeas," and "how to juice celery"…because we all want to look good and be healthy after the apocalypse, right?

Next on the popularity list are "how to make pandesal" and "how to make siopao." Even though I don't know what pandesal or siopao is, I suddenly feel my family is missing out during the pandemic and that I should be making them.

I tumble down the rabbit hole and google "what is siopao?", forgetting all about grooming the dog.

A week later, Looney looks more ragged than ever, but I've made siopao three times, so I go back on YouTube and start to type "how to…" and am glad to see the thoughts running through the heads of my demographic have lightened since last week.

All the doomsday survival searches are gone. People must be focusing on the escape day when the lockdown will be lifted, as "how to lose belly fat" is now the new number one. The survival researchers seem to have moved on to "how to save a life"… Maybe they've learned all they needed to know about survival and want to be sure they have friends to share their new reality with after the apocalypse has happened? Other new entries are "how to draw" and "how to basic"… What does "how to basic" even mean?

Unfortunately, "how to twerk" is still in the top fifteen searches, so the doomsday researchers are right: there really isn't any hope for humanity.

Izzy's tone changes. "Mam…"

I knew something bad was coming, I could see it in her eyes.

"I want to come home to you guys, home to Italy. I think I'm going to crack up in this apartment block. It is so noisy, I haven't slept more than three hours a night. They never turn off the TV next door. The guy on the other side works from home now, and all his clients are in the U.S., so his calls go on all night, and up above they seem to be constantly moving furniture and doing weights."

"Oh no, that's awful; you've always been a light sleeper. Even during my pre-natal scan you had your little fists over your ears."

This makes her smile. "I still sleep like that."

"I know you do."

"I'm just so lonely and bored, Mam. All my friends here live on the other side of town, so I don't even get to meet up with them in the park for a social-distancing walk. I ordered art supplies at the start but got stressed that I'd get paint on the furniture or floor. I tried to order a cross-trainer to keep fit, but the shop ran out of supplies. I bought recipe books, but I can't find all the ingredients needed in my local corner shop.

"Up to now, it's been okay, as I've been catching up on all the books I've been wanting to read. But now I'm just so bored and lonely."

"And tired." I can see the black rings under her eyes. Being apart from her while all this is happening is one of the most difficult things.

"It got so bad that I use all the plates, cups, and glasses I can throughout the day so I have a pile of washing up to do before going to bed, as it gives me some sort of strange routine. I spent an hour today watching three ice cubes melt in a glass of water."

I don't tell her what I already know, as it's nearly too cruel. Even though we are living here, Izzy is not a resident. She's our child, and alone, but she is now an adult and a resident of the UK. The only flights allowed are for repatriating Italian citizens and residents; it's near impossible to get into the country if you're neither. Perhaps if the bloody house sale had gone through we might have had more pull, as it would have been the *prima casa* of the family.

But if there is a way of getting her here, I will find it. I've never seen her look so sad, but for now I need to raise her mood.

"Do you know how I get through missing you? I pretend you have joined a convent or that you are on a Buddhist retreat somewhere exotic." She's laughing; result achieved.

"Leave it with me a few hours, baby. I'll figure out something, don't worry."

Gardening helps me think. I spend the rest of the afternoon repotting my seedlings into bigger pots. I had hoped I would be transplanting these into our own garden in Passignano. The thought of buying a house in Italy needs to become a distant dream again, and now we need to focus on helping Izzy.

"I've been on to the Italian embassy, and they said that, because we are not residents or citizens, border control could turn her back," says Ronan, coming out onto the terrace after spending an hour in a call queue.

"And if she lets the apartment go before leaving, which she will need to do as her lease is up in a month, she would literally have nowhere to go; all the Airbnbs and hotels are closed."

"I've texted Lucia and Giovanni to see if they've heard of any way to get her back. Perhaps a letter from the Comune to say that her family is here and she has nowhere else to go?"

"It's a long shot, but she could still be turned back at border control, and then what happens?"

"Perhaps she needs to think about it from a different angle. I think her main issues are loneliness and not being able to sleep. In the UK, people are permitted to leave their area if they're moving, so what if she gets a new apartment closer to where her friends are? She'll need to pay double rent until her lease is up, but we can help her with that," I say, thinking aloud with Ronan.

"That could work. It will give her something to focus on and some hope. Conte is announcing the first phase of reopening tomorrow, so perhaps it will include opening the borders again, or maybe those with family will be allowed to travel."

Izzy calls before I get a chance to call her back. "I've had a long bath and a good cry. I'm just going to have to suck it up and get through this."

"Not so fast..." I tell her the idea about the apartment, and we both start googling apartments for rent, feeling hopeful again.

Chapter 45

THE GOVERNMENT IN ITALY ANNOUNCE PHASE TWO, WHICH WE have all been anticipating for months. Complete nationwide confusion follows about what is allowed. To summarize:

You can visit family but not friends, and not a family group, and you must keep away from them.

You can walk beyond two hundred meters from your house with a maximum of one other family member in an area where you can keep two meters apart.

You can go to the park if you prove it is absolutely necessary or an emergency, and as long as it is in walking distance of your house.

If you are lucky enough to find masks for sale, you can't offer your children in exchange for them, no matter how tired you are of your kids at this stage. You can only pay fifty cents for them, but you must be wearing a mask to go in to buy the rare masks.

You can train if you are an athlete, but only if your sport is running or walking.

You can get takeaway food if the nice restaurants close to you decide to turn into fast-food outlets.

You can only bury people outside. (Was there a time when we buried them inside?)

So really nothing will change for anyone not involved in construction or manufacturing, other than the fact that you can now walk as far as you like on your own—which will make us all look like zombies, as hairdressers and beauticians are to remain closed.

While having my morning tea on the terrace, I water the sunflower seeds I planted the day before quarantine. They now have small leaves. I call them "my little pots of hope" because I envisage this period will be finished by the time they flower.

A lot of people are going around like headless chickens. We were not expecting this; we had no time to prepare ourselves physically or mentally. It's not like a holiday we were building up to, looking forward to, and planning for, so I'm being gentle with myself. I don't have to rush into doing all those things on my long-term to-do list, and I don't have to be positive all the time. I have gone through anxiety, stress, fear, and general shock that this is actually happening. Nobody is able to say when it will end. That is the scariest thing.

However, the thing I dread most is the call I have to make next week to the notary and the estate agents when their offices reopen. The call to say we can't go through with buying the house. I have tried to think of every way possible to make it happen, but now the loan company has sent an email to say that, due to the current extraordinary circumstances, they have to reconsider all loan applications that were not drawn down pre-Covid. They need bank statements showing income for the last two months and invoices for the coming months of monies due, neither of which we can produce. We won't get it. Nothing less than a miracle will make it happen now; we have to let our dream go.

After dinner, Izzy calls.

"I got my online bank codes."

"At last! Are you still okay for cash? Have they paid you? Do you need any money?"

"Emmm, yeah. I got into my account online and I was a bit confused, so I had to check a few things with Dave, my agent... You remember when I read my contract and I told you how much they were paying me for each series?"

"Yes, more than I make in a year. I hope you're not complaining?"

"Well, I got it wrong. They are not paying me that amount per series..."

"Oh, Izzy. I told you to let me check over the contract."

"Mam, they are paying me that amount per episode..."

I pause. "But there are ten episodes in a series..."

"Yes, Mam!"

In my head I add the required zero onto the amount she was originally expecting. "That can't be right."

"It is! I've double-checked with Dave. And do you know the first thing I am going to do?"

"Faint?" My heart is pounding and I'm hot all of a sudden. Bloody hell, I hope I don't have Covid. I could really do without that and just enjoy a moment for once.

"I'm buying you the house in Italy."

Chapter 46

OF COURSE, I SAY NO TO HER OFFER. THERE'S NO WAY I CAN accept.

"That is a lovely thought, but you need to invest your money. Buy a property to rent, for example, or start a business as a source of passive income, in case your acting career has a lull."

"Okay, so I'll buy that house and rent it to you," she says jokingly. "Mam, I'm being completely selfish. I want us to have a family home again. I want to see you doing all the things you love again, like making a cool house, knocking down walls—you are so good at that."

She wasn't being selfish; she was being ridiculously generous. And I knew she would dig her heels in.

"I'm doing it, Mam. You can't stop me. It's what I promised to do on those early-morning drives up to Dublin for my first job, do you remember?"

"Ha, buy me a villa in Italy when you were a non-famous actor? Yes, I remember. Look, I'm beyond touched that you thought of doing this, but you don't have to. Let's both sleep on it and I'll have a chat with Dad, okay?"

"I've already discussed it with him."

Ronan stands at the terrace door, smiling. Izzy is still on my phone screen, laughing. "Try to persuade him not to let it happen. Chat later, Mam," and she hangs up. I'm annoyed. Not at Izzy, but at Ronan.

"Ronan, we need to persuade her not to do this."

He looks like I just told him he can never watch football again.

"She's twenty-three. She needs to use the money to build her own future, not ours," I say, feeling frustrated that I have to explain it to him.

"Why do you always have to get in the way of your own happiness?" He raises his voice at me, a rare occurrence.

I can't answer, as I have no idea what he's talking about.

"It's always the same: something amazing happens and you always think of the negative. It's the same with your work. You should be writing or painting, but instead you sit at your computer fourteen hours a day doing a stressful job."

"Excuse me—if I didn't have that job, where would we be?"

"Probably here a lot quicker and you'd be a lot less stressed. You're a bloody martyr, that's what you are, and you want Izzy to be the same," he shouts, storming back down the steps and into the garden.

"What the hell is that supposed to mean?" I say, going after him in a fury.

He stops and sighs loudly.

"Rosie, we both want the best for Izzy, and I want the best for you too. The world is in crisis, going through a bloody pandemic, and yet I haven't seen you this happy in years. You aren't sitting at your computer all day, we're having conversations again, you're laughing, and you're being creative. That's the way you should be all the time. You can't keep up the pace of work that you have in the past. It's time to step away from this workaholic merry-go-round. Izzy has noticed it too. She is giving you a solution, a way out, and you are refusing it."

"This is not about me or us; it's about what is best for her."

"It doesn't have to be just about Izzy. It can be the best thing for her and for us at the same time. Why not?"

"I have my pride," I blurt out.

"Pride? Bloody pride has been the downfall of many. It's what kept Eileen with that asshole for years. It's what kept me bloody drinking—it's not always a good thing to have." His words empty my mouth and brain of any possible response.

I'm glad the neighbors don't speak English. We're shouting at each other, but to them it probably just sounds like a normal family conversation.

Ronan takes hold of my shoulders. "Our daughter has made it. We should be happy! Practically speaking, she has money that needs to be invested into something. The investment market is beyond dodgy at the moment, other than gold and property. We know that house is an absolute bargain. With one hundred and twenty thousand from Izzy and one hundred thousand for renovation from us, she would have a property worth nearly half a million when finished. That's doubling the investment within a year. What other investment out there at the moment would give that return?"

He has a point. It's the same point we've made to ourselves every time we've had the "Are we mad buying a twenty-one-room house?" conversation.

"Think about it. If she bought the house, it would leave us with our eighty thousand to renovate and money to live off for the rest of the year, and it would give us time to think of the best ways to make the house generate an income. It's doable. Very doable. Lose the pride."

"But something bad always happens, the rug gets pulled."

"It doesn't have to."

I start to tremble.

"She did joke about renting it to us, but that's actually not a bad idea. We could pay her rent, and that would be a passive income stream for her?"

"You see, there's my Rosie! You're already finding ways of making it work for her. Let yourself be happy about it, —you deserve it—and let Izzy have her moment too. She was bursting to tell you. Call her back. I'll go in and make you a cup of tea."

I sit under the apple tree trying to figure out what the catch is, where the carpet corner is that's waiting to trip us up. Can I let myself be happy for once without expecting it all to go wrong? I press the return-call button.

"If you really want to buy us the house, here are my conditions: we pay you rent at the same rate we are paying here, and we renovate it into something that will be worth at least triple your investment within two years."

"Whatever, Mam, but I am buying you the bloody house." My trembles turn to proper shakes. I'm filling up.

"Is this really happening?"

"Hell yeahhh! Go make us a home."

I wake up to the sound of traffic on the 4th May. It's a beautiful sound. Italy is alive again.

Instead of the dreaded "We can't buy the house" email, I message the notary to ask if I can start transferring the balance and if we can fix a closing date. I'm so excited my heart is pounding. I immediately think maybe that shouldn't be happening, maybe I'm having a heart attack, or maybe this is the rug-pulling moment when I die of Covid. I flex my mindset muscle and follow this with the thought that a negative doesn't always have to follow a positive, and I stop the invisible barrier from going up that I've nurtured and perfected all these years, the barrier that protects me from heartbreak but that has also stopped me from fully enjoying my own happiness. Italy has done a good job of sewing me back together again, and I need to let her finish the job.

Taking my cup of tea onto the terrace, I find myself whooping loudly at two cyclists going by, the first I've seen in eight weeks. I've missed them and their spandex race gear.

It's like one of those wildlife-rescue programs, when they release a captive ape back into the wild, and even when the cage door is open, he sits there for a while and then cautiously crawls out, staying near the "safety" of the cage, then realizes he's free and runs for it. I now know what that feels like.

I get up and, out of habit, do my usual walk around the field at the back of our house, as I've done every day of lockdown, before Ronan and Luca wake.

It's getting warmer, so we've ditched our winter coats, sunglasses have been dusted off, and summer clothes have been unpacked. I head out to the field, swishing my favorite long, layered summer skirt, butterflies fluttering ahead of my path. The wheat that was just seed when lockdown started in March is now up to my thigh. The birds are singing, and I feel like a Disney princess let out of her tower for an hour.

Hot and sweaty, I return to the house to do my emails. As I sit there, a beautiful memory is triggered, a flashback to when I was pregnant and felt my baby move in my belly for the first time. I look down and, indeed, my tummy moves slightly below my skirt. "Aww bliss," I think for a nanosecond at the memory, and then I am up on my feet, ripping my skirt off. Something from the field, something alive, is trapped in between the layers of fabric; I can see its dark shadow jumping up and down on my stomach. I run out in the garden in my knickers and T-shirt, skirt in hand. Thankfully it's only a grasshopper and not a scorpion, as I first imagined. Relieved and returning to the house, I wave at the cyclists.

I'm so happy to see life emerging again after the strict lockdown that I forget I am skirt-less.

We were going to wait until Tuesday to go out properly, just to let everyone else test the water first and see what happens, but we can't wait. As soon as Ronan is up and ready, we're in the car in no time.

I roll down the window, wave, and say "Ciao" to everyone we pass.

We drive to Passignano to check in on our house—well, almost our house. We open all the shutters for the first time and let the

sunlight stream in through the cobwebs. Ten years of grime and spar-
kly dust fills the air.

Roof still caving in? Check.

Walls still crumbling with damp? Check.

The returned doors still piled on the floor? Check.

Ronan putting his hand through glass pane when closing the window
   and miraculously not severing a vein? Check.

Sanity check as to why we are buying such a dilapidated house?
   Not checked.

We walk along the lakefront that runs behind the house; very few
people are out. We aren't doing anything wrong, but it feels similar to
ditching school. Are we supposed to be here? We got the date correct,
right? Why aren't there more people out? And then we realize it's one
thirty: all the Italians are inside, having their leisurely lunches or perhaps visiting their relatives for the first time since before lockdown.

I allow myself to think of the future: perhaps Izzy or Luca will
have kids some day and I'll walk this walk with them down to the
playground. Perhaps they'll come for the summer or live here for good
and make Italy their home. In the Sighing House, there will be plenty
of room for three or four generations.

I'll make it so beautiful that Izzy and Luca will never want to
leave, or at least, when they do, they'll want to come back often and
stay for a long time. It will be the place they think of when they think
of home. It's not too late for me to build a place for us to create memories in and to transport some of our old ones to. We will have a family

base at last, a constant, with no more talk of moving somewhere else in the future. It will be a home where I can have the life I imagined when I dreamed of Italy, with a courtyard and a big "Mamma mia" family dinner table.

We buy some kebabs at the only takeaway place in town and head back home. As we walk back to the car, I brush cobwebs off the back of Ronan's T-shirt and he does likewise for me, like true newly released zombies now that the quarantine has ended.

There's some weird Covid rule about two people traveling in a car together—the passenger should be in the back seat. So that's where I sit, so as not to draw attention to ourselves, which is difficult at the best of times, as our car is a right-hand drive with an Irish registration plate.

On the way back, there's a police checkpoint. Ronan rolls down the window and hands over the required self-certificates.

"You are Irish; are you resident here?"

"Yes… No… Yes, I am Irish, but not resident. We came. And then the virus," shouts Ronan.

The policeman looks sympathetic. "Ah, maybe in a couple of weeks you will be able to go back home."

He seems to speak perfect English, which is more than can be said for Ronan, who has always had the strange habit of shouting in broken English at foreigners, something he's continued to do so since we moved in Italy.

"No. We stay. We go buy a house in Passignano," he yells.

I'm confused at what Ronan is trying to say in his native language, and now the policeman also looks confused. "You are going or staying?"

"We stay. We stay in house five minutes here."

The policeman gives up trying to understand Ronan's broken English and waves us on.

In fairness, Ronan does attempt to talk in Italian now and then—his own version, where he just adds an "o" onto the end of English words. "Uno cuppo coffeeo" is probably one of his best combinations to date. He feels he is "too old" to learn the language but will just pick up what he needs to as time goes by.

He thought he had struck gold when he discovered Google's audio translator, which he used regularly to communicate with Giovanni when we first arrived. However, after a few months, it all went very wrong when the electric gate got stuck open and he needed to get Giovanni to come over to fix it so the dogs wouldn't get out.

Into the voice translator, he said in broken English (his default language when communicating with non-English speakers):

"Hi, Giovanni. Rosie is away. I am at home and the gate is stuck open. Will you come over?" He sent it, went inside, got his reading glasses, and read back over the translated message that was sent: "Hi, Giovanni. Rosie is away. I am at home and gay, stuck and open. Will you come over?"

Ronan called me in a panic, but all I could do was cry laughing for a full ten minutes.

Giovanni did not come over that day. Ronan managed to fix the gate and never used the voice translator again after that.

Chapter 47

THE FINAL SIGNING DATE IS FIXED FOR THE 26TH OF MAY, THE anniversary of when Eileen left this world.

As soon as the date is announced for the end of lockdown, I am on the phone to Mick Kelly to make appointments with all the tradesmen on the first day permitted, so that we can get quotes for the work that needs to be done. The date for the meetings is set.

It's the first time we will meet and speak face to face with anyone outside our family in over two months. The first to arrive are the architect and the builder. They know each other, and it turns out we know the builder: his name is Antonio, and he's the son of Giovanni, our landlord. Before they've even greeted each other, the architect is running his fingers through his hair (his own hair, that is) and asking the builder how he managed to get a haircut. They laugh. Mick Kelly translates: "I ask him how he got a haircut. He says he has a captive chopper." I think he means his wife is a hairdresser. Well, I hope that's what he means.

The electrician and plumber soon arrive too. We all, of course, wear masks and stand apart. Tradesmen and builders are different here, not a butt crack in sight. Instead, they all have starched, perfectly pressed shirts over fit bodies and clean-shaven, immaculate faces, they smell great, and they're all discussing their hair and their longing for a barber. I'm disappointed that Covid rules will keep me from giving them the Italian welcome kiss each morning when they arrive to work on the house.

One thing Italians and Dubliners have in common is that we add "o" onto the end of male names, the Italians at birth (Marco, Francesco, Mario), while we Dubliners tend to shorten two- and three-syllable male names and add the "o" during their teenage years (Anthony becomes Anto, Damien becomes Damo). Other examples would be Franko, Johno, Davo. It's like a rite of passage.

As I'm introduced to the posse who will become familiar faces for the next four months, I Dublinize their names, so now Damiano will be Damo, Antonio will be Anto, Tommaso will be Tomo, and Daniele will be Danny Boy. I miss the carpenter's name. He's the oldest guy and a bit grumpy, but I know he's a good carpenter, not because I have seen any of his work but because he's missing half of one finger. It's a sign that he's stuck to what he loves to do, even after learning the hard way to keep his fingers away from the saw. They whizz around looking at what's to be done and keep saying things like "It's a big house, a lot of work. You will live here alone, just one family?"

I have been learning my building terms in Italian so that I have some idea of what they're discussing. I know the words for things like "bricks," "plasterboard," "pipes," "windows," "doors," "broken," and "crazy Irish." There are some things that I don't even know the names of in English, such as the terra-cotta fascia under the roof, which I don't want destroyed. I discover the word for plinth is *"zoccolo,"* which seems appropriate, so I tell Michele, *"Voglio mantenere lo zoccolo del piccolo tetto"*—"I want to keep the plinth of the small roof."

But I haven't said that; I've said, *"Voglio mantenere la zoccola del piccole tette."* Not very different, you would think, but he blushes a little and begs, "Oh Rosie, you say the strangest things. Please say things in English; it is safer." After much persuasion, he explains that I've used the female versions of two of the words, which changes the meaning to "I want to keep the…emm…it's not a nice word…the whore with the small…boobies."

We decide it's best if only I go to the final deed meeting, as Ronan is diabetic and we're limiting exposure to people outside our safety bubble. Instead, he will drop me at the notary's office and drive to the house and wait for me there until the deed is done.

Betty meets me at the door. She smiles and leads me through her office to a large terrace with chairs set up, the perfect solution to the Covid rules; everyone can sit apart outside. I recognize the cousins from the last meeting, but there are two new additions. They all stand together, chatting and laughing as families do, having not seen each other in a long time. They're not throwing daggers as I'd expected. I'm guessing the bald, tanned cousin is Cousin Vinny, the thief. And the new token mystery woman for this part of the process must be the cousin from Milan. Lucia arrives beaming. "Izzy has been trying to call you. She has a flight booked for 4th of June."

Betty starts by announcing the names of everyone present, their dates of birth, and their addresses. The mystery woman confirms that she is Ella, and she makes a correction to her date of birth. As she's not one of the Milanese owners, that means the ownership has multiplied for the fourth time, now to nine owners. I want to sign right now before any more can pop up out of the woodwork.

Betty continues to read the twenty-page document at full speed. About halfway through, Riccardo's phone starts to ring, like the last time we met. Instead of turning it off and apologizing, he walks over to the terrace wall, away from the group, and takes the call. Betty gives him a glance but continues.

"I need my secretary to make the change to the incorrect date of birth, and then we will proceed with the signing," Betty says in English when she has finished reading.

Out of nowhere, Ella starts shouting, "If this isn't over soon, I'm leaving and not signing. I have an appointment somewhere else. I am not staying." Riccardo tells her to shut up, and Stefana tries to reason with her, but her whole body is twitching with impatience. At this point I don't understand what she has said, but I can see she is packing up her bag and getting ready to leave. Is the deal off? Next, Uncle Francesca, who has a seat inside the office next to the open French doors onto the terrace, pipes up and says something loudly to Betty. Betty doesn't have a chance to answer; instead, all the cousins shout at Uncle Francesca together, except for Vinny, who seems to have some dignity.

"Now what the hell is happening?" I ask Lucia.

"Basically, she does not want the checks handed over to some of them, as there is money owed from a previous inheritance."

"Not this again! Surely she can't stop Betty from giving them the money they are entitled to from this transaction because of something that went wrong in another transaction over forty years ago?"

"Exactly; that is what Betty is saying." I can hear Betty telling Francesca off like a mother scolding a child over the din of the cousins' shouting.

The pieces of the jigsaw are coming together. Is this why Uncle Francesca was so hesitant about changing the wording on the power of attorney? If she hadn't made the changes naming the exact parts of the house and land parcels, which Betty had requested of her three times, then it would have appeared on paper that she had power of attorney over the whole property; "It could cause problems in the future," as Betty had pointed out. Maybe this was the problem Betty foresaw and, with due diligence, avoided. Or perhaps Ella knows something was done incorrectly in the past, understood that this was going to be an issue Uncle Francesca could bring up, and decided to try to speed past it by having her tantrum?

While Paolo goes in and calmly talks to his aunt one to one, and Ella is in a huff over by her brother's invisible telephone box, Cousin Vinny skulks over to me. "I am sorry my English is not very good. I want to apologize for the furniture. I was just following family duty." He pokes his chin up in the direction of his aunt.

"Why the doors?"

"She is a...I don't know how to say it...*accumulatore*? Like a squigel."

"A squigel? Oooh, a squirrel! You mean she is a hoarder."

"She is a bit crazy—she tries to control everything in the family. Her parents and family went through the doors many times. To her, they hold memories of parties, events, growing up, so she did not want them destroyed. She told me you were going to put new ones. But everything is returned now. The furniture I put in the garden behind the house. I hope you have many years of happiness in the house. I now go and sign." Each of the cousins goes one by one into Betty's office to sign the deed and receive their check.

Laura arrives, and we are genuinely so happy to see each other again. Her family is in Piemonte, one of the worst-hit areas in Italy for Covid. They are all doing well, but she doesn't know when she will be able to see them again.

From the corner of my eye, I can see Uncle Francesca talking to Lucia and using dramatic hand gestures; Lucia dismisses what she's saying and walks away into Betty's office to sign her name as my translator, so Uncle Francesca comes over and interrupts me and Laura with a dramatic announcement. "She has a present for you," says Lucia, translating. She hands me a small parcel of reused blue wrapping paper. I open it to find two big old-fashioned keys with a label marked "*Cancello*" on them.

"They are the keys to the front gate," explains Laura.

"*Grazie.*" I'm genuinely touched by her effort to make it special. Maybe Uncle Francesca isn't as bad as everyone else seems to think. She returns to her seat and starts fumbling in her bag again. Having all signed and received their checks, the cousins begin to leave with a nod and an "*Arrivederci*" in my direction.

Uncle Francesca comes back over to me and Laura with a

crumpled piece of paper in her hand, which she gives to Laura, providing a long-winded explanation.

"Oh, is it the history of the house she promised?"

"No, it is not the history of the house. She says you can source that yourself through a company in Perugia," says Laura, translating while handing me the piece of paper. "This is the phone number of the local police. You need to call them, as the neighbors have reported you for not having the grass cut."

I'm astonished. I burst out laughing. "She has passed on a police record to me before I have even finished buying the house! What the hell?"

Uncle Francesca walks off to pack up her papers and bag, oblivious to what I have said.

Laura is smiling awkwardly. "This is unusual."

"This whole process has been unusual."

"So I will now say goodbye," says Laura.

"Please do come to the house at Christmas. I'd love to see you again, and hopefully I will be able to show you around what we have done... Oh, and Laura, it's 'uncle' for '*zio*' and 'aunt' for '*zia*.' So she is called Aunt Francesca."

"Ah, I see! Thank you... Why didn't you tell me before?"

"I thought it would be rude to correct you, and it was cute... Uncle Francesca suits the old biddy, although we probably should have called her Don Francesca."

We can't hug, so we just wave and give each other a smile from behind our masks.

I go in and join Lucia at Betty's desk. "*Mamma mia*," says Betty.

"It's a miracle. I have never had such a difficult family. Every step was a problem. Mamma mia!" She's holding her head in her hands. I hadn't realized her English was this good.

"She has gifted me with a complaint. I have to report to the police."

"She had said this to me," says Lucia. "And I told her it is nothing to do with you, as it is from before you have purchased the house, so if there is a fine to pay, she needs to pay it, not you."

"A fine?"

With that, Uncle Francesca pokes her head in the door to say goodbye. I probably would have given Uncle Francesca a hug had it not been for Covid. Even though she has caused problems and delays along the way, she made the whole process…interesting. I look towards Betty, who is putting her final official signature to the end of the very long document, which will go on top of the tall file of papers, ancient and new, concerning the succession of the property. "Congratulations. You are now the owner of a villa in Italy," she says, sticking out her elbow, as we cannot shake hands due to Covid.

The house is only two minutes away. "We Get Knocked Down, But We Get Up Again" comes on Lucia's car radio, a song that was a previous anthem of Ronan's and mine during the recovery years. It reminds me of how much we've been through and how far we've come. Lucia drops me at the gate and heads home to her chickens. Ronan is lying on the disputed wrought-iron bed smoking a cigarette, beside the car, with the same radio channel blasting. And in the shade of the apple tree Luca is putting the finishing touches on the table setting for lunch.

"Well?" asks Ronan.

"Done," I answer.

He takes me by the hand and leads me to the open front door. It's open. He bends forward. "Hop on."

"What are you doing?"

"I'm carrying you across the threshold."

It's been twenty-five years since he first swept me off my feet and lifted me without effort in his 'ms across the threshold of our first home; now with his bad back my extra pounds, a piggyback is much more practical.

Just inside the doorway, I slide off. I look ahead and finally realize why the Sighing House feels so familiar, with its central staircase, two rooms to the left and two to the right on each of the three floors, and a secret attic under the orangey-red roof. A heavy scent of perfume drifts past, and I find myself saying the words I couldn't say all those years ago at the Halloween bonfire: "I can fix you." At last I have my own dollhouse.

We are home.

READING GROUP GUIDE

1. Rosie plans her ideal home with her husband and son, with different "must-haves" on their lists. What is your ideal home? What is on your must-have list?

2. Rosie's sister, Eileen, marries someone Rosie is not a fan of. What do you do when a close friend or family member is in a relationship with someone you don't like?

3. Rosie encourages her children to set goals without restraint. What kinds of lofty goals would you set for yourself?

4. Eileen dies unexpectedly at a young age. How do Rosie and her family deal with her passing? What do you do if suddenly all your plans are upended?

5. In terms of houses, do you prefer a fixer-upper or something that's ready to move in?

6. Rosie, in one of her many trips to Italy, is given an "earthquake bag," an emergency bag of supplies that, in this case, happens to include wine. What would be in your earthquake bag?

7. While Rosie ultimately finds her place in Italy, her first impressions are less idyllic than she'd imagined. What happens when your dreams (or dream locations) don't turn out quite as you'd hoped?

8. In a particularly dark moment in Rosie's life, she hits rock bottom in terms of self-confidence and financial issues. Have you been in this spot before? How did—or would you—get through it?

9. Have you experienced travel disasters before? Has something appeared spectacular online but unfortunate in reality? How did you deal with the situation?

10. If you had to leave your home in a rapid move, what would you take with you? Only essentials? Or only extremely personal or treasured items?

11. How did you experience the COVID-19 quarantine, if you did? What did you do to get through it?

12. At the end of the book, someone unexpectedly offers to buy the house in Italy for Rosie. What do you think of her reaction? How would you react to such a generous gift from a loved one?

A CONVERSATION WITH THE AUTHOR

What was the process of writing this book like? Did you have notes to look back on, or did you write it from memory?

This book started as a blog on the 10th March 2020—the first day of lockdown in Italy. All our wedding clients postponed or canceled their weddings, so the Covid Lockdowns gave me the time I always wanted but never felt I could afford to take to write.

It started as a Covid Lockdown memoir, and then I thought I should add "a chapter or two" about how we ended up coming to Italy. However, when I started writing those two chapters I couldn't stop, and they developed into twenty chapters. There were a lot of big life-changing events that are just very clear and needed to get onto a page.

By the time I was finishing writing the book, I realized people wouldn't be interested in all the Covid stuff, as the whole world had been through lockdowns at that point and were sick of hearing about it. The house purchase was happening while I was writing the book, which was a comedy show in itself, so parts of the book were happening as I wrote it.

What do you think of the events that happened in this book as you look back on them now?

Ohhh, it depends which events you are talking about. The book deals with a lot of different types of loss, a move to a different country, a house purchase, and a pandemic. Whenever major things—bad or good—have happened in my life, I've always said "that is another chapter for the book." Having put some order to events on paper, looking back now, I see how chaotic my adult life has been. I'm just so glad that I actually have got around to writing "the book."

Do you see yourself as a different person from who you were back then?

There's a lot of back story to when I was in my twenties and thirties and dealing with huge life issues. When you are in your twenties and thirties, you think you can deal with everything that life throws at you and at everyone else that you love. And you can, in a way. I look back and give that me a big hug. I could not deal now with what that version of me dealt with then. The version of me now is stronger in different ways, but softer in others. She is kinder to herself and in less of a panic to get on to the next chapter of her life. She enjoys living in the moment a lot more.

What do you want people to take away from your story?

You don't need to have lots of money in the bank to make your dreams come true. Actually, the more broke you are makes getting to where you want to be more "interesting." Life is short and an adventure. Keep it interesting, even the crappy parts. Wading through the sludge gets you to the more enjoyable chapters of your life.

What was your path to becoming a writer?

I am one of those people who always wanted to write books and create magazines about things I was passionate about: social issues, animal rights, and travel.

When I was eleven years old, I used to write numbers in ledgers for a bookkeeper neighbor who was losing her sight. She gave me an old travel typewriter one evening, and I thought I was going to write the most amazing books on it. I got my first story published in a magazine when I was fifteen and got paid £25. My mother told me that as I had been paid for my writing, I was a professional writer. I had made it! It took me over thirty years before I made money from fiction again.

When I was nineteen, I traveled around the States and I saw a street magazine called *Spare Change* in Boston and one called *Street News* in New York. So at twenty-one I returned to Ireland, did a one-year journalism course, and started working on creating a street magazine that would give homeless people an income. I heard of a guy called Ronan, who had a similar idea, and we got together with a few other people and created *The Big Issues* magazine in Ireland. We also got married.

I worked as a magazine writer and editor for ten years, and then I started a destination wedding business, so I could travel and see amazing places while earning a living. That is how I got to see a lot of Italy before we moved here.

The Covid Lockdowns gave me the empty time I needed to follow my someday dream of writing books. I would never have given myself the "luxury" of time to do it otherwise.

What is your writing process like?

I wake about 7 a.m. most mornings. I log on to a shared social media group and write with two writing friends, Elizabeth Reed in LA and Jordan Barnes in Hawaii. They are night writers, whereas my brain is more creative in the morning. We do writing sprints of twenty-five minutes and chat for two to ten minutes in between sprints, depending what's happening in our lives. I write until about 11 or 12 noon or until I have at least one thousand words written. It hasn't always been like this, but once I found the formula that worked for me, writing and finishing books became easier. I write most days and if I'm not writing, I'm thinking about it, listening to a craft of writing podcast or class.

What are you reading right now?

I always have about four books going at the same time—a mix of fictional and nonfictional. So at the moment I am nearly finished reading an eye-opening book called *Unwell Women* by Elinor Cleghorn. Every woman and man should read it. *Surrender* by Bono—I grew up on the Northside of Dublin and went to the same school as U2 so I am enjoying the Memory Lane of the places and the teachers he refers to.

I have lots of renovation jobs to do in the house and garden, so audiobooks are my savior when I don't have time to sit and read—I am currently enjoying listening to Sophie Kinsella's *Twenties Girl* and *The Signature of All Things* by Elizabeth Gilbert.

ACKNOWLEDGMENTS

MANY THANKS TO ERIN McCLARY OF SOURCEBOOKS FOR HAVING belief in this book and to Sourcebooks for risking their team on me, and to my agent, Emma Parry, for her encouragement.

To Annie and Sullivan, my little pebbles that have rolled up to become my rocks. To my husband, Ronan—thank you for not reading my books. You probably would divorce me if you read everything I write about you.

To Ingrid, Aoife, Conor, and Sophie for always having a welcoming kitchen table and a cuppa to escape to during all the highs and lows and drastic decisions. To Sharon, Gary, Archie, and Tabby for making moving abroad seem possible and helping us so much along the way.

I'd like to thank Santa for gifting the younger me the big clunky secondhand typewriter, where I sweated over my first novel-writing efforts in true Jack Kerouac style, and my Mam and Dad, who always encouraged my writing and creativity.

To my lifelong friend Denise Bryan for being my guinea-pig reader of the first draft. This would have been a very different book without her initial insight. To our dear friend Lucia, who welcomed us to Italy and is now like family to us.

Many thanks to the readers of my blog posts and those who interacted with me on social media during Covid, encouraging me all the way: Yvonne Farrell, Glen Martin, Lisa Chiodo, Lucy Hayworth, Rosemary Beard, Sara Pietrelli, and so many more. Also, all those who have written reviews—honestly, without your kindness and encouragement, I would never have continued writing. Thank you to Suzy Pope for helping me fine-tune my first efforts into something readable.

Thank you to my morning writing buddies, Elizabeth Reed and Jordan Barnes. To Fatima Fayez and everyone in the Clubhouse Author group who share their invaluable wisdom daily. They made me realize being a full-time author was possible and not just a someday dream.

Uncle Francesca (her name has been changed) and the family who made the purchase of the Sighing House eventful enough to make me feel it needed to be written about.

And to Jamsie, my wonderful brother who first spotted the house, I know you worked your angel magic to make this lifelong book dream of mine come true. Love you to Star Trek Galaxies and back.

ABOUT THE AUTHOR

Dubliner Rosie Meleady has been a magazine publisher and editor since 1994. She won the International Women in Publishing Award in 1996 at the ripe old age of twenty-four. She couldn't attend the award ceremony in London, as she'd decided it would also be a good day to give birth.

In her A Rosie Life in Italy series, she writes about buying a derelict villa in Italy by accident, renovating it, and living in Italy.

She now lives happily ever after in Italy, renovating the villa and writing long into the night.

Follow Rosie on her blog and social media at:
www.rosiemeleady.com

ALSO BY ROSIE MELEADY

A Rosie Life in Italy 2: What Have We Done?
A Rosie Life in Italy 3: Should I Stay or Should I Go?
A Rosie Life in Italy 4: Potatoes, Pizza, and Poteen
A Rosie Life in Italy 5: Romulus and Seamus

MYSTERIES:
A Nun-Holy Murder
A Brush with Death